THE DEMON'S BROOD

Also by Desmond Seward

The Hundred Years War
The Wars of the Roses
The Last White Rose

THE DEMON'S BROOD

DESMOND SEWARD

Constable • London

Constable & Robinson Ltd
55–56 Russell Square
London WC1B 4HP
www.constablerobinson.com

First published in the UK by Constable,
an imprint of Constable & Robinson, 2014

A copy of the British Library Cataloguing in Publication Data
is available from the British Library

ISBN 978-1-78033-177-5 (hardback)
ISBN 978-1-47210-564-6 (ebook)

Printed and bound by
CPI Group (UK) Ltd, Croydon, CR0 4YY

1 3 5 7 9 10 8 6 4 2

For Frederick, Kristin, William and Julian

Acknowledgements

Among those who helped, I should particularly like to thank my agent Andrew Lownie for encouraging me to persevere with so daunting a project. I owe another debt to my copy-editor, Elizabeth Stone, for helping me to make the book more readable. I am also grateful to the staff of the London Library for unfailingly courteous and imaginative assistance, and to the staff of the British Library.

Contents

Family trees   ix
Introduction: The Demon and Her Heirs   xvii
Timeline   xxi

Part 1
The First Plantagenets

1 The First Plantagenets   3
2 The Eagle – Henry II   8
3 The Lionheart – Richard I   32
4 The Madman – John   44
5 The Aesthete – Henry III   66

Part 2
Plantagenet Britain?

6 The Hammer – Edward I   91
7 The Changeling – Edward II   117

Part 3
Plantagenet France?

8 The Paladin – Edward III   147
9 The Absolutist – Richard II   170

10   The Usurper – Henry IV   192
11   The 'Gleaming King' – Henry V   210

Part 4
Lancaster and York

12   The Holy Fool – Henry VI   233
13   The Self-Made King – Edward IV   251
14   The Suicide – Richard III   271
15   Postscript – The Kings in the National Myth   289
     Notes   295

     Index   313

THE PLANTAGENET DESCENT
OF EDWARD III

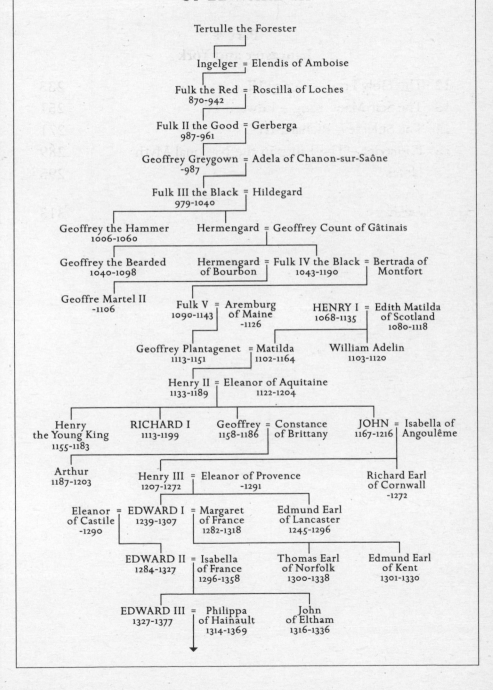

Tertulle the Forester

Ingelger = Elendis of Amboise

Fulk the Red = Roscilla of Loches
870-942

Fulk II the Good = Gerberga
987-961

Geoffrey Greygown = Adela of Chanon-sur-Saône
-987

Fulk III the Black = Hildegard
979-1040

Geoffrey the Hammer   Hermengard = Geoffrey Count of Gâtinais
1006-1060

Geoffrey the Bearded   Hermengard = Fulk IV the Black = Bertrada of
1040-1098   of Bourbon   1043-1190   Montfort

Geoffre Martel II   Fulk V = Aremburg   HENRY I = Edith Matilda
-1106   1090-1143   of Maine   1068-1135   of Scotland
                        -1126   1080-1118

Geoffrey Plantagenet = Matilda   William Adelin
1113-1151   1102-1164   1103-1120

Henry II = Eleanor of Aquitaine
1133-1189   1122-1204

Henry   RICHARD I   Geoffrey = Constance   JOHN = Isabella of
the Young King   1113-1199   1158-1186   of Brittany   1167-1216   Angoulême
1155-1183

Arthur   Henry III = Eleanor of Provence   Richard Earl
1187-1203   1207-1272   -1291   of Cornwall
                                                         -1272

Eleanor = EDWARD I = Margaret   Edmund Earl
of Castile   1239-1307   of France   of Lancaster
-1290   1282-1318   1245-1296

EDWARD II = Isabella   Thomas Earl   Edmund Earl
1284-1327   of France   of Norfolk   of Kent
            1296-1358   1300-1338   1301-1330

EDWARD III = Philippa   John
1327-1377   of Hainault   of Eltham
            1314-1369   1316-1336

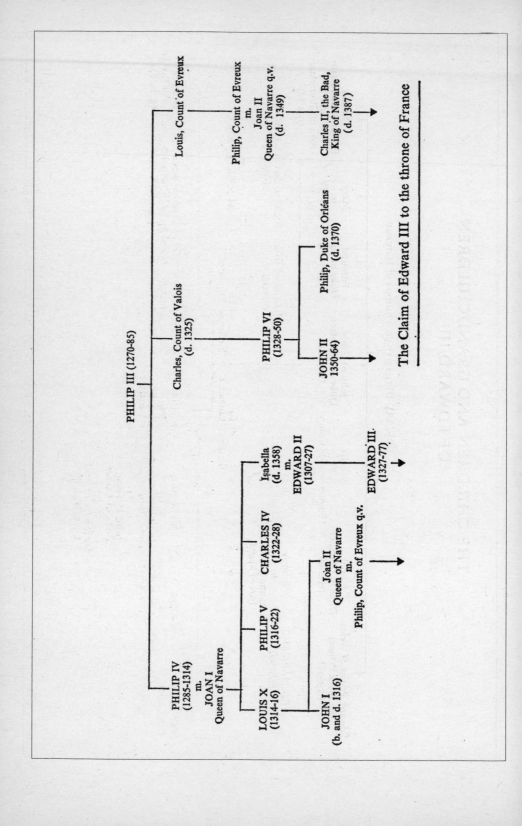

The Claim of Edward III to the throne of France

PHILIP III (1270-85)

PHILIP IV (1285-1314) m. JOAN I Queen of Navarre

Charles, Count of Valois (d. 1325)

Louis, Count of Evreux

LOUIS X (1314-16)

PHILIP V (1316-22)

CHARLES IV (1322-28)

Isabella (d. 1358) m. EDWARD II (1307-27)

PHILIP VI (1328-50)

Philip, Count of Evreux m. Joan II Queen of Navarre q.v. (d. 1349)

JOHN I (b. and d. 1316)

Joan II Queen of Navarre m. Philip, Count of Evreux q.v.

EDWARD III (1327-77)

JOHN II 1350-64

Philip, Duke of Orléans (d. 1370)

Charles II, the Bad, King of Navarre (d. 1387)

THE CHILDREN AND GRANDCHILDREN OF EDWARD III

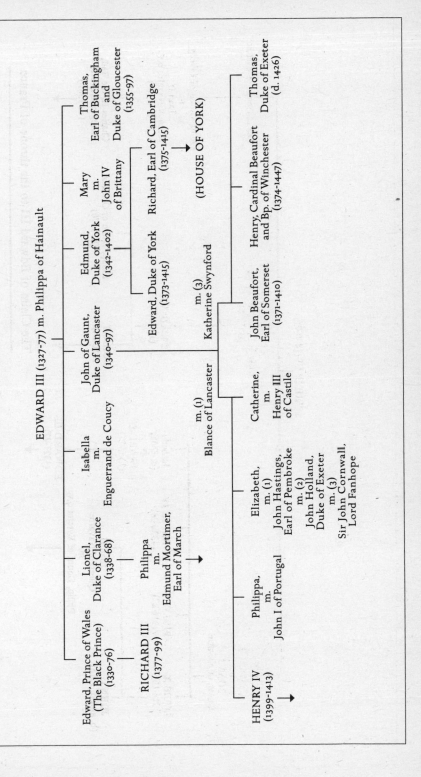

EDWARD III (1327-77) m. Philippa of Hainault

Edward, Prince of Wales (The Black Prince) (1330-76)

Isabella m. Enguerrand de Coucy

Lionel, Duke of Clarence (1338-68)

Philippa m. Edmund Mortimer, Earl of March →

RICHARD III (1377-99)

John of Gaunt, Duke of Lancaster (1340-97)

m. (1) Blance of Lancaster

m. (3) Katherine Swynford

Edmund, Duke of York (1342-1402)

Edward, Duke of York (1373-1415)

Richard, Earl of Cambridge (1375-1415) →

(HOUSE OF YORK)

Mary m. John IV of Brittany

Thomas, Earl of Buckingham and Duke of Gloucester (1355-97)

Henry, Cardinal Beaufort and Bp. of Winchester (1374-1447)

John Beaufort, Earl of Somerset (1371-1410)

Thomas, Duke of Exeter (d. 1426)

Catherine, m. Henry III of Castile

Elizabeth, m. (1) John Hastings, Earl of Pembroke m. (2) John Holland, Duke of Exeter m. (3) Sir John Cornwall, Lord Fanhope

Philippa, m. John I of Portugal

HENRY IV (1399-1413) →

HOUSES OF LANCASTER, BEAUFORT AND TUDOR

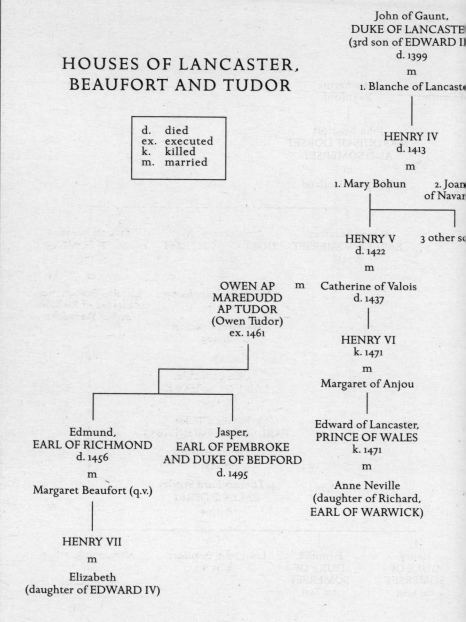

d.   died
ex. executed
k.   killed
m.   married

John of Gaunt,
DUKE OF LANCASTE[R]
(3rd son of EDWARD I[II])
d. 1399

m

1. Blanche of Lancast[er]

HENRY IV
d. 1413

m

1. Mary Bohun   2. Joan[?]
                          of Navar[re]

HENRY V   3 other so[ns]
d. 1422

m

OWEN AP   m   Catherine of Valois
MAREDUDD   d. 1437
AP TUDOR
(Owen Tudor)
ex. 1461

HENRY VI
k. 1471

m

Margaret of Anjou

Edmund,   Jasper,   Edward of Lancaster,
EARL OF RICHMOND   EARL OF PEMBROKE   PRINCE OF WALES
d. 1456   AND DUKE OF BEDFORD   k. 1471
                       d. 1495
m   m

Margaret Beaufort (q.v.)   Anne Neville
                                              (daughter of Richard,
                                              EARL OF WARWICK)

HENRY VII

m

Elizabeth
(daughter of EDWARD IV)

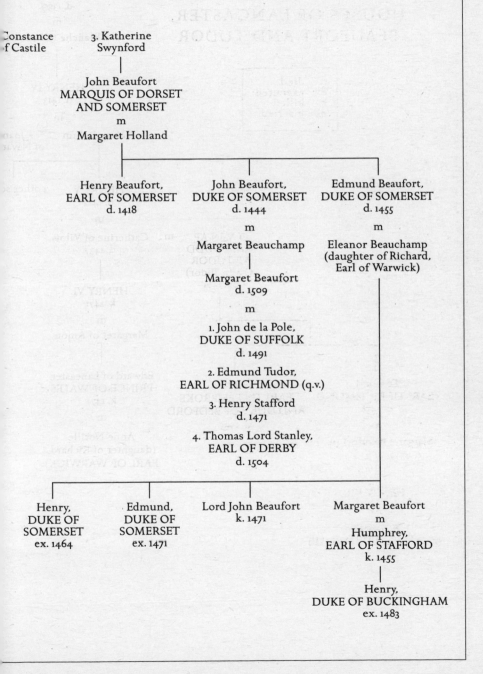

Constance
of Castile

3. Katherine
Swynford

John Beaufort
MARQUIS OF DORSET
AND SOMERSET
m
Margaret Holland

Henry Beaufort,
EARL OF SOMERSET
d. 1418

John Beaufort,
DUKE OF SOMERSET
d. 1444
m
Margaret Beauchamp

Edmund Beaufort,
DUKE OF SOMERSET
d. 1455
m
Eleanor Beauchamp
(daughter of Richard,
Earl of Warwick)

Margaret Beaufort
d. 1509
m

1. John de la Pole,
DUKE OF SUFFOLK
d. 1491

2. Edmund Tudor,
EARL OF RICHMOND (q.v.)

3. Henry Stafford
d. 1471

4. Thomas Lord Stanley,
EARL OF DERBY
d. 1504

Henry,
DUKE OF
SOMERSET
ex. 1464

Edmund,
DUKE OF
SOMERSET
ex. 1471

Lord John Beaufort
k. 1471

Margaret Beaufort
m
Humphrey,
EARL OF STAFFORD
k. 1455

Henry,
DUKE OF BUCKINGHAM
ex. 1483

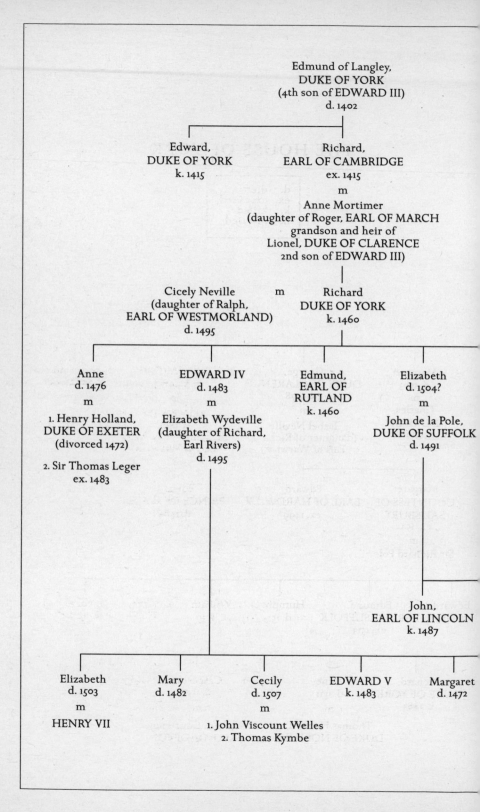

Edmund of Langley,
DUKE OF YORK
(4th son of EDWARD III)
d. 1402

Edward,
DUKE OF YORK
k. 1415

Richard,
EARL OF CAMBRIDGE
ex. 1415
m
Anne Mortimer
(daughter of Roger, EARL OF MARCH
grandson and heir of
Lionel, DUKE OF CLARENCE
2nd son of EDWARD III)

Cicely Neville   m   Richard
(daughter of Ralph,   DUKE OF YORK
EARL OF WESTMORLAND)   k. 1460
d. 1495

Anne   EDWARD IV   Edmund,   Elizabeth
d. 1476   d. 1483   EARL OF   d. 1504?
m   m   RUTLAND   m
1. Henry Holland,   Elizabeth Wydeville k. 1460   John de la Pole,
DUKE OF EXETER   (daughter of Richard,   DUKE OF SUFFOLK
(divorced 1472)   Earl Rivers)   d. 1491
                    d. 1495
2. Sir Thomas Leger
ex. 1483

                                                          John,
                                                          EARL OF LINCOLN
                                                          k. 1487

Elizabeth   Mary   Cecily   EDWARD V   Margaret
d. 1503   d. 1482   d. 1507   k. 1483   d. 1472
m   m
HENRY VII   1. John Viscount Welles
                            2. Thomas Kymbe

THE HOUSE OF YORK

d. died
ex. executed
k. killed
m. married

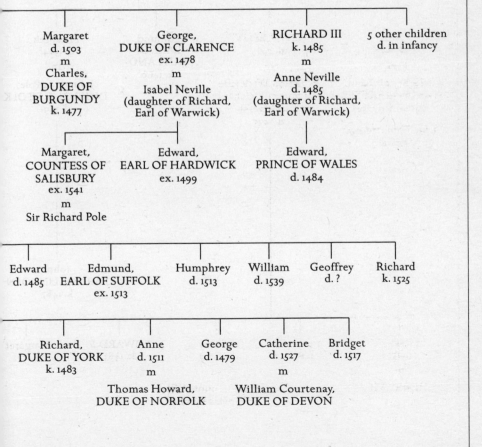

Margaret
d. 1503
m
Charles,
DUKE OF
BURGUNDY
k. 1477

George,
DUKE OF CLARENCE
ex. 1478
m
Isabel Neville
(daughter of Richard,
Earl of Warwick)

RICHARD III
k. 1485
m
Anne Neville
d. 1485
(daughter of Richard,
Earl of Warwick)

5 other children
d. in infancy

Margaret,
COUNTESS OF
SALISBURY
ex. 1541
m
Sir Richard Pole

Edward,
EARL OF HARDWICK
ex. 1499

Edward,
PRINCE OF WALES
d. 1484

Edward
d. 1485

Edmund,
EARL OF SUFFOLK
ex. 1513

Humphrey
d. 1513

William
d. 1539

Geoffrey
d. ?

Richard
k. 1525

Richard,
DUKE OF YORK
k. 1483

Anne
d. 1511
m

George
d. 1479

Catherine
d. 1527
m

Bridget
d. 1517

Thomas Howard,
DUKE OF NORFOLK

William Courtenay,
DUKE OF DEVON

Introduction:
The Demon and Her Heirs

The French Kings of England rose . . . to an eminence which
was the wonder and dread of all neighbouring nations.

Lord Macaulay[1]

In 999 a Plantagenet forebear, Count Fulk the Black of Anjou,
had his young wife, Elisabeth of Vendôme, burned alive in her
wedding dress in the marketplace at his capital of Angers, in
front of the cathedral, after catching her in flagrante with a goatherd.[2] A few days later, all Angers went up in flames, torched by
unknown hands, and the townsmen suspected Fulk. There is no
record of what happened to the goatherd.

The Black Count was just as merciless on campaign, slaying
and destroying, robbing and raping. When, as an old man, he
put down a rebellion by his equally ferocious son, Geoffrey the
Hammer, he made him crawl around the floor in front of his
courtiers, saddled and bridled like a horse, begging for mercy,
while his father screamed, 'You're broken in, broken in!' Yet on
pilgrimages to the Holy Land Fulk ordered his servants to flog
him through the streets of Jerusalem as he howled for God's

forgiveness. The Angevins decided that a devil's blood must run in the veins of their sinister lord.

A story grew up that, while hunting in the depths of a forest, Black Fulk's father or grandfather had met and married on the spot a lady of unearthly beauty but mysterious origin, called Melusine, who bore him four children. She shocked her husband and his court by rarely attending church – if she did, she left Mass after the reading of the Gospel, deliberately missing the most sacred moment, the Consecration. Finally, her husband ordered his knights to intervene: next time she tried to leave they seized hold of her cloak. Melusine reacted by slipping out of the cloak to fly up into the air, vanishing through a church window, with two sons under her arm. Neither the demon countess nor the boys was ever seen again.[3] But she left behind the other sons.

This is the account given by Gerald of Wales, who was a courtier of Henry II and his son Richard I. Gerald's friend, Walter Map, tells a similar tale in his *Courtiers' Trifles*, but tactfully does not mention the Plantagenets. He describes the 'loveliest of girls' who captured the heart of 'Henno with the Big Teeth' and bore him four beautiful children. She too always left Mass before the Consecration, until, when bathing with her maid, her mother-in-law spied on her and, seeing them both change into dragons, had them sprinkled with holy water by a priest, whereupon they shrieked horribly and disappeared through the roof.[4] (Behind this lie two very ancient European myths, those of the wood or water sprite and of the succubus – a female demon who seduces men in dreams.)

According to Gerald of Wales, the tale of Melusine was frequently told by King Richard, who said that with such an ancestor it was not surprising that he and his brothers quarrelled. 'We come from the Devil and we'll end by going to the Devil', joked the Lionheart.[5] What might be termed diabolical genes were part of the family inheritance. 'The things we call aristocracies and reigning houses are the last places to look for masterful men,' John Buchan suggested, just after the First World War. 'They began strongly, but they have been too long in possession. They have been cosseted and comforted, and the devil has gone out of their blood.'[6] Yet until the very end the devil never abandoned Plantagenet blood.

The royal family who reigned longest over the English, descendants of Fulk and the demon, had a strange surname – Plantagenet – which they took from a twelfth-century count who wore a sprig of broom-flower (*Planta genista* in medieval Latin) on his cap. Although the family did not adopt it as a cognomen until 1460, it is used throughout this book to stress the continuity of the line. Academics restrict 'Plantagenet' to the kings from Henry II to Richard II, but the Lancastrians and Yorkists were no less members of the dynasty.

These men from Anjou, who ended as the most English of the English, not only spearheaded the merger of Normans and Anglo-Saxons into a nation but saved the country from disintegrating into separatist parts. Henry II rebuilt England after the anarchy left by King Stephen, although there were further attempts to undo this good work, not least with the revolt of Henry's sons in the 1170s; and even as late as the fifteenth century rebel magnates allied with the Welsh leader Owain Glyndwr to divide England between them, to be defeated by Henry IV. The Plantagenets began the colonization of Ireland and conquered Wales, if they failed to absorb Scotland. During the Hundred Years War they overran north-western France, creating an Anglo-French dual monarchy – Paris was occupied for nearly fifteen years, Normandy for thirty. However, it all ended in defeat abroad and bankruptcy at home. Divided between Lancaster and York, the family was destroyed by the series of dynastic murders and battles that became known as the Wars of the Roses, its last king dying at Bosworth in 1485.

Although they produced gifted rulers, four Plantagenets were murdered, two came close to deposition, and another was killed in battle by rebels – as Richard I had predicted, there was a diabolical streak until the end. Shakespeare's tragedies have shaped the way in which we see no less than six of them.

This book is an attempt to provide non-specialists with a short, readable, easily accessible overview of the whole dynasty in one volume. It is based on the major contemporary sources and also reflects recent research – I use quotations from earlier historians when they are more telling than those from modern academics. At the same time, it is a very personal interpretation of my reading across the years – and no doubt, some people may disagree with how I see Henry V or Richard III.

Timeline

1152   Henry Fitz-Empress marries Eleanor of Aquitaine

1153   Treaty of Wallingford – King Stephen recognizes
Henry as heir to the English throne

HENRY II

1162   Thomas Becket becomes Archbishop of Canterbury

1164   Constitutions of Clarendon
Thomas Becket goes into exile

1166   Assize of Clarendon

1170   Murder of Thomas Becket

1172   Henry conquers Ireland

1173   Rebellion of Henry's son, the 'Young King'

1174   Defeat of the Young King's rebellion

1187   Henry quarrels with his son and heir, Richard

1189   Richard openly rebels, aided by Philip II of France –
death of Henry II

RICHARD I

1190–2   Richard on Crusade

1193   Richard, a captive of the emperor

1194   Richard's return to England

1194–9 Richard's war in France against Philip II

1199   Death of Richard I

JOHN

1203   John murders his nephew, Arthur of Brittany

1204   Philip II conquers Normandy, Anjou, Maine and most of Poitou

1205   English barons refuse to help John reconquer his lands in France

1207   Stephen Langton made Archbishop of Canterbury – John refuses to accept him

1208   Pope Innocent III places England under an interdict

1210   John campaigns in Ireland

1211   John subdues Llewelyn ap Iorwerth in north Wales – Llewelyn counter-attacks

1212   English barons plot to murder John

1213   John becomes the pope's vassal

1214   John's campaign in France wrecked by his German allies' defeat at Bouvines

1215   John forced to grant Magna Carta

1216   Civil war between John and the barons, who invite Louis of France to replace him

1216   Death of John

HENRY III

1216   Henry crowned at Gloucester

1217   William Marshal routs the barons and the French at Lincoln

        Louis of France concedes defeat

1219   Hubert de Burgh becomes justiciar

1230	Henry's unsuccessful campaign in France
1231	Systematic attacks on papal tax collectors in England
1232	Dismissal of Hubert de Burgh
	Stephen de Segrave becomes justiciar – government run by Peter des Roches
1234	Henry rules as his own first minister
1242	Henry's defeat at Taillebourg
1255	Henry accepts the crown of Sicily for his son Edmund
1258	The Provisions of Oxford
1264	The Mise of Amiens – Louis IX decides in favour of Henry
	Simon de Montfort refuses to accept Louis's decision
	Henry defeated at Lewes by Simon, who rules England as Lord Steward
1265	The Lord Edward defeats and kills Simon de Montfort at Evesham
1270	Edward goes on Crusade
1272	Death of Henry III

EDWARD I

1275	First Statute of Westminster
1277	Defeat of Llewelyn ap Gruffydd
1279	Statute of Mortmain
1282	Final conquest of Wales
1285	Statute of Merchants
1290	Expulsion of the Jews
1291	Parliament of Norham to discuss Scottish succession
1294	Philip IV invades Gascony
	Rebellion of Madog ap Llewelyn
1296	Edward conquers Scotland

1297	William Wallace defeats the English at Stirling
	Barons refuse to fight in Gascony
1298	Edward destroys Wallace's army at Falkirk
1304	All Scotland submits to Edward
1306	Robert the Bruce revolts against English rule
1307	Death of Edward I

EDWARD II

1308	Exile of Edward II's favourite, Piers Gaveston
1312	Murder of Gaveston
1314	Scots defeat the English at Bannockburn
1318	Edward accepts ordinances limiting his power
1322	Earl of Lancaster defeated at Boroughbridge and executed
1322	Edward defeated by Scots at Old Byland
1322	Despensers' tyranny
1326	Queen Isabella and Mortimer invade – fall of the Despensers
1327	Edward II abdicates

EDWARD III

1329	Treaty of Northampton recognizes Scottish independence
1330	Edward III overthrows Mortimer
1333	English archers annihilate the Scots at Halidon Hill
1337	Edward claims the French crown
1340	Edward defeats the French fleet at Sluys
1346	English defeat the French at Crécy
	English defeat the Scots at Neville's Cross

1347	English capture Calais
1348	Black Death
1349	Ordinance of Labourers
1355	Black Prince's campaign in France
1356	Black Prince defeats the French at Poitiers, capturing King John II
1360	Treaty of Brétigny gives Aquitaine to the English
1369	Charles V 'confiscates' Aquitaine
1372	Castilians defeat English fleet off La Rochelle
1373	Failure of John of Gaunt's campaign – loss of Aquitaine
1376	Death of the Black Prince
1377	Death of Edward III

RICHARD II

1381	The Peasants' Revolt
1387	Royal army defeated by Lords Appellant at Radcot Bridge
1388	The Merciless Parliament purges Richard's supporters
1389	Richard regains control
	Peace with France
1394	Richard's Irish campaign
1397	Murder of Thomas, Duke of Gloucester
	Richard's revenge on the Lords Appellant
1398	Richard's despotism
	Gaunt's son, Bolingbroke, is exiled
1399	Gaunt dies and his estates are confiscated
	Richard's new campaign in Ireland
	Bolingbroke seizes the throne

HENRY IV

1400	Owain Glyndwr's revolt
1403	Henry defeats the Percys at Shrewsbury
1405	Archbishop Scrope's rebellion
	Henry struck down by disease
1407	French invade Gascony, unsuccessfully
1408	Northumberland and Lord Bardolf defeated and killed at Bramham Moor
1409	Surrender of Harlech Castle – defeat of Owain Glyndwr
1411	English expedition to help Burgundians against Armagnacs
1412	Henry quarrels with his heir, Prince Henry
1413	Death of Henry IV

HENRY V

1414	Lollard plot
1415	Southampton plot
	Battle of Agincourt
1417	Henry invades Normandy
1419	Rouen falls to Henry
	John, Duke of Burgundy, assassinated – Burgundians ally with England
1420	Treaty of Troyes – Charles VI recognizes Henry as 'Heir and Regent of France'
	English occupy Paris
1422	Death of Henry V

HENRY VI

1424 Duke of Bedford, Regent of France, routs the
      Dauphinists at Verneuil

1429 Joan of Arc relieves Orléans

1431 Joan of Arc burned at Rouen
      Coronation at Paris of Henry VI as King of France

1435 Treaty of Arras – Burgundians abandon alliance with
      England

1436 French recapture Paris

1444 Truce of Tours between French and English

1445 Henry marries Margaret of Anjou

1447 Death of Humphrey, Duke of Gloucester

1448 English surrender Maine

1449 French invade Normandy – Rouen falls

1450 English defeat at Formigny – loss of Normandy
      Jack Cade occupies London

1451 English lose Gascony

1452 Duke of York's rising
      Lord Talbot reoccupies Gascony

1453 Talbot defeated at Castillon – Gascony finally lost
      Henry VI goes insane
      Birth of Henry's son, Henry of Lancaster

1454 Duke of York becomes Lord Protector
      King Henry regains his sanity

1455 First Battle of St Albans, won by York
      York's second protectorate

1456 End of York's second protectorate

1459 'Rout of Ludford' – York and his allies flee from
      England

1460   Yorkist victory at Northampton
        Parliament recognizes York as heir to the throne
        York defeated and killed at Wakefield
1461   Yorkist victory at Mortimer's Cross
        Lancastrian victory at second Battle of St Albans
        Edward, Earl of March, proclaimed king in London

EDWARD IV

1461   Edward IV wins a decisive victory at Towton
1462   Surrender of last Lancastrian garrisons in
        Northumberland
1464   Edward IV marries Elizabeth Wydeville
        Duke of Somerset's rebellion defeated at Hexham
1465   Capture of Henry V in Lancashire
1469   Edward survives plot by the Earl of Warwick and the
        Duke of Clarence
1470   Warwick's reconciliation with Margaret of Anjou
1470   Flight of Edward IV and restoration of Henry VI
1471   Edward defeats and kills Warwick at Barnet
        Edward defeats last Lancastrian army at Tewkesbury
        Murder of Henry VI
1475   Edward invades France but makes peace with Louis XI
1478   Murder of the Duke of Clarence
1483   Death of Edward IV – Duke of Gloucester becomes
        Protector

EDWARD V

1483   Deposition of Edward V

RICHARD III

1483   Gloucester becomes Richard III
        Failure of Buckingham's rebellion
1485   Richard III killed at Bosworth
1499   Execution of the Earl of Warwick, last male
        Plantagenet

PART 1

The First Plantagenets

1

The First Plantagenets

Fulk Nerra, Fulk the Black, is the greatest of the Angevins, the first in whom we can trace that marked type of character which their house was to preserve with a fatal constancy through two hundred years

John Richard Green[1]

A little knowledge of their ancestors helps us to understand the first Plantagenets. The earliest to make his mark was a Breton outlaw called Tertulle the Forester, half woodman and half bandit, who, in the ninth century, fought Viking invaders from a stronghold in the dense woods overlooking the Loire known as the 'Blackbird's Nest'. Although he and his son Ingelger are semi-mythical figures, Ingelger's son Fulk the Red (*c.*870–942) certainly existed, acquiring the old Roman hill town of Angers and becoming Count of Anjou.

The savagery of the wife-burner Fulk III (987–1040) shocked contemporaries. In 992 the Black Count defeated the Bretons, killing their duke with his own hands, while in 1025 he reduced

Saumur to ashes, massacring its inhabitants after capturing its lord, the Count of Maine, by false promises. These were only the best-known victims during a saga in which he and his son, Geoffrey the Hammer, transformed an obscure county into one of the most powerful feudal lordships in France. Eastward, they conquered Blois and Tours, southward Saumur and Chinon, won by battles or sieges, held down by tiny garrisons in small stone towers – Fulk's favourite lair in old age was the tower of Durtal near Baugé.[2]

Geoffrey the Hammer was succeeded by his son-in-law, Geoffrey of Gâtinais, whose heirs inherited Black Fulk's wolfish qualities. If they paid homage to the French king as overlord, the Counts of Anjou were independent of a monarch whose real authority was restricted to a small area around Paris.

Geoffrey V (called 'Plantagenet' from his broom-flower badge) became Count of Anjou in 1129 after his father, Fulk V, left France to become King (by marriage) of Jerusalem. Geoffrey's barons thought a pleasant-mannered boy of fifteen must be easy game and so they rebelled; but he soon disillusioned them by marrying the widow of the Holy Roman Emperor Henry V, Matilda, who was also the daughter of Henry I, King of England and Duke of Normandy. Ten years older, a beautiful virago, she made the same mistake as the barons and tried to bully her young husband. As a result she was sent back to England. After much wrangling, her father King Henry made Count Geoffrey take her back – she was now sufficiently tamed to produce children, although after she had done her duty the couple lived apart. Henry hoped the marriage would defuse the quarrel with Anjou over the county of Maine, but when the king died in 1135 Geoffrey was contemplating invasion.

Geoffrey had matured into a tall, yellow-haired, handsome man, a fine soldier, with a taste for books rare in somebody who was not a cleric. His worst fault was self-indulgence where girls or hunting were concerned. There was a streak of the Black Count in him – any magnate who disputed his authority received short shrift – and he was determined to preserve his son's inheritance in both England and Normandy.

It was generally expected that Matilda would succeed her father Henry I on the English throne and at Rouen. A huge personality who roared out his commands, this last Norman king had made his barons and prelates swear loyalty to Matilda after the drowning of his only legitimate son, William, in the *White Ship*. Even though they had no say in the matter, his Anglo-Saxon subjects may well have approved the succession. They knew that her mother, another Matilda (originally Edith), had been the daughter of King Malcolm of Scots and his English Queen Margaret – sister of Edgar Atheling and granddaughter of the heroic King Edmund Ironside.

Henry never forgot the example of his father William I, who had claimed to be Edward the Confessor's heir. Despite replacing the old Anglo-Saxon aristocracy by Normans, the Conqueror declared, 'It is my will and command that all shall have and hold the law of King Edward in respect of all their lands and all their possessions.'[3] Like William, Henry took the old coronation oaths, promising to keep the Confessor's laws, and ruled through Anglo-Saxon hundred and shire courts. He gave the son who predeceased him the title 'Atheling' borne by pre-Conquest heirs to the throne, while his choice of an English wife irked courtiers so much that they nicknamed the royal couple 'Godwy and Godgifu'. Although the Conqueror had introduced feudalism (which, basically, meant military service in return for land tenure), by preserving pre-Conquest legal tradition, Henry hastened the transformation of Norman settlers into Englishmen.

But when Henry died in 1135, it was not a direct heir that took up claim to the throne but Stephen of Blois, Count of Boulogne, whose mother had been a daughter of William the Conqueror, hurried over to London and persuaded the council to let him take the throne. The great Anglo-Norman lords, the tenants-in-chief, rejected Matilda, partly because they did not

care to be ruled by a woman and partly because they had suffered from her husband's raids on Normandy. Stephen was even
accepted as king by Matilda's bastard half-brother Robert, Earl
of Gloucester, the richest magnate in England.

At first, the new king ingratiated himself by his friendliness,
sitting down to eat with all comers, regardless of rank.[4] Yet he
turned out to be a disaster – 'a mild, good humoured, easy-
going man, who never punished anybody', says *The Anglo-Saxon
Chronicle*,[5] and let his Flemish, Breton and Basque mercenaries
plunder to their hearts' content. Squandering the treasure left
by the Norman kings (including gold vases filled with rubies,
emeralds and sapphires), he ran out of money and debased the
coinage. The Archdeacon of Huntingdon writes, 'there was no
peace in the realm [of England] but all was destroyed by murder, burning and rapine, with the sounds of war, wailing and
terror everywhere'.[6] *The Anglo-Saxon Chronicle* tells the same
story: 'In the days of this king there was nothing but strife, evil
and robbery.'[7] He confiscated castles from barons he disliked
and upset bishops by questioning their privileges.

Then Stephen made the mistake of quarrelling with Robert
of Gloucester, who invited Matilda to take the king's place; her
supporters, meanwhile, were rebelling all over England. The
'Lady of the English' (an old Anglo-Saxon title) as she styled
herself, landed at Arundel in 1139. Two years later, the king
was defeated and captured at Lincoln, and imprisoned at Bristol
while Matilda occupied London. Walter Map says she was partly
good, but mostly evil. Her haughtiness upset the Londoners and,
instead of granting their petition for lower taxes, she ordered
them to pay more. Just as the Lady of the English was sitting
down to dinner at Westminster soon after her arrival, an armed
mob marched on the palace and chased her out of London.

Behind King Stephen stood another fearsome virago, his
queen (also called Matilda), who was determined he should
keep the crown and hand it on to their son Eustace – who had
recently married Louis VII's sister. After Stephen was taken

prisoner at Lincoln, angered by the Lady's refusal to let Eustace inherit even his father's original patrimony on the other side of the Channel, the queen gathered a new royal army to fight for the king's restoration.

The Lady of the English had re-established her court at Winchester, the old royal capital, but, in the wake of these events, was driven out in September 1141, riding astride like a man. Terrified, she continued her flight in a litter hung between two horses, looking like a corpse – some said she hid inside a coffin. Robert of Gloucester was captured and exchanged for King Stephen, who returned to his capital. But Matilda regained her nerve. In December 1142, while besieged at Oxford, she muffled herself in white during a blizzard and was let down by ropes at night on to the frozen moat. With three white-clad knights as escort, she slipped through the enemy lines, walking through the snow to Abingdon, where they found horses and made good their escape.

Stalemate ensued. A time-server with 'the mouth of a lion and the heart of a rabbit' (in King Stephen's view),[8] Robert stayed on the defensive in his city of Bristol, while the Lady sulked in her castle at Devizes which, although Henry of Huntingdon thought it the most splendid in Europe,[9] was scarcely a capital. The king kept only the south-east and some isolated outposts. His opponents ruled the West, the Welsh border and East Anglia, while the Scots occupied Northumberland, Cumbria and northern Lancashire.

Central government had collapsed, replaced by warlords whose mercenaries operated from 'castles' – stockades with wooden watchtowers on top of mounds or Iron Age hill forts. The chronicles are full of atrocities committed by 'castle-men', who left people eating dogs and horses. 'Never did a country endure more misery,' wrote a Peterborough monk in the final pages of *The Anglo-Saxon Chronicle*. 'If the ground was tilled the earth bore no corn, for the land was ruined by such doings; and men said openly that Christ and his saints slept.'[10]

2

The Eagle – Henry II

The painting shows an eagle with four of its young perching
on it, one on each wing with a third on its back, tearing the
parent with beaks and talons, while a fourth just as big as the
others stands on its neck, waiting for a chance to peck out
its eyes

Gerald of Wales[1]

The first campaign of Henry fitz-Empress

In spring 1147, just after his fourteenth birthday, a red-headed,
freckle-faced boy landed at Wareham in Dorset, to wage war on
the king who had stolen his heritage. His troops were young
cronies and a few mercenaries – he must have been very eloquent for them to risk their lives on a perilous adventure when
he could offer only promises in lieu of pay.

Marching inland, he attacked two Wiltshire castles, Cricklade
and Purton, whose garrisons were threatening his mother at
Devizes. However, Cricklade easily repulsed his scratch force,

as did Purton. Unpaid, his men began to desert. Henry rushed to Devizes, begging his mother for money, but she was penniless. His uncle, Robert of Gloucester, refused to help. Finally, he wrote and asked the king for funds. Hoping to get rid of the boy, Stephen paid him to go home to France, instead of trying to catch a rival who, despite his youth, was already dangerous. By the end of May 1147 Henry was back in Normandy.

If his expedition was a mere teenage adventure, to his adherents he became a king over the water. Yet no other English monarch had to fight harder for his inheritance than Henry fitz-Empress. And, after he succeeded, his achievement was nearly destroyed by his rebellious sons, the young eagles who were depicted in a mural at Winchester.

The pretender

Henry was born at Le Mans on 5 March 1133. His first visit to England began in November 1142 when he was brought over from France by his Uncle Robert. Landing at Wareham, they fought their way ashore, recapturing the port from Stephen's supporters before marching to Bristol. There the boy saw plenty of military activity, the Earl Robert's troops regularly raiding areas controlled by the king. Henry stayed at the castle, tutored by a Master Matthew and the canons of the local abbey, before returning to Anjou towards the end of 1143. He then received an education of a sort given to few laymen, learning to read, write and speak Latin. Throughout his life he remained fond of books, fluent Latin helping him to understand the law and communicate on equal terms with bureaucrats.

Meanwhile, having overthrown Stephen's regime in Normandy and been formally accepted as duke by right of his wife, Geoffrey Plantagenet ruled Normandy ruthlessly. (When the canons of Séez elected as bishop a certain Arnulf, of whom Geoffrey disapproved, he had him castrated, making the chapter process through the city carrying Arnulf's severed member in a basin – to show he was a eunuch and could not function as a bishop – then blandly denied any involvement.[2]) But in England, despite hopes raised by Henry's foray, Matilda's cause seemed lost when Earl Robert died. Early in 1148 the 'Lady of the English' went to Normandy where she remained in pious retirement until her death in 1167.

King Stephen was never secure, as a result of his own sheer ineptitude. One example of this was his clumsy persecution of prelates whom he suspected of supporting the empress – when he banished Archbishop Theobald of Canterbury, the archbishop simply moved to Norfolk, an area outside royal control.[3] Moreover, Geoffrey's conquest of Normandy put the English barons in a quandary. If they remained loyal to Stephen their Norman estates would be forfeit, but if they supported Geoffrey they would lose their lands in England.

During spring 1149 Henry fitz-Empress returned to England, to Carlisle where he was knighted by his great-uncle, David I, King of Scots. Several English magnates joined them, planning to attack York, but scattered when Stephen appeared with an army. The king set up roadblocks along the main roads to catch Henry, fleeing south from Lancashire; however, he avoided capture by using byways under cover of darkness. Learning Henry was on his way to Bristol, Stephen's son Eustace marched through the night in pursuit, mounting three ambushes, but, somehow, Henry reached Bristol. When he moved to Dorset, where he harried royal supporters, the king marched westward, hoping that the boy would give battle. Wisely, Henry's advisers persuaded him to go back to Normandy.

Soon after, Count Geoffrey gave Henry the duchy of Normandy, and Henry was duly invested as duke at Rouen Cathedral, with the ducal lance, sword and coronet. Louis VII initially refused to recognize the investiture, summoning Eustace to help him evict the new duke, but their campaign failed dismally. Louis finally accepted the situation and in the summer Henry went to Paris, where he did homage to the king for the duchy. Geoffrey then announced that he would invade England. However, he died in September, aged only thirty-nine, leaving Anjou, Maine and Touraine to Henry, save for a handful of castles he bequeathed to his second son. Henry erected a tomb to his father in the cathedral at Le Mans, surmounted by his effigy on a superb enamel plaque. But Geoffrey's best monument is his name – 'Plantagenet'.

In 1152 Stephen attempted to have Eustace crowned king, to ensure his succession. 'Open-handed wherever he went, he enjoyed being generous,' the *Gesta Stephani* says of Eustace. 'Because he took after his father, he treated men as equals.'[4] But the same writer admits that Eustace had a vicious streak, ordering his troops 'to show the ferocity of wild beasts'. An evil man is how *The Anglo-Saxon Chronicle* sees him: 'Wherever he went he did more evil than good – he robbed the land, levying heavy taxes.'[5] Whatever the truth of the matter, Pope Eugenius forbade the English bishops to crown Eustace.

Henry's position grew stronger when Eleanor of Aquitaine became his wife in 1152. Her marriage to Louis VII had recently been annulled, on grounds of consanguinity, although in reality because she had failed to produce a son. Lurid rumours surrounded her, such as her having slept with her new husband's father – credited by Walter Map, who thought that in marrying Henry she was committing incest and brought a curse on their children. None the less, 'incomparable' is how the monk Richard of Devizes describes Eleanor. 'Beautiful but gracious, strong but kind, unpretentious but wise, an unusual mixture in a woman.'[6] Her assets outweighed her bad name as Aquitaine stretched from Poitou to the Pyrenees, meaning that Henry now ruled more of France than King Louis. Within a month he was at Barfleur, preparing to invade England.

Suddenly, however, joined by Eustace, Louis struck at Normandy, while Henry's brother, another Geoffrey, rose in Anjou. 'Nearly all the Normans thought Duke Henry would lose everything,' wrote the Abbot of Mont Saint-Michel.[7]

They were mistaken. Reacting so fast that some of his men's horses dropped dead, Henry laid waste Louis's lands across the Norman border with such savagery that the French king asked for a truce; Henry then swung south and crushed Geoffrey.

In the meantime, Stephen was trying to eliminate Plantagenet strongholds before the invasion, tightening his blockade of Wallingford Castle in north Berkshire, whose garrison implored Henry to send a relief force or let them surrender. His response was to come in person, landing on Epiphany 1153 with 140 knights and 3,000 foot soldiers. Entering a church for Mass, the first words he heard were Psalm 71, 'Give to the king thy judgment, O God: and to the king's son thy justice', which he took as a good omen. He then attacked Malmesbury in Wiltshire, one of Stephen's own strongpoints, laying siege to the castle. This forced the king and Eustace (who had hurried back from France) to leave Wallingford and confront Henry.

Beneath a freezing downpour the two armies faced each other across the swollen River Avon, rain blowing into the faces of Stephen's troops, whose hands became so cold that they could scarcely grip swords dripping with water. The king lost his nerve, retreating to London, aware that his barons had reached secret agreements with the duke, who was threatening their Norman estates. A truce was negotiated, leaving Wallingford in peace for six months and letting the Malmesbury garrison march out in safety.

Henry then marched through the Midlands, capturing fortresses and being joined by more and more barons. In July he began demolishing the enemy's siege works at Wallingford, until the king and Eustace arrived with a bigger army. But Stephen's barons refused to fight. Like the *Gesta Stephani*'s author, even those who supported the king saw Henry as the lawful heir to the throne. Reluctantly, Stephen agreed to open negotiations for a lasting peace.

Infuriated, Eustace ravaged East Anglia, trying to provoke Henry into fighting. In August he arrived at Bury St Edmunds, wrecking the abbey's lands when it refused to lend him money, after which he dined in its refectory – and choked to death. Queen Matilda was dead and, although he had other sons, Stephen gave up. All he wanted was to die on the throne. In November he met the duke at Winchester, agreeing that Henry should succeed him and that stolen lands should be restored to those who had held them in 1135.

In December Stephen issued a charter recognizing the duke as his heir and promising to demolish over 1,100 castles. The settlement did not go smoothly, Henry grumbling that the king was slow in pulling down the castles. When some Flemish mercenaries plotted to kill him, Henry went back to Normandy, staying there until Stephen died from a haemorrhage in October 1154.

The restorer

All over England crowds thundered 'Vivat Rex' when Henry II was crowned by Archbishop Theobald of Canterbury at Westminster Abbey on 7 December 1154. Londoners gaped at the short French cloak worn by this battle-scarred veteran of twenty-one, calling him 'court-mantle', which shows how foreign he seemed. Yet, although a Frenchman from top to toe, Henry was a great-great-grandson of the hero King Edmund Ironside through his grandmother (Henry I's queen), and as early as 1139 a Norman chronicler had claimed he represented England's old rulers. 'Nowadays, no earl, bishop or abbot is an Englishman', the great monk-historian William of Malmesbury who was himself half-English, had written thirty years before. 'Newcomers eat up the riches and the very guts of England, nor is there any hope of ending such misery.'[8] But by 1154 speaking French was a sign of class rather than race.[9]

Whatever their class or race, Henry's subjects would have been struck by his appearance. Stocky, bull-necked, slightly above average height, with coarse, reddish skin and bulging eyes, he had red hair that was close-cropped. His clothes were as rough as his looks, his one jewel a gold signet ring engraved with a lion. If quiet-spoken, his manner was brutally direct.

Presumably, he inspected his new capital. William fitz Stephen described it later in the reign, boasting of the Tower and the Palace of Westminster upstream, of walls with seven double gates and many towers, of thirteen great churches and 126 smaller ones. He praises its spacious gardens and healthy air, tells how it was bordered by pastures, cornfields and meadows and a forest full of deer, and how the Thames teemed with fish. He mentions cook shops where it was possible to get venison, sturgeon or guineafowl, and extols the capital's pleasures – tournaments on the river, hunting and hawking outside the walls. But, recalling Le Mans and Rouen, the king may not have been so enthusiastic, while the queen no doubt missed Paris and Poitiers.

Henry soon left London, travelling all over the kingdom to rebuild government. The administrative framework of Henry I's day still existed: the most senior official was the justiciar (regent in the king's absence overseas), a role often filled by the chancellor, who, with other senior royal servants, formed the court of the Great Council (*Curia Regis*), which met at Westminster Hall, hearing appeals and controlling finances. To help him, the king appointed a new chancellor, a flamboyant canon-lawyer named Thomas Becket, who had studied at Paris and was recommended by Archbishop Theobald.

Within months William Peverell of the Peak lost his huge estates, retiring to a monastery, while William of Aumale, who controlled Yorkshire, surrendered his strongholds, as did Hugh de Mortimer and Hugh of Hereford on the Welsh Marches. Many lesser lords were tamed. By 1157 the king had expelled the Scots from the northern counties and retaken castles seized by the Welsh. Demolishing illegal fortresses, he frightened 'castlemen' into leaving the country 'so quickly, they appeared to vanish like ghosts', writes William of Newburgh. William adds, 'his primary concern was restoring order and he took care to ensure the law's full strength returned to England, where under King Stephen it seemed dead and buried. He appointed men to administer proper justice in every region of the realm and see laws were kept, keeping down criminals and deciding disputes . . . if they got it wrong or were too lenient, he put matters right with a royal ordinance.'[10]

The Exchequer at Westminster (so called from a black and white cloth on the table around which its officials sat) looked after the revenue. In Henry I's time it had met only at Easter and Michaelmas, chaired by the king or the justiciar, to audit accounts and question sheriffs about tax discrepancies, although it also supervised the collection of income from royal estates and forests, using notched wooden tally sticks as receipts and sheepskin scrolls as records (the Pipe Rolls). Under the new king it centralized financial control and, from an occasional committee, became an institution with a permanent staff.[11] Royal estates lost under Stephen were recovered while sheriffs who pocketed taxes were prosecuted.

More and more English wool was being sold to Flemish weavers, so in 1158 merchants were given a better currency – silver pence containing 10 per cent more bullion than before. (In 1180 another new coinage appeared, with an even bigger silver content.) To help credit facilities the king encouraged Jewish moneylenders to settle in English cities.

What made Henry rich, however, was the legal system, to which he made a lasting contribution, introducing circuit judges, writs and twelve-man juries. He was determined England should be ruled by custom and precedent as under his Anglo-Saxon predecessors. Realizing that a central legal system would increase the Crown's authority and its revenue, he combined into one the royal court (*Curia Regis*), the shire courts and the hundred baronial and manorial courts. He sent out Exchequer officials as his personal representatives; they travelled the country with armed escorts and sat in the courts next to the sheriffs, trying criminals, and dealing with disputes over land and property. All serious offences – murder, rape, robbery – were heard by these royal 'justices in eyre', forerunners of today's circuit judges. Procedure was standardized, so that there could be no confusion about the law's meaning.

Echoing Anglo-Saxon tradition, the justices summoned a panel of twelve reliable men to report anyone suspected of ill-doing and asked it if those 'presented' were guilty, a practice that became the jury system. Some justices stayed at Westminster, forming a tribunal – the origin of the courts of King's Bench and Common Pleas. Recovering land stolen during Stephen's reign was solved by the sheriffs issuing writs: one writ ordered the offender to give it back – if he refused, another summoned twelve neighbours to declare on oath who was the rightful owner. The main document setting out these reforms was the Assize of Clarendon, drawn up early in 1166, and supplemented a few years later by the Assizes of Northampton. Clarendon marks the beginning of the Common Law.[12]

After Clarendon, annual royal income rose from £13,000 to over £20,000, largely thanks to fines levied under the new system. Another source was feudal dues, collected more efficiently following a survey of the Crown's major tenants. Instead of summoning knights to serve in his army or garrison his castles, the king made them pay shield money (scutage) and ward-money, which enabled him to hire mercenaries. His castles became treasure houses in which dungeons were crammed with bullion.[13]

Government had never broken down in Normandy and Anjou, while southwards it did not exist, authority belonging to the local aristocracy. Henry's problems here were rebellious barons and protecting his frontiers. When his brother Geoffrey, whom the Bretons had chosen to be their ruler, died in 1157 he succeeded him as Duke of Brittany, diplomacy securing the border castles of the Vexin and giving eastern Normandy a vital line of defence. A campaign to add Toulouse to his territory was a failure, but one he would rectify within a few years.

The man

Two stories explain why his subjects liked Henry II. When he called Bishop Roger of Worcester a traitor for not coming to court, the bishop (who was Robert of Gloucester's son) retorted that the king was ungrateful after all his brothers had done to help him gain the Crown – he had taken away three-quarters of the family estates, letting one brother grow so poor that he had been forced to join the Hospitallers: 'That's how you repay family and friends, that's what people get for helping you.' When some sycophant rebuked Roger, Henry told the man he was an oaf: 'Don't think that because I speak as I like to my cousin the bishop it gives you a right to insult him.' Then he asked Roger to dinner, during which they had a very friendly discussion.[14]

Bishop Hugh of Lincoln angered the king by excommunicating a royal forester who ill-treated peasants. Next time he came to court, Henry, sitting on the ground and stitching a finger-stall, ignored him. Calmly taking a seat next to the king, Hugh whispered, 'You look like your cousins at Falaise' – alluding to William the Conqueror's mother, daughter of a tanner. Henry laughed so much that he rolled on the ground, before explaining the joke to his courtiers.[15]

Because Henry fascinated chroniclers, we know a lot about him. Gerald of Wales recalls bloodshot eyes flaming with rage, a big paunch, a mania for hunting, inattention at Mass. He says the king regularly broke treaties, comparing his greed for money to that of Elisha's covetous servant, Gehazi. Even so, Gerald praises Henry's humanity, his pity for those who fell in battle and preference for a peaceful solution; for example, when things went badly, nobody was more courteous. Gerald also states that Henry never altered his opinion of anyone he disliked on first sight and rarely changed his mind about somebody to whom he took a liking.

'In making laws and improving government he showed extreme intelligence, very clever at finding new, unexpected ways of getting what he wanted,' says Walter Map, Gerald's fellow courtier. 'He was always affable, polite, unassuming. In troubled times, he never complained. But on his endless journeys he travelled like a common carrier and did not bother about accommodation, showing no consideration for his entourage . . . He spent whole nights without sleep, seemingly tireless . . . personally, I think his excessive activity was not so much due to lack of self-control as fear of growing fat.'

Map stresses the king's accessibility. 'Whenever he went outside, he was mobbed by crowds, pulled this way and that, dragged along. Astonishingly, he listened patiently to what they were saying even when being yelled at or violently shoved and pushed, never rebuking anybody or using it as an excuse to lose his temper. If the pestering became really unbearable, he stayed calm, retreating to a quieter place. He was never proud or puffed up . . .'[16]

Map also describes how Henry reimbursed skippers wrecked while shipping his court across the Channel. Courtiers dreaded these crossings in tiny, clinker-built transports, particularly during winter. So did the king, who had his own ship, the *Esnecca* ('Sea-Snake'), and went to confession before embarking – sailing on lucky feast days such as Candlemas or postponing a voyage because of an ill omen. Such fears are understandable. In March 1170, 400 courtiers, including the royal physician, were drowned en route from Normandy.

On land, Henry lived on horseback as his realm stretched from the Tweed to the Pyrenees, from the Shannon to the verge of the Ile de France. Much of his time was spent hearing law cases and drafting charters. His entourage dropped from exhaustion, his secretary Peter of Blois recalling how the king stopped at places with shelter for himself but none for courtiers. After wandering by night for miles through dense woodland, they would come to blows over who should sleep in a pigsty.

Clarendon and court life

One of the places in England where Henry could relax was Clarendon, 'in which I delight above all other'.[17] On a low hill amid woodland, 3 miles from Salisbury, this was a hunting lodge he transformed into a palace around a courtyard, with chambers where he could sulk, an aisled hall 50 ft wide and 80 ft long for assemblies, wooden cloisters where he walked in wet weather, and a huge wine cellar. Yet Clarendon can have been scarcely more comfortable than his castles. Rooms reserved for royal privacy were mere closets, while, save for a few portable windows of oiled cloth, there was no glazing, only wooden shutters, which in winter meant choosing between rain, snow or darkness. The air was thick with smoke, its sole exit through holes in the roof.

A large deer park contained the fallow buck that was the principal game, although red deer, boar and hare were also hunted. Henry set off at daybreak, riding into the woods and up into the hills, says Gerald of Wales. From Shrovetide to midsummer he pursued the otter. Walter Map comments on his knowledge of hawks as well as hounds, and he flew peregrines and gyrfalcons, possibly even sea eagles. Brutal game laws cowed poachers of whatever class in the royal forests (game parks) that covered a third of England

Yet, as a Frenchman who spent only a third of his reign in England, Henry's favourite residence in his entire lands was not Clarendon but Chinon. On a low hill over the Vienne before it flows into the Loire, this key stronghold was the nerve centre of Plantagenet France and the 'defensive pivot' of his empire.[18] He replaced its old buildings with a massive fortress, from whose tall keep (the 'Tower of the Mill') watch could be kept for miles around.

Gifted men were attracted to Henry's court, hoping for a bishopric or a lucrative office, although Gerald of Wales called it a hell. It was regulated with impressive ceremony, by heralds who blew trumpets and marshals with wands. Despite preferring rough clothes, on formal occasions Henry wore rich robes and, from the 1170s, was '*rex dei gratia*' in charters – addressed as 'Lord King' in French or Latin, or 'God hold thee, King' in English.[19] Petitioners knelt before him or threw themselves on their faces.

There were men at court who discussed Plutarch between the hunting and the drinking bouts. Henry enjoyed their conversation while they respected his intellect. Gerald praises his memory and knowledge of history, Map his command of languages, Peter of Blois his fondness for reading and learned discussion. (Like all medieval men he read aloud, to himself.) Fifteen books are known to have been dedicated to him, which shows their authors thought he might at least look at them. The authors included the Exchequer official Richard fitz-Neale, the jurist Ranulf Glanville and four chroniclers. Admittedly, Gerald of Wales grumbled he had wasted his time by writing his *Topography of Ireland* for Henry.

What really interested Henry were legends of King Arthur and Merlin's prophecies, popularized by Geoffrey of Monmouth's *History of the Kings of England*, translated as the *Roman de Brut* by Wace (who dedicated it to Queen Eleanor) and by Marie de France's *Lais*. According to Gerald, Henry unearthed Arthur's bones at Glastonbury, informing the monks that a bard who sang of ancient Britain had told him the body would be found 16 feet down, in a hollowed-out oak tree.

Court life was colourful, with tournaments and banquets where roast crane was served. Entertainment went on until after midnight. Music was provided by harpers, viol players and minstrels, stories were told by professional storytellers and jesters, there were jugglers, tumblers and clowns. A certain Roland le Fartère was given a small manor in Suffolk by the king on condition that every Christmas he gave a jump, a whistle and a fart before Henry and his courtiers. (*Unum saltum et siffletum et unum bumbulum.*)[20] So many prostitutes flocked to the court that a 'marshal of the whores' was appointed to control them.

Before a marriage producing seven children Henry fathered a number of bastards, the most notable being Geoffrey Plantagenet. He also seduced several ladies, one of whom married Roger Bigod, Earl of Norfolk, after bearing the king a son. Even before the birth of his last child by Eleanor, he began an affair with Rosamund Clifford. Little is known about her except that she was the daughter of a knight from the Welsh Marches, young and very beautiful, and that the king kept her at the royal palace of Woodstock, within easy reach of Clarendon. When she died at the nunnery of Godstow in 1176, Henry buried her in a tomb before the high altar, a shrine at which, on his instructions, the nuns burned candles.

Henry terrified the toughest courtier. His rages verged on insanity, like the tantrum described by Becket in 1166 when he ripped off his clothes and ate the straw on the floor. However, what frightened them more was his inscrutability. As W. L. Warren (his best biographer) put it: 'He was no godlike Achilles, either in valour or in wrath; but in cunning and ingenuity, in fortitude and courage, he stands not far below the subtle-souled Odysseus.' [21]

A disputed succession

England had never known such prosperity, while the Plantagenet territories in France were unusually peaceful. Yet Henry nearly destroyed it all by announcing what would happen after his death – his eldest son Henry would rule England, Normandy, Anjou and Maine; Richard Aquitaine; Geoffrey Maine; and John Ireland.[22] The flaw was that each son had set his heart on inheriting everything. Henry did not expect them to rebel and the mural at Winchester Castle mentioned by Gerald shows how much the discovery of their treachery hurt. 'The eagle's four young are my sons, who won't stop tormenting me till I'm dead,' was how he explained the mural. 'The youngest of whom I'm so fond will hurt me more painfully and fatally than the rest put together.'²³ What encouraged the boys to rebel was Henry's moral defeat by Thomas Becket.

Becket

Although genuinely devout, giving alms to the poor on a large scale, the king was determined to rule the Church in his territories, ignoring Pope Adrian IV's grumble in 1156 that he would not let clerics appeal to Rome. When the Bishop of Chichester declared in his presence that no bishop might be deposed without papal authority the king commented, 'Quite right, a bishop can't be deposed', then gestured as if pushing with his hands: 'But he can be ejected with a good shove.'²⁴ It is unsurprising that his relations with the bishops were deteriorating by the time Theobald of Canterbury died in 1161.²⁵

The pope at the time of Theobald's death, Alexander III, was threatened by an anti-pope, 'Victor IV'; this enabled Henry to secure his chancellor Thomas Becket's election as primate in 1162, after a hasty ordination. Forty-four years old, the big, hawk-nosed Norman (who had actually been born in London in Cheapside) was so congenial that Henry could not do without his company; he even rode into Becket's hall, jumping his horse over the high table, then dismounting and demanding food. Henry thought that, as his best friend, the new archbishop would do whatever he wanted. But during the last century the great reforming pope Gregory VII had insisted that clergy were immune from the laws governing laymen; a view with which Becket agreed.

Judges told Henry that theft, robbery and murder were committed by clerics, who included not just priests but church doorkeepers and even church sweepers. They could only be tried by ecclesiastical courts, whose harshest penalties were defrocking or flogging. Henry was outraged by four cases in particular: those of a Worcestershire cleric who raped a girl and knifed her father; a Bedfordshire canon who murdered a knight; a Wiltshire priest who had also committed murder; and a London clerk who stole a silver chalice.[26] Becket refused to surrender them to the secular authorities, but had the canon banished and the clerk branded, sentencing the priest to lifelong penance in a monastery. It did not mollify the king.

King versus archbishop

In January 1164, during a council at Clarendon, Henry introduced laws stipulating that clergy and laity must settle disputes in the royal courts, and that clerics found guilty by church tribunals must be defrocked and handed over to his own courts. Appeals to Rome were forbidden. The 'Constitutions of Clarendon' took Archbishop Thomas by surprise. While refusing to put his seal on the document, he reluctantly gave verbal assent. Then he changed his mind, arguing that to try clerics in lay courts amounted to a double trial. Henry responded by using Becket's refusal to let a vassal be tried by a lay tribunal as grounds for arraigning him for contempt of court, besides suing him for 'debts' incurred when chancellor. Summoned before a council of the realm at Northampton in October, the defiant bishop was so awe-inspiring that the assembled magnates dared not pronounce sentence, and he fled to Flanders.

From abroad Becket excommunicated Henry's ministers, calling on the king to atone for the harm he had done the Church, and threatening to excommunicate him too. But the English bishops supported the king, allowing clerics to be tried by lay courts. Henry attempted to obtain Rome's support, so unsuccessfully that he swore he never wanted to see a cardinal again, if it meant turning Muslim. Finally, Pope Alexander placed England under an interdict, which forced Henry to let the archbishop return at the start of winter 1170. Ominously, the king refused to exchange the kiss of peace with him.

Before he left France, Becket excommunicated the Archbishop of York and two bishops for crowning Henry's son without his permission. In Normandy, when, during Christmas 1170, York warned Henry he would never have peace while Thomas lived,[27] the king bellowed that courtiers whose careers he had made were traitors in letting him be treated so disgracefully. Four knights immediately set off for Canterbury where they surrounded the archbishop in his cathedral. Although he could have escaped, he let them hack him to death, one blow slicing off the top of his skull and spilling his brains on the paving.

Henry reacted more like a friend than an enemy. In tears, he kept to his room for three days, refusing to eat. Aware that the Church would use the universal horror to wring concessions from him, he avoided Pope Alexander's commissioners by going to Ireland.

Ireland

In 1155, at Henry's request, Pope Adrian IV had granted him the entire country of Ireland, sending an emerald ring in token of investiture, in the hope that conquest would bring the Irish Church under papal control. But the king had deferred an invasion. What forced his hand now was a group of Anglo-Norman barons from Wales led by Richard, Earl of Clare ('Strongbow'), who, except in the mountains and bogs, easily routed Irish tribesmen armed with axes, javelins and long knives. Now, having subdued all Leinster, Strongbow was acting as an independent prince.

Henry arrived in October 1171 with an army on 400 ships, staying for six months, most of the time in a wattle-and-daub palace at Dublin. Strongbow and the barons submitted to Henry's lordship – and were thus regranted the lands they had conquered – while many native kings paid homage, although not the High King, Rory O'Connor. At Cashel, Henry presided over a council of Irish bishops, who swore fealty. Without fighting a single battle, when he left in April he was recognized as 'Lord of Ireland' by three-quarters of its rulers.

He came back to find Europe blaming him for Becket's martyrdom. At Avranches Cathedral in spring 1172 he admitted before the papal legates that he had been unwittingly responsible, swearing on the Gospels how deeply he regretted it and promising to accept any terms. These were: sending 200 knights to defend the Holy Land, cancelling the Constitutions of Clarendon and restoring the see of Canterbury's lands. After public penance, Henry received absolution. But while the English clergy regained their legal immunity, the king lost very little. Within a decade, most of the disputes for which Becket died had been resolved by negotiation.[28]

The Young King's rebellion

The Becket affair misled Henry's enemies in England and France into thinking he was insecure. A Lincolnshire knight, Roger de Estreby, claimed that St Peter and the Archangel Gabriel had told him to warn Henry that if he went on Crusade and obeyed their commands, he would reign gloriously for another seven years – otherwise, he would die within four. Among the commands were to condemn no one to death without fair trial, ensure every man entered into his inheritance, dispense justice without bribes, reward services to his ministers and officials, and expel all Jews minus their money and bonds.

In May 1170, to ensure an undisputed succession Henry had had his fifteen-year-old eldest son, also named Henry, crowned king at Westminster by the Archbishop of York. Unfortunately the '*Rex Filius*' or 'Henry III' was greedy. Hoping to take his father's place, he went to his father-in-law King Louis for help, joined by his brothers Richard and Geoffrey, who had been secretly encouraged by their mother. In 1173 rebellions in favour of the 'Young King' broke out on both sides of the Channel, while Louis attacked Normandy and the Scots raided down into the Midlands. Northampton was sacked, Nottingham and Norwich went up in flames, and for a time there was anarchy in London.

Among those who rebelled were the Earls of Norfolk, Chester, Derby and Leicester (son of the king's justiciar), with many lesser lords. In the words of Ralph de Diceto, a future dean of St Paul's, they did so because the Old King 'punished oppressors who plundered the poor'.[29] Young Henry offered lavish rewards. In England old Hugh Bigod, Earl of Norfolk, who looked back to the 'freedom' of Stephen's reign with nostalgia, was to have a bigger chunk of East Anglia; William, the King of Scots would take the three northern counties (as in Stephen's time) and his brother Cambridgeshire; while Philip of Flanders was promised all of Kent. Normandy, the revolt's real centre, was going be carved up in the same way.

But in October Hugh de Lacy routed Leicester's Flemish mercenaries at Fornham in Suffolk, where peasants with bad memories of foreign 'castlemen' from the previous reign massacred 3,000 fugitives, drowning them in the marshes. Confined to the North and Midlands, the rebels had no proper strategy while the Old King possessed better troops. His hand was strengthened when Queen Eleanor was caught fleeing to Paris – dressed as a knight and riding astride – as a consequence she was unable to mobilize her barons in Aquitaine.

Next spring, having routed his Breton enemies the Old King dealt with the Scots. Before doing so, he had himself flogged by the monks of Canterbury at Becket's shrine; within twenty-four hours some Yorkshiremen had captured King William in a Northumberland fog, whereupon the rebellion in England collapsed. Henry then returned to Normandy, driving out Louis. By autumn 1174 all his enemies had sued for peace.

Henry allowed the Young King two castles in Normandy with an annual allowance of £15,000, besides providing for Richard and Geoffrey. The King of Scots was released after acknowledging Henry as overlord and surrendering five key strongholds. The biggest loser was Queen Eleanor, who spent several years in confinement. Meanwhile, as the war reminded people of the miseries of Stephen's time, Henry had no more trouble in England.

Abroad, it would be different. One-eyed, red-faced, unkempt, charmless, a timid young man fearful of assassins and hard-mouthed horses, Philip II of France was a brilliant statesman who dreamed of making his kingdom what it had been in Charlemagne's day, and was determined to conquer the Plantagenet lands. He acquired a war chest by expelling Jews from his territory and seizing their money.

Only seventeen, Henry's second son Richard, as titular Duke of Aquitaine, had been given the job of cowing the barons of the Angoumois, Limousin and Périgord. He did so savagely, Gerald of Wales commenting that Richard was only happy when marking his steps with blood. He was also accused of 'abducting his vassals' wives, daughters and women folk, and using them as concubines before handing them on to his troops'.[30]

Egged on by Geoffrey, the Young King told the Aquitanian barons that he would make a kinder duke than Richard. The Old King tried to defuse the situation, commanding his three sons to make peace. Early in 1184 he told Richard and Geoffrey to do homage to their oldest brother. Richard refused, saying he was his mother's heir, whereupon the Young King and Geoffrey seized his city of Limoges. Their father spent all Lent trying to evict the pair, his horse being hit by a crossbow bolt on one occasion.

Leaving Limoges, the Young King plundered the shrines at Rocamadour and Grandmont (where he knew his father wanted to be buried) to pay his troops, but contracted dysentery, which killed him in June. He had been so handsome and eloquent that Walter Map called him 'a little lower than the angels', while adding he was like Absalom, a parricide who desired his father's death.[31] Even so, Henry threw himself on the ground and howled on hearing of his death. When the king asked the rebel troubadour Bertran de Born, 'You used to boast of your brains

– what's happened to them?' and Bertran answered, 'I lost them the day you lost your son', he burst into tears.[32]

Besides wrecking Henry's plans, the Young King's death unsettled his brothers even further. Geoffrey and John each hoped for the Crown despite their father announcing that Richard had taken the Young King's place as heir and would be responsible for Normandy, Anjou and England – Geoffrey was to continue in Brittany, while John would take over in Aquitaine. However, Henry had not bothered to explain this to Richard, who fled to Poitou and gathered troops, refusing to leave. For the moment his father accepted the situation, but Richard did not trust him.

Another problem was Alice of France, Philip's sister, to whom Richard had been betrothed since 1169, and who lived at the English court. Henry was rumoured to have fathered a bastard on her, which was why he would not let the marriage take place. In any case, Richard, repelled by the girl's ugliness, wanted to marry Berengaria of Navarre. Trying to set all three sons against each other, Philip offered to cede the Norman border territory of the Vexin in perpetuity if Henry granted it to a son who married Alice.

The Old King hoped John at least would be satisfied by becoming King of Ireland. Now eighteen, John set off for his new kingdom in April 1185, Pope Urban III sending a crown of peacocks' feathers set in gold for his coronation. It never took place. When he landed, John upset the Irish chieftains, pulling their beards and jeering at them, after which he replaced veteran Anglo-Norman commanders by young cronies whose campaign swiftly ended in defeat. Taking refuge in the coastal towns, he spent his time drinking and whoring until Henry recalled him in September. In retrospect, it is possible that John's behaviour may have been deliberate, to avoid spending the rest of his life in Ireland.

In the month John sailed for Ireland, Henry ordered Richard to hand Aquitaine back to Eleanor, who had been released from captivity. Although this looked like a setback for Richard, it guaranteed his succession to the duchy, as he and his mother were devoted to each other. Despairing of Aquitaine, next year his brother Geoffrey sought Philip's help in securing Anjou. A small, swarthy man, he is referred to by the chronicler Howden as that son of perdition (the name given to Judas by the Gospel) while Gerald of Wales calls him a smooth-tongued hypocrite, always stirring up trouble. But in Paris, plotting against his father and brethren, Geoffrey was kicked to death by a horse during a tournament. There is no record of Henry showing any grief.

The betrayal

As the oldest surviving son, Richard saw himself as heir to the entire Plantagenet empire. But, some time during 1187, he learned that Henry had written to King Philip, suggesting Alice should marry John, who would inherit Aquitaine and Anjou. Suspecting that his disinheritance was being planned, Richard allied with Philip, who invited him to Paris, where they slept in the same bed. War was averted in January 1188 by news that Saladin had captured the Holy City: Henry, Richard and Philip all swore to go on Crusade. However, the expedition was delayed by rebellion in Poitou and by war between Richard and Raymond of Toulouse – both secretly set in motion by King Philip.

In summer 1188 Philip intervened openly. In response, Henry assembled an army of Anglo-Norman knights and Flemish mercenaries. (Among them was the famous William Marshal, who had been head of the Young King's military household.) Instead of a battle there was a meeting between the two kings in August under an elm tree near Gisors, which the French king left on the pretext of sunstroke – in order to prolong hostilities without fighting. Henry and Richard continued the campaign until Henry ran out of money and disbanded his army. All this time Philip was playing upon Richard's paranoia.

At a meeting in November between the English and French

kings at Bonsmoulins in Normandy, when his father refused to acknowledge him as heir, Richard cried, 'Now I know what I thought impossible!' Then he publicly did homage to Philip for Normandy, Anjou, Maine and Aquitaine. An attempt at reconciliation next Easter failed because Henry still refused to acknowledge Richard as heir. Meanwhile, Aquitaine supported Richard and Brittany was in revolt.

By now Henry was increasingly unwell. Early in June 1189, the two kings and Richard met at La Ferté-Bernard, joined by a papal legate who was anxious for the Crusade to start. Philip demanded that Henry let Alice marry Richard and guarantee his succession, while John must go on Crusade. Richard made the same demands. Henry proposed, instead, that John should marry Alice and take over Aquitaine, which was rejected out of hand. When the legate threatened to put France under an inter-dict if Philip did not make peace, Philip accused him of taking bribes and ended the conference.

Philip and Richard now invaded Maine, catching Henry by surprise at Le Mans on 11 June. Its people fired the suburbs, but the French rode through the flames into the city and Henry fled, pursued by his own son. His escort included William Marshal, who deliberately charged at Richard. 'For God's sake, don't kill me, Marshal,' he begged. 'I'm not wearing armour.' 'No, I will not kill you,' replied William as he ran his lance into Richard's horse. 'I shall leave that to the devil.'[33]

'O God, today you humiliated me by stealing the city I loved most on earth, where I was born and bred!' cried the Old King. With his bastard son Geoffrey and a few followers, he fled into the forest, reaching Chinon before he collapsed. Then Philip captured Tours, another key stronghold. Feverish with blood poisoning from a wounded heel, Henry met the French king at Villandry, where he was further shaken by a bolt of lightning that just missed him. Held up in his saddle, he agreed to make his barons swear allegiance to Richard, pay a cash indemnity and go on Crusade with Philip. Exchanging a kiss of peace with

Richard, Henry whispered in his ear, 'God grant I don't die before I have my revenge on you!'[34]

Returning to Chinon, Henry learned of the desertion of John, whom he had contemplated making his heir. He moaned, 'Shame on a conquered king!', calling down God's curse on his sons. He died on 6 July. Before his burial in the abbey church at Fontevrault Richard came to see the corpse. A torrent of blood flowed from its nostrils, enraged even in death.

Retrospect

Henry II's most enduring monument is not the battered effigy at Fontevrault, but in England, where no ruler has ever left a deeper, more lasting mark.

In accepting pre-Conquest legal customs, the Normans had unknowingly committed themselves to becoming Englishmen, and Henry made certain they would do so by creating the Common Law.

3

The Lionheart – Richard I

Queen of kingdoms while King Richard lives . . . your position is secure under so great a helmsman . . .

Geoffrey of Vinsauf[1]

The Crusader

The sudden collapse of the Crusader states in 1187 caused the same sort of horror among Christians that Jews might feel today were they to hear that the Israeli armed forces had been wiped out and Jerusalem lost, with the remnant of Israel's population huddled in one or two beleaguered seaports. Every major Western ruler took an oath to go on the Third Crusade and rescue the Holy Land. Among them was England's new king.

In 1860 a statue of Richard I was erected outside the Palace of Westminster, although some Victorians did not think he deserved one. 'His subjects, fortunately for themselves, saw very little of him,' wrote Stubbs. 'His ambition was that of a mere warrior: he would fight for anything whatever, but he would sell everything that was worth fighting for.' As late as 1974, *The Oxford*

History of England argued that his only use for his kingdom was to finance ambitions overseas, a generally accepted view until his convincing rehabilitation in 1991 by John Gillingham. While he may have been essentially a Frenchman and 'No Englishman' (Stubbs's phrase), he valued his kingdom. Nor did his English subjects feel any resentment, idolizing him as the leader who saved Christian Palestine.

One of Richard's first acts was to pardon William Marshal who only recently had nearly killed him. He also gave William the hand of the greatest heiress of the day, Isabel de Clare, so the landless knight from the Kennet Valley became Earl of Pembroke and Lord of Leinster. 'The Marshal', as everyone called him, was the most celebrated knight of the age, a hero of the tournament and the battlefield, who rose through sheer ability and ended his career by uniting England behind the Plantagenet dynasty.

After Richard's investment as Duke of Normandy, he was crowned King of England at Westminster on 3 September 1189. The coronation was marred by the crowd outside, who attacked and killed a deputation from the Jewish community when it tried to present the new king with gifts. The incident turned into a pogrom that spread from London to as far north as York, and many Jews were murdered or even burned alive. Richard tried to save them, from greed rather than compassion – he wanted to fleece the entire community to help pay for his Crusade.

Even so, he did not forget the oaths sworn at his coronation; his remark 'I would sell London if I could find a buyer' was only a witticism.[2] If he sold offices and lordships to finance his Crusade, he made the Welsh princes swear not to attack in his absence and guarded the North by selling Roxburgh and Berwick back to the Scots. Marrying his brother John to Isabel of Gloucester, heiress to the great earldom of Gloucester, giving him other English estates and creating him Count of Mortain in Normandy, was less of a risk than leaving him dissatisfied.

In July 1190 Richard joined his fellow crusader Philip II at Vézelay, with 4,000 men-at-arms and as many foot soldiers.

A hundred ships took the soldiers from Marseilles to Messina where they waited for King Richard before sailing on to Sicily. No English monarch had brought so large an expedition on such a long journey. To preserve discipline Richard issued a list of penalties – anyone who killed a man was to be thrown overboard tied to his victim's corpse, anyone who drew blood in a quarrel was to lose his hand, and thieves were to be tarred and feathered.

He himself went overland with a single knight – and was nearly lynched in Calabria for stealing a peasant's falcon. On arrival, he found that his sister Queen Joanna, William II of Sicily's widow, had been imprisoned by King Tancred. A usurper, Tancred lived in fear of Emperor Henry VI, who had married the heiress to the throne, Constance of Hauteville. After the English king sacked and occupied Messina as a punishment for Tancred refusing to admit him, Tancred, desperate to avoid making another dangerous enemy, hastily freed Joanna, signing a treaty by which he agreed to pay her compensation. In return, Richard promised that one of Tancred's daughters should marry his nephew Arthur of Brittany, whom he had adopted as his heir.

During the winter at Messina, Richard told King Philip he could not marry Alice of France because of her reputation. Instead, he would wed Berengaria of Navarre, whom Queen Eleanor was bringing to Sicily. The insult did not improve relations between the two men.

The man

Handsome and well built if a bit plump, with reddish-blond hair, Richard, despite having been born at Oxford in 1157 (presumably just outside, in Beaumont Palace), had become a man from south of the Loire, whose languages were Poitevin, Provençal and Latin. He knew no English and complained of his kingdom's cold and rain.

'Well aware of what a filthy life he had been leading and

regretting it, he summoned all the archbishops and prelates to Reginald de Moyac's chapel in Messina where, throwing himself naked at their feet, he openly confessed to God his filthiness', Roger of Howden tells us.[3] In token of repentance, the king held three scourges. What was Richard's sin? Some historians, but only since John Harvey in 1948 and without any evidence, have suggested he was homosexual, citing his failure to produce an heir. Yet Berengaria may have been barren, as Richard fathered at least one bastard and had raped captive ladies in Aquitaine.[4]

The overall picture from chronicles is of a man with enormous self-confidence and dynamism. (His only physical handicap was malaria, caught before he went to the Holy Land – during bouts he shook all over.) In Palestine and France he proved to be a magnificent soldier, who inspired loyalty in his men and terrified his enemies. His one fault was rashness, behaving as though he bore a charmed life.

Contemptuous of most prelates, Richard respected Hugh of Lincoln, remarking 'If other bishops were like him, no one would dare to argue with them.'[5] Occasionally cruel, he could also show breathtaking magnanimity. The name *'coeur de lion'* was bestowed in his lifetime, Gerald of Wales writing of 'our lion, our more than lion', even before he became king, which gave rise to the tale of Richard reaching down a lion's throat and pulling out its heart. Only an unusually impressive personality could inspire such a legend.

Cyprus and Palestine

En route for the Holy Land in April 1191 Richard's fleet ran into a storm and many ships were wrecked off Cyprus. Survivors were imprisoned by its ruler, 'Emperor' Isaac (a dissident Byzantine), who invited Queen Joanna and Berengaria to land when they anchored off Limassol. They wisely declined so he refused to let their boat take on fresh food or water. As soon as Richard arrived, he stormed Limassol, then conquered the whole island within days and imprisoned Isaac, adding a vast booty to his war chest.

While the mountains of the Holy Land could be seen from Cyprus, it was sufficiently far away to be safe from Muslim invasion. Aware that it could give the Crusade a base from which to bring in reinforcements and supplies, almost immediately Richard sold the island to the Templars. When they did not pay, he presented it to Guy de Lusignan, the former King of Jerusalem.

Before setting out on the last lap of his journey, he married Berengaria at Limassol. He also had her crowned as Queen of the English, instead of waiting for a coronation at Westminster, which shows that he was hoping for an heir. (By all accounts, Berengaria was an unusually pleasant if not very good-looking lady.) Then he sailed for Palestine, which he reached only just in time to save the Second Crusade.

'Outremer', as Anglo-Normans called the Kingdom of Jerusalem, had disintegrated. While always under threat from Muslim neighbours, it had been a thriving little country for ninety years, with a French nobility, an Italian bourgeoisie and a Christian Arab underclass. But now, having lost its entire military manpower and its capital in 1187, it was reduced to a few toeholds on the coast. Even so, there was bitter rivalry for the lost Crown between the ex-king, Guy de Lusignan, and the Marquis of Montferrat, who was eventually elected to take his place, only to be murdered in 1192.

When King Richard joined the camp near Acre (once Outremer's biggest seaport) on 8 June 1191 he found a siege that had already lasted so long that the besiegers were comparing it to the siege of Troy. Handpicked by Sultan Saladin, the Muslim garrison knew the Crusade would collapse if they held out. Even Christians admired Saladin. A Kurd who had united Syria and Egypt, and wiped out the Crusader army at the Horns of Hattin in 1187, he was renowned for magnanimity, generosity and bravery, and it seemed inconceivable to the defenders that he would not rescue them.

Weakened by epidemics and starvation – they were eating their horses – the besiegers could not take Acre, despite Philip II's arrival. But everything changed when Richard came. After capturing a big enemy ship bringing reinforcements, he added his siege engines to those already in place and, when he went down with malaria, had himself carried in a litter to the walls, sniping at the enemy with a crossbow. His determination restored morale.

Soon such large areas of the walls collapsed that, despite having sworn to fight to the death, the defenders surrendered on 12 July, the two kings' banners flying in triumph from the citadel. When Duke Leopold of Austria had his own banner hoisted, the English threw it down into the ditch, an affront he did not forget. Richard moved into the former royal palace where his men drank like fishes amid the braying of horns and trumpets.

At the end of July Philip went home. Richard stayed on as undisputed leader of the crusaders, whose aim was to recapture Jerusalem. The lives of the Acre garrison had been spared in return for 2,000 dinars, 1,500 Christian captives and the Holy Cross. However, when it became clear that the ransom would not be paid, in the most shameful crime of his entire career Richard massacred his prisoners – and, as some of them had swallowed gold coins, they were disembowelled.

Richard then set out for Jaffa on 25 August, marching along the shore and supplying his army from the sea. When Saladin's much bigger army attacked at Arsuf on 7 September, the king had difficulty holding back his knights. Finally, the Hospitallers disobeyed, charging the enemy. Richard saved the day by riding with them and then regrouping to launch further charges. In the end, the enemy broke. Not only had Richard won an overwhelming victory but he had destroyed Saladin's reputation for invincibility.

His dilemma was to recover Jerusalem or rebuild the Christian kingdom on the coast. Besieging the Holy City meant exposing his supply lines, so he offered Saladin's brother, al-Adil, the coastal cities and his sister Joanna as wife if he would convert to Christianity. 'To get what he wanted, he used force first, then smooth talk,' says one of Saladin's officers. 'We never had a bolder or more crafty opponent.'[6]

Early in 1192 Richard stormed Ascalon, which he refortified, cutting Saladin's communications with Egypt. In June, the sultan sent a big, heavily escorted caravan to revictual the Holy City. When it camped for the night near the wells of Kuwaifa, the king, after reconnoitring in the darkness disguised as a Bedouin, attacked at dawn, seizing the entire caravan and its valuable cargo – once more humiliating Saladin.

In July the enemy captured Jaffa, but its citadel held out. On 1 August a flotilla of Christian ships sailed into the harbour, led by Richard in a red galley with a red sail and, wading ashore with a small force, he drove the astonished Muslims out of the city. Four days later Saladin came in person with a large army. Richard's troops were a mere 2,000 foot soldiers and fifty-four knights, only fifteen of whom were mounted, but his spearmen and crossbowmen fought on from behind a barrier of tent-pegs until he charged out with his handful of cavalry and cowed the attackers. A Muslim eyewitness recalled how fearsome he appeared: 'The King of England, lance in hand, rode along the whole length of our army from right to left, and none of our soldiers dared to leave the ranks.'[7]

In the end, the Palestinian barons convinced the king that Jerusalem was beyond his reach. Having done all he could, in August 1192 he signed a treaty with Saladin by which the Christians kept the territory they had recovered and were given access to the Holy City. Although he had failed to regain Jerusalem, Richard had restored the kingdom of Outremer, if much reduced in size, with Acre for its capital.

Because Western Christians were so obsessed with the Crusade, everybody heard of Richard's heroic deeds in the Holy Land, from the sermons of the parish priests who obtained their information from his letters to the bishops. If Englishmen were groaning beneath the Saladin Tithe, they knew that Richard had given them value for their money.

Captivity

Leaving Palestine in October 1192, Richard's ship was driven by contrary winds into Corfu. Here, with twenty followers and disguised as a Templar, he took passage on a small pirate vessel, only to be wrecked between Aquileia and Venice. Twice arrested and twice escaping, the king was caught in a brothel near Vienna – cooking a leg of lamb – by the Duke of Austria's men and imprisoned at the castle of Dürnstein.

On Palm Sunday 1193 Richard was handed over to Emperor Henry VI, who had him tried at Speyer on a charge of betraying the Holy Land, King Philip's agents claiming that he had organized the Marquis of Montferrat's murder and poisoned the Duke of Burgundy. He defended himself so eloquently that Henry withdrew the charge. Even so, Richard remained in captivity. (Regrettably, there is no truth in the story of the minstrel Blondel recognizing the king when he sang a song they had written together.)

Meanwhile Philip II attacked the Plantagenet empire, capturing the great castle of Gisors. John, who hoped he would help him seize the English throne, did homage to the French king, surrendering eastern Normandy and the key strongholds of Touraine. In England John's men occupied royal castles while he invited the Welsh and Scots to overthrow his brother. But the English magnates stayed loyal to Richard.

In June 1193 the emperor agreed to release his prisoner for £100,000 (double the English Crown's entire revenue.) Although this meant a tax as heavy as the Saladin Tithe, it was raised without complaint. Early in 1194 Henry freed his captive, rejecting bribes by Philip and John to keep him prisoner. 'Look to yourself,' Philip warned John. 'The Devil is loose.'[8]

The castellan of St Michael's Mount, who was one of John's supporters, died of fright when he heard of Richard's imminent return.

Rebuilding the Plantagenet empire

The king had left his chancellor, William Longchamp, in charge, a good administrator but intolerably heavy-handed, 'with a sneer, a savage grin and contempt in his eye'.[9] In 1191 William was dismissed by an angry assembly of barons and bishops at St Paul's, cheered on by 10,000 Londoners, led by their first mayor, who complained that William had insulted the English nation. Richard had already sent Walter of Coutances, Archbishop of Rouen, to take his place. Meanwhile, panic-stricken, John fled to France.

During the two months he spent in England, Richard prepared for war with Philip II. To ensure that reinforcements and supplies reached his troops across the Channel, he began Portsmouth's long career as a naval base, granting it a charter. He used the port as a harbour for a fleet of galleys, modelled on those he had seen in the Mediterranean. Another innovation was naming specific localities (Salisbury, Stamford, Warwick, Brackley and Blyth) where tournaments – more like miniature pitched battles than the tilting yard duels of later days – were to be held regularly. These were supervised by two experienced knights and two clerks, to whom participants paid a fee graded according to their social standing. The purpose was to provide a steady supply of well-trained men-at-arms.

Richard did not confine himself to the war effort; he also witnessed charter after charter, chose bishops and appointed sheriffs. He made sure that forest laws were maintained – convicted deer poachers must lose their eyes and virility 'as in the days of Henry, grandfather of our lord the king'.[10] He established a customs service that levied a tenth of the value on all goods for export at every port in his domains. Since these included

London, Southampton, Bristol, Dublin, Nantes, Rouen, La Rochelle, Bordeaux and Bayonne, it became a valuable source of royal revenue. The Welsh were cowed while peace was made with the Scots. Finally, he appointed a superb administrator, Hubert Walter – about to become Archbishop of Canterbury – to rule in his absence.

In summer 1194 he sailed to Normandy. When he arrived, John threw himself at his feet. 'Don't worry,' Richard told him, 'you're just a child who has had bad advisers.' Next year, he restored the twenty-eight-year-old 'child' to his county of Mortain and English estates.[11] To show repentance, having installed a French garrison at Evreux John invited its members to a dinner where he had them murdered and their heads stuck on poles.

The war – a struggle for the area between Paris and Rouen – involved endless fighting for control of the bridges and fords over the Seine, and for strategically sited castles. Inspired by the Byzantine strongholds he had seen in the East, Richard built a huge fortress on a rock above the Seine at Les Andelys, Château Gaillard, whose functions were safeguarding the road to Rouen and enabling his troops to raid deep into French territory. Neither side could win decisively because neither could afford to maintain an army in the field for long enough.[12]

Even so, Richard won a string of minor successes. Often led by a Provençal mercenary named Mercadier, who had been with him in the Holy Land, his army's unexpected attacks after forced marches or from sailing barges demoralized the enemy. Mercadier raided Beauvais, taking prisoner its bishop, while in September 1198 Richard nearly captured King Philip during an ambush in eastern Normandy. A bridge at Gisors collapsed beneath Philip as he fled in terror across the River Epte – he had to be pulled out of the water by the legs while twenty of his knights were swept away. 'We heard reports that he had to drink from the river', Richard wrote in a letter to the Bishop of Durham.[13] Through relentless campaigning and diplomacy, by the end of 1198 he had recovered everything lost during his captivity.

Then an obscure Limousin baron, Achard of Chalus, dis-covered a buried treasure, said to be a gold model of a Roman emperor and his family sitting around a golden table, together with a hoard of gold coins. Unwisely – and illegally – he refused to let Richard have it all, keeping back part at his little castle. In March 1199, with Mercadier, the king besieged Chalus which, although defended by only fifteen men, refused to surrender. Reconnoitring without his armour, the king was hit in the shoul-der by a crossbow quarrel and the wound turned gangrenous. When the castle fell, he had the garrison hanged, except for the crossbowman, who turned out to be a mere boy.

'What harm have I done you, to make you kill me?', the dying Richard asked the boy, who was called Pierre Basile. 'You slew my father and my brothers with your own hand, and you meant to slay me too – so revenge yourself in any way you like,' answered Pierre. 'I forgive you for my death, live on,' replied the king, ordering his release. After Richard died on 6 April, despite the pardon, Mercadier had the boy flayed alive before hanging him.[14]

A Frenchman until the very end, the king left instructions for his body to be buried in the abbey church at Fontevrault, at the feet of the father he had betrayed, and for his heart to be interred at Rouen. Queen Berengaria was so grief-stricken, 'almost heartbroken', that Bishop Hugh of Lincoln journeyed through a wild and dangerous forest region to comfort her,[15] which refutes the stories that Richard neglected his wife.

Always objective, despite his admiration for the late king, Roger of Howden notes an enemy's comment: 'Valour, avarice, crime, unbounded lust, foul famine, unscrupulous pride and blind desire have reigned for twice five years.' But Roger also quotes another verdict, 'His courage was undaunted by count-less mighty obstacles, his advance never checked by any barriers, whether raging, roaring seas, the abysses of the deep or towering mountains'.[16] The *History of William Marshal* records Marshal's opinion of the king – 'the best prince in all the world'.[17]

Retrospect

If Richard I failed to regain Jerusalem for Christianity, he ensured that at least part of the Holy Land survived as a Christian kingdom for another century, fed from Cyprus. He also kept the Plantagenet empire intact. A recent historian of warfare in the West during the High Middle Ages does not hesitate in calling him 'the greatest commander within this period'.[18] In England, despite his absence overseas, well-chosen justiciars improved the laws and administration left by his father. The kingdom continued to prosper.

The name 'lion heart' was justified. Richard had become a folk hero for all Western Europe and a demon in Arab legend. The English never forgot him. He really does deserve that statue at Westminster.

4

The Madman – John

a trifler and a coward

Lord Macaulay[1]

The foulness of John

John is arguably the worst king in our entire history. 'Foul though it is, Hell itself is defouled by the foulness of John,' wrote Matthew Paris.[2] Yet, in a negative sense, he is one of the most important. As well as for Magna Carta, he deserves to be remembered for speeding up the Plantagenets' transformation into Englishmen, by losing the empire left by his brother.

The Victorians took a particularly poor view of John, Kate Norgate crediting him with almost superhuman wickedness. Twentieth-century historians differed, and for fifty years it was orthodoxy that the real-life John had not been so bad as he was painted by chroniclers, that closer study showed him as effective and much better-hearted. Recently, however, it has been generally accepted that the chroniclers were telling the truth.[3]

Losing an empire

Despite having named Arthur as his heir when in Sicily, Richard left his throne to John. Archbishop Hubert Walter told William Marshal he thought Arthur should be king, but reluctantly agreed to support John. 'Marshal, you'll never regret anything in your life so much as you will this,' he warned.[4]

Meeting at Angers, the barons of Anjou, Maine and Touraine recognized the fifteen-year-old Arthur as their lord, on the grounds that an elder brother's son had a better right than a younger brother, and John narrowly escaped capture at Le Mans. He had no trouble in Normandy, however, where he was invested as duke in April, while in England he was crowned king in May. His mother made sure of Aquitaine. During the ceremony at Rouen some cronies sniggered when the lance (part of the Norman regalia) was placed in his hand and, turning to join in their laughter, he dropped it. Many spectators thought this a bad omen.

Like the Angevins, the Bretons declared for Arthur. (The Barnwell annalist tells us they hoped he would be a second King Arthur and destroy the English.[5]) However, when John invaded Maine in September, William des Roches, constable of Anjou, Maine and Touraine, went over to him. At Le Goulet in May 1200 John reached an agreement with Philip II, who, in return for minor territorial concessions and a 'relief' (inheritance tax) of 20,000 marks, recognized him as heir to all lands once ruled by Henry II.

The agreement earned him the name 'John Soft Sword'.[6] Accepting Philip's feudal overlordship by paying the 'relief' was an admission of weakness – neither his father nor brother ever paid one – as was abandoning a war Richard had been winning. Another was swearing not to help his nephew Otto of Brunswick or the Count of Flanders or any French lord should they attack Philip, which deprived him of allies.

In 1200 (having divorced his barren wife, Isabella of Gloucester, for consanguinity) John married another Isabella, the Count of Angoulême's twelve-year-old heiress, ignoring her betrothal to Hugh of Lusignan, Count of La Marche, despite the fact that betrothal in thirteenth-century canon law was almost as binding as marriage. This reopened the war for the Plantagenet succession since, instead of compensating Hugh, John confiscated La Marche. Hugh then appealed to their joint overlord, King Philip, who summoned John to Paris to answer a charge of oppression. He declined, so in April 1201 Philip proclaimed him a 'contumacious vassal', announcing that his lands were forfeit and Arthur was their rightful lord.

Next month, Philip attacked north-eastern Normandy, seizing strongholds along the Seine. Without waiting for the Bretons, Arthur and his ambitious mother joined the Lusignans and invaded Poitou. Learning Queen Eleanor was at the little town of Mirebeau on the Angevin border, they tried to capture the old lady, who took refuge in its minute citadel from where she sent for help to John at Le Mans, 80 miles away. He arrived at dawn, within forty-eight hours. Catching the besiegers off guard, he captured Hugh de Lusignan, together with his brother and over 200 knights.

However, John threw away his victory by the way he treated his prisoners. Although Hugh de Lusignan, the most dangerous, was allowed to ransom himself, the rest were shipped to England, where some were blinded and twenty starved to death, which made bitter enemies among their friends and relatives. At the same time, the king alienated William des Roches by refusing to let him have custody of Arthur.

A worse mistake was murdering his nephew. John offered to let Arthur go if he would abandon Philip, but he told his uncle to hand over England to him, with all Richard's other territories. Angrily, the king sent him to Rouen under close guard and 'shortly after, the said Arthur disappeared'.[7] Everyone in France thought John had killed him with his own hands. Probably he did so when drunk, throwing the body into the Seine, weighted with a heavy stone. (One source claims he grabbed the boy by his hair and drove a sword into him.) By April 1203 Arthur was known to have vanished. Brittany rose in revolt at the news, accusing his uncle of murder, and King Philip again summoned John to Paris for trial.

Philip invaded eastern Normandy again in 1203, as in feudal law John had forfeited the duchy by refusing to answer the charges, and a Breton army attacked from the south-west. Besieging a town or a castle, Philip invited its defenders to accept him as lord or be hanged or flayed alive, one defiant castellan being dragged to execution at a horse's tail. Garrisons gave in without putting up even token resistance. Few Norman barons would fight for John. Those in the east had flirted with Philip II's overtures for years while John had antagonized many in the south by his treatment of their kinsmen captured at Mirebeau. Now he alienated those in the centre by employing mercenaries who plundered the property of local knights and raped their wives.[8] In any case, he was crippled by lack of money, able to extract only half the taxes that the duchy had paid his brother.

Throughout, John showed pathological inertia, spending Christmas 1203 at Caen where he feasted daily with his queen and slept until long after everybody else had risen. If told a town or fortress had fallen to Philip, the king muttered, 'Whatever he captures now, I'll get back tomorrow.' Some said a spell had been cast on him.[9] In August he found the energy to besiege Alençon, but he retreated as soon as Philip's troops appeared. At the end of the month he sent boats along the Seine to revictual the great castle of Château Gaillard, to be thwarted by adverse river tides. (He had not led the flotilla in person, remaining safely at Rouen.)

Warned that the Normans planned to hand him over to King Philip, who would punish him for Arthur's murder, John's paranoia became so intense that he travelled by night, and Ralph of Coggeshall heard he was 'incapable of relieving the besieged, terrified his own subjects might betray him'.[10] The only troops with whom he felt safe were his bodyguard or his mercenaries. More Normans deserted every day, despite the barrels of silver coin he spent on trying to buy their loyalty; the French telling beleaguered castellans they had been abandoned and that Philip was a better ruler. In December, John left for England, with only the Cotentin, Mortain, Rouen and a few castles still holding out for him. In March 1204 Château Gaillard surrendered, no further attempt having been made to relieve it. In June Philip rode into Rouen. He had conquered the entire duchy of Normandy.

When Queen Eleanor died in April many Poitevins went over to Philip, who entered Poitiers in August 1204. Led by William des Roches, the barons of Anjou, Maine and Touraine followed suit. That winter, Philip even threatened to invade England. In January 1205 a terrified John ordered every male over twelve to swear to defend the realm, under the command of shire, hundred and parish constables, or a specially appointed 'city constable' – anyone failing to do so would be proclaimed a public enemy. Forty-five galleys were hired to guard the south coast and East Anglia, from whose ports no ship could sail without the king's written permission.

John's recovery

In an astonishing mood swing, John suddenly regained his nerve, convinced he could not only defeat a French invasion but reconquer his lands in France. He began assembling an army and an armada, and in March held a council at Oxford, demanding oaths of loyalty from his barons, whom he insisted must join the expedition. They joined very half-heartedly, after making him swear to respect their rights.[11]

Although Chinon's surrender at Easter 1205 meant he had lost his last foothold in Anjou, John went on with plans to invade Normandy and Poitou. After six months of preparation,

14,000 men assembled at Portsmouth in June, ready to go on board 1,500 ships. At the last moment Archbishop Hubert and William Marshal begged John to call off the expedition, saying he would be outnumbered and that, because of his performance in Normandy, his barons would not fight.

However, after he had approached each magnate personally, with threats or bribes, some agreed to come with him, and in June 1206 he and his fleet sailed into La Rochelle, which was still loyal. Nearly all Poitou had gone over to Philip, but John did recover the south-west. Marching into Anjou, he occupied Angers for a week before striking north towards Maine, devastating the lands of Angevin barons who had deserted him, but retreating when he heard that Philip was coming. In October both kings agreed to accept the status quo: John keeping Gascony, southern Poitou, the Angoumois and the Saintonge (a small, seaboard province beyond the Garonne). Given his supine performance three years before, it was a surprising achievement, largely due to Savari de Mauléon and the Archbishop of Bordeaux, Hélie de Malemort.

One factor had been the area's commercial interdependence, based on rivers and the sea. Moreover, John had retained La Rochelle, Bordeaux and Bayonne, ports that, with the Channel Islands, formed a sea lane to England. The campaign confirmed his interest in shipping, as a defence against invasion as well as a link with Poitou and Gascony. By 1208 he had created an organization that amounted to an admiralty. In 1209–12 twenty galleys and thirty-four other vessels would be launched for the king; if he did not make England a maritime power, he certainly gave her a navy.[12]

The impact of losing Normandy on the greater English magnates cannot be exaggerated. In 1204 there were over a hundred tenants-in-chief in England with manors in Normandy,[13] who now had to choose between an English or a French king, losing lands and castles in one or other country – they could not pay homage in both.

The man

Born at Oxford at Christmas 1166, John bore no resemblance to Richard, being swarthy if high-coloured and only 5ft 5ins tall (a reasonable height in the twelfth century), while in middle age he grew fat and lost his reddish hair. Because of his childhood in Poitou, he was most at home with Poitevins, neither liking nor trusting Englishmen. As a youth, he possessed all Melusine's diabolical charm: his parents were devoted to him. Richard, although with few illusions about his brother's capacity, made him his heir: 'My brother John is not the man to conquer a country if anybody puts up the slightest resistance', he had commented on hearing of his revolt in 1193.[14]

In those days John had been alarming in his drunken rages, his face distorted and dark red, foaming at the mouth, eyes blazing. Now, he was terrifying – there is a wolfish quality in his face on the effigy at Worcester Cathedral. His mental health was unsound and throughout his career he showed pathological lack of self-control, as he did during the fall of Normandy. When Archbishop Geoffrey of York visited him in 1207 to appeal against a heavy new tax, Geoffrey threw himself at his feet, imploring him to have mercy. In response, John threw himself at the archbishop's feet and cried mockingly, 'Look, Lord Archbishop, I'm doing just what you did!' Then, sniggering, he sent him away. That is not the conduct of a man who was wholly sane.[15]

Although highly intelligent and often hard-working, he was also gluttonous, and would, besides, drink to excess. He kept numerous mistresses and begot five known bastards, and his predatory attitude towards his barons' wives and daughters was notorious – he was infuriated when Eustace de Vesci put a common woman in the royal bed instead of his wife. A note on the royal expenses for 1204 states, 'The wife of Hugh de Neville promises the lord king two hundred chickens if she is allowed to spend one night with her husband.'[16]

Matthew Paris alleges that Isabella of Angoulême, eighteen

years younger, was as lustful as her husband, 'an incestuous and depraved woman, so often guilty of adultery that the king gave orders for her lovers to be throttled on her bed'.[17] While there is no evidence of her infidelity, she was undoubtedly arrogant. Even so, between 1207 and 1215 she gave the king three sons and three daughters who reached maturity. If he gave her a lavish dress allowance, she was treated meanly, deprived of her revenues. In 1208 she was placed in close custody at Corfe Castle, while on several occasions she was left at Marlborough Castle with Hugh de Neville, husband of John's mistress. One shudders to think how someone as formidable as Isabella reacted. 'The wives of Plantagenet kings may have been quick tempered and hell to live with,' writes Nicholas Vincent. 'Dull they never were.'[18]

Like his father, John had an insatiable love of hunting and hawking, partly to keep down weight. He, too, pursued the otter along the rivers. He pampered his falcons, ordering that a cherished gyrfalcon called Gibbon be fed plump hens and well-fed goats, supplemented once a week by a hare. He was unusually clean, taking baths and owning a dressing gown, and his clothes were magnificent, even for a king, some made from Byzantine or Arab fabrics. He was fond of backgammon, and he had a small library (among them a Pliny) that went with him on progress. He collected rings and gems that also accompanied him. Most must have been lost crossing the Wellstream in 1216, but a hoard found at Devizes Castle after his death included 111 rings set with sapphires, 107 with diamonds, twenty-eight with rubies, fifteen with diamonds and nine with garnets.

But the qualities that stand out most are not love of luxury or self-indulgence. They are treachery, cruelty, vindictiveness and avarice. He was suspicious to the point of mania.

The quarrel with the Church

Adam of Eynsham records that John did not receive the sacraments at Easter 1199 or at his coronation. 'Close friends said he had never done so since reaching adulthood.'[19] He hunted on fast days and ate meat on Fridays. Yet in his odd way he believed, hearing Mass regularly, giving alms, making offerings at shrines, and wearing a relic on a gold chain round his neck. He had a particular devotion to the Anglo-Saxon saint, Wulstan of Worcester.

With typical perversity he enjoyed teasing the saintly Bishop Hugh of Lincoln. When Hugh drew his attention to a sculpture of the Harrowing of Hell, he pointed to a carving of souls in Paradise, saying 'You ought to show me those over here, as they're the ones I shall be with.'[20] While the bishop was saying an Easter Mass, he ostentatiously pocketed the gold coins he was meant to offer, and during a sermon asked him three times to keep it short as he wanted his dinner. Even so, John venerated Hugh, sitting by his deathbed and helping to carry his coffin; he was so moved by his death that he founded Beaulieu Abbey.

Probably he was unaware of Hugh's prophecy – that Philip II would take revenge for Queen Eleanor's desertion of his father and wipe out the English royal family. 'Three of Henry's sons, two of them kings and one a count, have already been destroyed by the French, who will only give the fourth a brief respite.'[21] So long as John lived, Philip fought an unending duel with him.

One of the few men who could handle John, Archbishop Hubert Walter, died in July 1205, much to the king's pleasure. Besides resenting Hubert's dictatorial guidance and sheer ability, John had even suspected him of being in French pay. By now he was on bad terms with his other great supporter, William Marshal, whom he also suspected of treachery. In consequence, he took his sons hostage, confiscated his castles, and told household knights to challenge him to mortal combat. Wisely, William went off to expand the vast territory he had inherited in Leinster. His advice might have avoided the next catastrophe.

Among the rare Englishmen whom John trusted was his secretary John de Gray, Bishop of Norwich. Adept at raising money, de Gray, who had worked for him since before he came to the throne, was a boon companion. John wanted John de Gray to succeed Hubert Walter at Canterbury, but the monks of the cathedral chapter elected their sub-prior, sending him to Rome to obtain confirmation. The king was so angry that the monks gave in and elected de Gray, with the English bishops' approval. After examining the case the pope, Innocent III, appointed a distinguished theologian living in Rome, Cardinal Stephen Langton, whom he consecrated in June 1207. The king refused to accept Langton, turning the monks out of their priory and seizing the cathedral's revenues.

When Innocent placed England under an interdict in 1208, John's reaction was to promise that if any clerics arrived from Rome, including the pope himself, he would send them back with their noses slit and no eyes. He also sent threatening letters to Innocent. But the bishops enforced the interdict, which meant there were no church services other than baptisms or the last sacraments for the dying, while the dead were buried in ditches without funeral rites.

However, John saw an opportunity to amass funds for his war chest. Seizing all Church property, from parish glebes to cathedral and abbey lands, he left just enough for the clergy to live on – women who lived in presbyteries, whether housekeepers or mistresses, were arrested and released only on payment of a fine. Monks had to pay heavily to keep their abbeys, although John did stay on good terms with one or two abbots, such as Sampson of Bury St Edmunds. To some extent the interdict's impact was softened by Mass being said at monasteries or in fields.

Later it was estimated that the king took 100,000 marks (£66,666) from the Church, although some clerics thought the real figure to be much higher.[22] He dragged out negotiations with the pope to prolong the windfall, sending Langton back to France when he arrived at Dover. Innocent III then excommunicated John, and every bishop save one fled abroad. The king was unworried. When a cleric, Geoffrey of Norwich, announced that a clergyman did not owe loyalty to an excommunicate, he had Geoffrey wrapped in a lead cope that killed him. In 1211 he promised to hang Langton if he set foot in England.

John's heyday

In his erratic way the king improved administration, which he saw as a means of increasing his power, and spent hours sitting on the bench with Exchequer officials, discussing financial problems and new ways of adding to the revenue. For the first time proper archives were kept, with dated documents. He also created a new office, the Wardrobe (originally a royal clothing closet), where he kept his private seal so that he could enforce his will more swiftly.

Possessing a detailed knowledge of the law, he asked his judges for their opinion on innumerable cases, as 'his goal was to assert the continued primacy of royal justice'.[23] Always on progress, he travelled twenty or thirty miles a day, meeting sheriffs, castellans, barons and abbots, joining the justices who rode with him in hearing disputes. He could be merciful – immediately pardoning a small boy charged with killing another by accidentally throwing a stone – and was tireless in hearing pleas, listening to plaintiffs in court and giving them private audiences. Barons might complain but most of his subjects got good treatment in his courts.

However, John's taxation was ruthless. He extorted scutages for non-existent campaigns, racked up reliefs (death duties), and sold wardships, heiresses and rich widows to the highest bidder – increasing the sum paid by those who did not want to remarry. He levied 'gracious aids' on personal goods and tallages on royal manors, and enforced forest laws more severely. Jews did not escape, and both sexes were tortured to make them pay – when a Bristol Jew defied him, the king had one of his teeth pulled out every day until he gave in. Mercenaries were made sheriffs or justices, mulcting rich landowners with writs of false charges. In consequence, John amassed treasure exceeding any possessed by his predecessors. In 1208 he had 40,000 marks stored at Winchester, and in 1212 50,000 marks at Nottingham. This was a fraction of his wealth in coin, which in 1212 amounted to somewhere in the region of 200,000 marks – billions of pounds in today's money.

Frontier policy

In 1209, John accused the King of Scots of sheltering his enemies. William the Lion hastily made peace 'since he knew the English king was prone to all kinds of cruelty',[24] handing over his daughters as hostages, surrendering castles and paying an indemnity. In 1210 John dealt with the Irish Anglo-Normans, leading an army of English knights and Flemish infantry on a short campaign that brought them to heel – but left Anglo-Ireland facing a threat from native kings with whom he failed to reach a settlement, endangering the entire future of English rule.[25] During 1211 he starved Llewelyn ap Iorwerth out of Snowdonia.

'In Ireland, Scotland and Wales no man dared to disobey the King of England, which we all know was never the case under his predecessors, and appeared successful in every way he wanted, except for being robbed of his territories overseas and under the ban of the Church,' wrote a chronicler.[26]

Uniting the barons – in opposition

At the end of 1211 Llewelyn burst into central Wales, killing English settlers. Bent on retaliation, next autumn, John gathered a great army at Nottingham where he hanged twenty-eight hostages who were the sons of Welsh chieftains. But letters came from his daughter Joan (Llewelyn's wife) and the King of Scots, warning of a plot to use his excommunication as an excuse for handing him over to Llewelyn. The flight of Robert FitzWalter, Lord of Dunmow, and Eustace de Vesci, Lord of Alnwick, confirmed the warning. In a panic, the king dismissed the army, barricading himself inside Nottingham Castle for a fortnight, after which he arrested several magnates.

There was bound to be conflict with the barons, whom John had saddled with debts to the Crown or to Jewish money lenders, and with inflated feudal dues. In 1203 a 'gracious aid' had taken a seventh of their movable property and in 1207 another aid a thirteenth. Their biggest grievance, however, was the huge duties they paid to inherit their patrimony.

One means of cowing them was taking sons or nephews as hostages. In 1208 William de Briouze, a henchman who had lost favour, offered to surrender his three grandsons, but when royal officers came to collect them, his wife Matilda refused, shouting, 'I'm not going to hand over any children to King John, who murdered his nephew Arthur.'[27] After hunting her down in 1210, John had Matilda starved to death at Windsor with her eldest son – one report says they were given a flitch of bacon and a sheaf of oats, and that, driven mad by thirst, she gnawed the boy's cheeks before she died. They were murdered because Matilda knew what had happened to Arthur.[28]

Besides henchmen who had served him well in France, he employed Flemish and Welsh bodyguards, who were lavishly paid to put down any opposition. 'There were English barons whose wives or daughters had been raped by the king', writes Roger of Wendover, adding that he reduced many to poverty with unlawful taxes, driving others into exile and seizing their estates. 'Above all and behind all he was secretive and suspicious, over-sensitive to the merest flicker of opposition, relentless in revenge, cruel and mocking when he had men in his clutch.'[29] Understandably, 'the king's enemies were as many as his barons'.[30]

While a small landowner could appeal to the king against a baron and have his case settled by a jury, there was no way a baron could appeal against the king – 'the under-tenant had access to a system of justice which was far more predictable than that available to the great man opposed to his equal in the king's court . . . The magnate in the king's court was altogether less certain and secure.'[31] For John would seize the estates of a baron who failed to pay fines or feudal aids, when humbler men could not be dispossessed without judgement against them in the courts.

During 1212 the king was terrified by a Yorkshire holy man, Peter the Hermit, who foretold he would be dead by Ascension Day next spring. Shaken by this and by other signs of his unpopularity, he relaxed forest laws and remitted a number of taxes. Then William Marshal came to the rescue, urging Irish barons to swear an oath of loyalty to John. Realizing he had at least one dependable supporter, he recalled William, who suggested he could strengthen his position by reaching a settlement with Pope Innocent.

The pope had been on the point of deposing him and asking Philip of France to take his place when his envoys reached Rome. Even so, Philip went on with plans for invasion and in May 1213 an English army gathered near Canterbury to be ready when it landed. However, John's bastard half-brother the Earl of Salisbury destroyed Philip's fleet off the Flemish coast. The king then made peace with Rome, agreeing to everything the pope demanded – Langton as archbishop, reinstatement of exiled clerics, return of Church property and payment of compensation. He also placed England and Ireland under papal overlordship. At the Templar commandery of Ewell, kneeling at the papal legate's feet, on 15 May he surrendered the kingdom to the pope, receiving it back as his feudatory.

Finding himself still alive on Ascension Day, John had the clairvoyant Peter the Hermit, who had prophesied his imminent death, drawn behind a horse's tail till he died, marking the occasion with a great feast for the court.

At Winchester Cathedral on 20 July Archbishop Stephen Langton publicly absolved the king, ending his excommunication, while John swore to bring back the laws of the English kings before him, especially Edward the Confessor's. The interdict stayed in force for another year, until John repaid the Church. However, Innocent let him keep two-thirds of the money he had plundered.[32]

The last campaign in France

Now was the moment for the king to recover his lost lands in France, the motive behind all his policies. But there was a new obstacle. Peace with the Church forced him to allow the return of Robert FitzWalter and Eustace de Vesci, who had posed as martyrs for religion, and now led the magnates in insisting on better government. They had absorbed the pre-Conquest belief that the king should rule according to the advice of his witan.

A council of bishops that convened at St Albans in August to discuss compensation for the Church was joined by not only earls and barons but by humbler men who demanded a return to the laws of Henry I. In London, at St Paul's, Langton showed a group of magnates the old king's coronation charter with its promise of good laws. Unfortunately for John, his justiciar Geoffrey FitzPeter died at this moment, a man whose tact might have calmed the situation. 'When he gets to hell, he can go and say hello to Hubert Walter, whom he's bound to find down there', John joked inanely, adding, 'By God's feet, for the first time I really feel I'm King of England and the master.'[33] Led by Eustace de Vesci, the barons of northern England then announced they did not have any duty to fight in Poitou or pay for troops. John marched north to crush them but was persuaded by Langton to compromise at a parley at Wallingford on 1 November. Later that month he summoned his magnates and four knights from each shire to an unsatisfactory meeting at Oxford.

But he was ready for his great overseas campaign. While he attacked Philip II from the south-west, Otto of Brunswick (now Emperor Otto IV), the Duke of Brabant and the Counts of

Boulogne, Flanders and Holland, would invade France from the north. He sent his half-brother Salisbury to reinforce them, then sailed for Poitou on 2 February 1214, with an army of mercenaries, taking gold, silver and gems for use as bribes. He left England in the hands of a justiciar, the Bishop of Winchester, a former knight from Touraine who had been the only prelate to stay loyal to him during the interdict.[34]

The expedition was welcomed at La Rochelle, which depended on English trade. Hoping to win over the barons of Aquitaine, John spent two months marching through Angoulême, La Marche, the Limousin and Gascony, securing the Lusignan clan's homage through bribery. Early in summer he struck north, defeating a French army and capturing Nantes, the Breton capital. In June he occupied Angers as an Angevin count, holding court. Encouraged, he prepared to attack Paris, which Philip II – in the north, trying to intercept the Emperor Otto's invasion – was unable to defend. En route, he besieged the castle of Roche-au-Moine near Angers, the last obstacle to his advance.

When it was about to surrender, Philip's son Louis arrived from Chinon with 800 knights and the Poitevin lords, whose troops formed a substantial part of John's army, refused to fight him. Losing his nerve, the king returned to La Rochelle, where he waited anxiously for news of his northern allies. Despite frantic pleas, the barons of England refused to come to his aid.

On 27 July on some marshy fields near Bouvines, a village between Lille and Tournai, 24,000 imperial troops confronted Philip's slightly smaller army and a confused battle was fought until Otto's wounded horse ran away with him and the French won a crushing victory. This ended all John's hopes, if at first he did not realize it, sending money to the emperor and ordering Peter des Roches to hire 300 Welsh mercenaries for a fresh campaign. In September, however, he accepted a truce from Philip based on the status quo. Next month, he sailed into Dartmouth, humiliated. Normandy and Anjou were lost for ever.

Magna Carta

When at La Rochelle John had demanded financial compensation from magnates who had failed to accompany him while his justiciar, Peter des Roches, had outraged the entire baronage by abusing the law. Further taxes were the last straw for the northern lords led by Eustace de Vesci, who refused to pay despite Peter's threat to confiscate their estates. Nor were they more amenable after John's return. Protests came from East Anglia, led by Robert FitzWalter, then from all over England. In autumn 1214 the barons assembled at Bury St Edmunds to voice their grievances and at Epiphany 1215 met in London, fully armed, demanding reforms. The king promised to discuss their complaints at Northampton on the Sunday after Easter, but they did not trust him.

Early in the spring of 1215, five earls and forty barons – almost the entire nobility – elected FitzWalter 'Marshal of the army of the Lord and Holy Church', then gathered at Stamford before marching south. Their army consisted of 2,000 knights, with many more sergeants (mounted men-at-arms) and foot soldiers. Occupying Northampton, they besieged the castle but, failing to take it, advanced on London. En route, they renounced their feudal homage to the king – questioning his occupancy of the throne.

However, John had powerful allies in the Earls of Chester, Derby, Devon, Salisbury, Surrey and Warwick, who were the richest magnates in England, and in William Marshal. He was also backed by Archbishop Langton, eight other prelates, the Master of the Temple and the papal legate. He could rely, too, on lesser but extremely able men, such as Hubert de Burgh and Peter des Roches. On Ash Wednesday 1215 the king swore an oath to go on Crusade, which secured Innocent III's support. Early in May he gave the city of London a charter allowing its citizens to elect their mayor annually.

John's anxiety to avoid armed confrontation shows in a draft that historians call the 'Unknown Charter of Liberties', drawn up before June. Referring to Henry I's coronation charter, this contains such concessions as scaling down feudal dues, granting freedom of inheritance, abolishing scutage and military service overseas, cancelling debts to Jews and relaxing forest laws. 'Why don't the barons ask for my entire kingdom?', he had commented. 'What they're demanding is stupid and altogether unrealistic, with no sort of logic behind it.'[35] Yet the document shows he was ready to grant a good deal.

At Windsor on 9 May he announced that the dispute would be settled by eight arbitrators, four chosen by each side. When the barons rejected this, he ordered the sheriffs to seize their goods, which was impossible. On the morning of Sunday 17 May, when most citizens were at Mass, the barons entered London, where they took the opportunity to rob and kill Jews. There was trouble elsewhere, rebels capturing and occupying Exeter. Negotiating a truce through Archbishop Langton, John played for time in which to assemble a really large army. Finally he accepted that he must give way if he was to avoid deposition.

The two sides met on 15 June at Runnymede meadow, between Staines and Windsor, a draft treaty having been agreed as a basis for negotiation. 'Through the Archbishop of Canterbury's mediation, and that of some of his fellow bishops and several barons, a species of peace was concluded', says Ralph of Coggeshall with a certain understatement.[36] What was agreed after nearly a week's discussion was a reaffirmation of ancient law and custom applying to every freeman in England.

The real importance of the 'Great Charter of the Liberties of England and of the Liberties of the Forest' lies of course in the clause that no freeman can be imprisoned or dispossessed of his land or liberty, or outlawed or exiled or punished in any way, except by judgement of his peers or the law of the land. Translated into French in 1219 so that ordinary men could understand it, the Magna Carta was re-issued over 30 times – the last occasion being in 1423 – and, if many clauses have been repealed, is still on the statute books. As a twentieth century

Master of the Rolls, Lord Denning, famously put it, the charter is 'the greatest constitutional documents of all times – the foundation of the freedom of the individual against the arbitrary authority of the despot.'

The charter covered a bewildering number of grievances. There were clauses on the freedom of the Church, death duties, feudal aids (scutage, wardships, dowries, taxes, fines and marriage of heirs), widths of cloth, measures of wine, fish traps, debts to Jews, London liberties, free passage for merchants in war time, releasing Scottish hostages, exiling foreign mercenaries and relaxing forest laws – poachers would no longer risk losing their private parts. The last clause provided for a committee of twenty-five barons, chosen by those present at Runnymede, who were to seize the king's castles and lands if he failed to remedy all grievances listed within forty days.

Summoning John to settle a law case while he was ill, the twenty-five insisted he came in a litter, refusing to rise to their feet when he arrived. In any case, an investigation by another committee of twelve knights into the 'evil customs' of sheriffs, foresters and their officials (extorting money) made cooperation impossible – the king needed the revenue. Archbishop Langton did his best to reconcile the two sides but a letter from Pope Innocent released John from his oath, annulled the Charter as diabolical, and called Langton and the English bishops worse than Saracens for trying to depose an anointed king.

Civil war and death

Roger of Wendover and Matthew Paris (who continued Roger's chronicle) often exaggerate. Yet as monks of the great abbey of St Albans near the capital on the road north they met well-informed travellers and their accounts contain a basis of truth. Wendover may talk nonsense in claiming that after Runnymede John spent three months at sea as a pirate, but we can believe that he was in great agony of mind. Matthew adds that John imagined people saying behind his back, 'Look at a king without a kingdom, a lord without land!' While he smiled in public, in secret he 'ground his teeth and rolled his eyes, grabbing sticks and straws from off the floor which he chewed or tore in shreds with his fingers'.[37]

Warning castellans of the royal castles (there were nearly 150) to be on the alert, he sent to Flanders for more mercenaries, as he had few troops beside his bodyguard – Wendover says that only seven English knights remained with him. He expected them to arrive at the end of September, but their fleet ran into a gale and their bodies were washed up all along the Norfolk coast. When he heard the news he seemed out of his mind.

Collecting a scratch force from his garrisons, in October John laid siege to Rochester Castle, defended by William of Aubigny (one of the twenty-five barons) that barred the way to London. Instead of marching to William's relief, the barons occupying the capital spent their time 'gambling at dice, drinking the very best wines, which were freely available, and indulging in all the other vices.' The only action they took was to send envoys to Philip II's son, Louis, offering him the throne since he had a claim to it through his wife Blanche of Castile, who was a grand-daughter of Henry II.[38]

Eventually, foreign troops joined John (Poitevin and Gascon knights under Savaric de Mauléon who brought Flemish cross-bowmen) and Rochester was starved into surrender at the end of November. The king was encouraged still more in mid-December by Pope Innocent excommunicating thirty barons for rebellion – the document reached England in February, to be read from pulpits throughout the country. No other baronial stronghold put up a fight and, in control of the south and the West Country, John occupied East Anglia and the north, the revolt's real centres.

In the north he made his men set fire to towns and hedgerows as they marched, burning baronial manors and farms, torturing people of all classes until they paid a ransom. They ransacked towns and villages, hanging victims by their hands or roasting them. Markets and trading ceased, agriculture came to a standstill. Yet the king preferred money to revenge, extracting £1,000 from York, while rebels could purchase a pardon. By the spring of 1216 he had restored his authority across the whole country save London.

Invasion

The situation altered dramatically in May when Louis of France came with an army to claim the throne, landing on the Isle of Thanet. John made no attempt to intercept him. Leaving Dover Castle to be defended by Hubert de Burgh, he withdrew to Winchester, before establishing his headquarters in Dorset at Corfe Castle, which was almost impregnable. In August the sixteen-year-old Alexander II of Scots – whom John called 'the little, sandy fox-cub'[39] – took Carlisle and then marched to reinforce Louis, who was besieging Dover. Next month Alexander did homage to Louis at Canterbury, as King of England.

Louis quickly overran eastern England, where the only fortresses that held out for John were Dover, Lincoln and Windsor. Even so, the Cinque Ports supported him, while in Kent and Sussex there was guerrilla resistance in his favour, led by 'Willikin of the Weald', and on Whit Sunday 1216 Cardinal Guala Bicchieri, the papal legate, excommunicated Louis. But in June the Frenchman was welcomed by the Londoners as their King. John's position looked desperate. Winchester, the ancient capital, fell next and Windsor was closely besieged. The Earl of Salisbury, his half-brother, went over to Louis, with the Earls of Albemarle, Arundel and Warren, who together mustered 430 knights. The king retreated westward, as far as Radnor in Wales, where he hired Welsh archers.

Nonetheless, a third of the baronage stayed loyal and in late summer the Earl of Salisbury rejoined him. The rebels' relations with Louis were strained, since the French saw the war as a second Norman Conquest – in London a dying French nobleman warned that Louis had sworn to banish them after he won, for betraying their king. Taking Savaric de Mauléon as military adviser, in September John tried to relieve Windsor but, outnumbered, withdrew to ravage East Anglia. Chased off by the French, he went north to relieve Lincoln. Then he marched south, devastating Norfolk.

But after a feast at King's Lynn, John contracted dysentery and realized he was seriously ill. (Revealingly, he granted a Briouze lady leave to found a religious house to pray for the souls of her kinswoman Matilda de Briouze and her son.) On 12 October he took a short cut across the Wellstream, part of the Wash, where he 'lost all his carts, wagons and pack horses, with his money, plate and everything of value, because the land opened in the middle of the waters and whirlpools sucked them down, men and horses'. He was lucky to escape with his life.[40] He spent the night after at Swinehead Abbey, stuffing himself with peaches and new cider that made his dysentery worse. He struggled on to Newark in a litter of willow branches or clinging to a slow paced nag. Here, in the Bishop of Lincoln's castle, he received the last sacraments, making a short will in which he asked to be buried in St Wulstan's cathedral at Worcester and named William Marshal as his principal lay executor. The king died at midnight on 18 October, during a whirlwind.

Retrospect

If the Barnwell annalist thought John a great prince, no doubt, but hardly a lucky one, every other chronicler agreed with Matthew Paris that he was too bad even for Hell. He left England in chaos. Louis ruled London, Winchester and the home and eastern counties, the Welsh occupied Shrewsbury, the Scots held Northumberland, Cumberland and Westmorland and most barons remained in revolt. Whatever revisionists claim, a reign that saw the loss of Normandy and the Angevin patrimony, ending with civil war and foreign occupation, can scarcely be called a success.

5

The Aesthete – Henry III

A thriftless, shiftless king

Frederick Maitland[1]

An aesthete at bay

On 14 May 1264, after two warhorses had been killed under him, and reeling from sword and mace blows, Henry III staggered down from the battle on the Downs above Lewes to take refuge in the Black Monks' priory. Simon de Montfort's men surrounded it, shooting flaming arrows that set fire to the roof of its great church (bigger than Chichester Cathedral) until the king sent out an envoy to ask for terms. He then agreed to everything for which the rebels had asked, becoming a crowned figurehead; his son Edward was hostage for his behaviour.

Usually remembered only for his struggle with Simon, Henry is one of our most interesting kings, an aesthete (if the term can be used of a medieval man) who built on the grand scale, and even if it was no thanks to him he left the parliamentary system. Prouder than any previous post-Conquest ruler of being heir to the Anglo-Saxon kings, he was the most English monarch since 1066.

The boy king

Since the enemy occupied London and Winchester, the nine-year-old Henry was crowned at Gloucester, with a plain gold circlet. But by then, ten days after John's death, Louis seemed more like a French conqueror than Magna Carta's saviour, and many who had opposed John saw no reason why a small boy should lose his inheritance to a foreigner. His father's will won papal support by urging compensation for the Church and help for the Holy Land.

On his deathbed the late king had begged his supporters to make William Marshal regent. 'For God's sake, beg the Marshal to forgive me', John had told them. 'I know he is truer than any other man and I beseech you to make him my son's guardian and see he takes care of him – my son can never keep these lands without the Marshal's help.'[2] Reluctantly (he was nearly seventy) and only after a great deal of persuasion, William accepted, saying he felt as though he was sailing on a bottomless sea with no prospect of landfall, but, if need be, would find refuge in Ireland and take the boy there on his shoulders. His council included Hubert de Burgh, holding out at Dover, and Peter des Roches, who became the king's tutor.

On hearing John was dead, Louis thought he had won. But the rebels were angered by his giving English estates to Frenchmen and by atrocities committed by his troops, whom the chroniclers call refuse and scum. William Marshal reissued Magna Carta with a new Charter of the Forest, demolishing the rebels' platform, and during Louis's absence in France in Lent 1217 the barons began to desert him. In May, while Louis was besieging Dover, William's troops stormed Lincoln, killing or capturing half his army. Then a fleet bringing reinforcements from France was destroyed off Sandwich.

When King Philip, Louis's father, heard William Marshal was in command, he said that his son had lost. In September Louis agreed to stop helping the English rebels and to give back the Channel Islands, the regency council paying him over £7,000 to go home. Rebel barons went unpunished. By the time William Marshal died in 1219, the old hero had restored some sort of law and order, and in 1221 Henry was crowned for a second time, at Westminster with the crown of St Edward. Yet the monarchy was still very weak and there was no guarantee Louis might not invade again. The Crown was heavily in debt, while the magnates had little respect for its authority.

The chief justiciar, Hubert de Burgh, governed England for more than a decade. A man on the make from the petty gentry who was turning himself into a magnate by acquiring castles and estates, he grew increasingly unpopular. Nevertheless, aided by Archbishop Langton and lawyers such as Henry de Bracton, he ensured the monarchy's survival. In a full-scale campaign, he put an end to the Earl of Albemarle's seizure of other men's castles, while he checked the ravages of Falkes de Breauté (a Norman who had been King John's favourite commander) by storming his stronghold at Bedford and hanging eighty of his men. For lack of money Hubert was unable to relieve La Rochelle when Louis VIII besieged it, and in consequence by autumn 1224 Gascony alone remained from the Angevin empire. Even so, Hubert stayed in power after Henry came of age in 1227, becoming Earl of Kent.

The man

Stockily built and 5 ft 6 in tall, Henry III had long, thick, yellow hair cut just below the ear, a beard and a moustache, with a drooping eyelid that hid half his left eye. We know exactly what he looked like from the effigy on his tomb in Westminster

Abbey; its fine, handsome features are based on his death mask. He was quiet voiced with a stammer, gentle in manner except when angry. His sharp intelligence was unbalanced by too much imagination and sensitivity, by bouts of ill health and nervous attacks. He had a naïve streak which, combined with a sardonic sense of humour, could give unintentional offence. Not a strong character, he fell under the spell of foreign favourites, who were disliked by everyone else.

'Accomplished, refined, liberal, magnificent; rash rather than brave, impulsive and ambitious, pious and, in an ordinary sense, virtuous, he was utterly devoid of all elements of greatness', wrote Stubbs. 'Unlike his father, who was incapable of receiving any impression, Henry was so susceptible of impressions that none of them could last long; John's heart was of millstone, Henry's of wax.'[3]

Yet he had unusual gifts. His lasting memorial is Westminster Abbey if his palace next door and apartments at the Tower have gone. Clarendon, too, went long ago, but excavation gives us some idea of how he rebuilt the woodland palace in the new Gothic style until it covered more than 8 acres. Using stone from Caen, his masons erected halls and chambers lit by stained glass – its earliest domestic use in England – and warmed by fireplaces, with walls, ceilings and wainscots painted in bright colours. There were gilded stone carvings over the fireplaces and doorways, and tiled pavements with lions and griffins. Henry's bedroom had frescoes of the four Evangelists, while there was a carving of the twelve months over the hearth in the queen's. The two chapels, one for the king, the other for the queen, were especially magnificent. There was a 'great garden', together with herb gardens, covered alleys bordered by flower beds, and stabling for 120 horses. He also made extensive additions at Winchester, Marlborough and Windsor, turning them into palaces as well as castles.

Henry resembled his father in his sudden (if rarer and milder) rages, on one occasion throwing a jester into the Thames for an unfortunate joke. Yet he was good natured, constantly giving presents to his household and alms to the poor: 5,000 paupers were fed in Westminster Hall on Edward the Confessor's day, while in his palaces were frescoes of the parable of Dives and Lazarus with the motto 'He who does not give what he cherishes shall not obtain his desire'. Henry grew devoted to his wife and family – and did not take mistresses. 'The "simplicity" so often mentioned by Matthew Paris and others was a kind of innocence which remained with him throughout his life and explains a curiously attractive quality.'[4]

Born at Winchester, the ancient capital and brought up in England, Henry was obsessed with his Anglo-Saxon predecessors. Choosing the Confessor for his patron saint, he named his eldest son after him and his second after the East Anglian martyr king, St Edmund. Genuinely devout, he made many pilgrimages to the Marian shrine at Walsingham in Norfolk, and endowed over thirty friaries. When Louis said that he often heard a sermon instead of going to Mass, Henry replied that he preferred to see a friend rather than hear someone talk about him.

Still an Angevin

At the same time, Henry III saw himself as an Angevin, mistakenly believing that Prince Louis had promised to persuade Philip II to return the lost Plantagenet lands, and that the old Marshal had missed a real chance of recovering them by failing to capture Louis in 1216–17. Unfortunately, the Capetians now ruled all France, while the Lusignan family who controlled Poitou were their loyal subjects.

Henry's obsession with the lost lands was fostered by his tutor from Touraine, Peter des Roches. Peter hoped to set him against Hubert de Burgh, whose policy was peace at all costs – with the barons, with Scots, Welsh and French. When in 1229 Hubert told the king not to invade across the Channel, Henry was so angry that he half drew his sword and called him a traitor. Ignoring Hubert's warnings, in 1230 he led an expedition to Brittany, where he was welcomed by its count, Peter of Dreux, a dissatisfied Capetian. 'The king stayed in the city of Nantes for most of the time, doing nothing but spend money' was what Roger of Wendover heard. 'Since Hubert, the king's justiciar, did not want them to wage war, his earls and barons entertained each other over and over again in a true English way, eating and drinking as if keeping Christmas.'[5] In despair, Henry led a meaningless *promenade militaire* down to Bordeaux, before returning to England.

Trouble with the Church partially – but only partially – explains what happened next. John's reliance on Innocent III had enabled papal officials to establish themselves in England, where they appropriated benefices whose revenues went to clergy in Italy, depriving landowners of the right to appoint relatives or friends. In 1231 a group of gentry began kidnapping and robbing Roman tax collectors, who in any case were disliked as foreigners.

When the king came home after recovering nothing more than the island of Oleron, Peter des Roches told him his failure was Hubert's fault. Henry thus dismissed Hubert in 1232, on the pretext of allowing the Roman tax collectors to be persecuted. (He was also accused of poisoning the Earl of Pembroke.) The new justiciar was Stephen de Segrave, a 'yielding man'. Real power lay with the new treasurer Peter de Rivaux, behind whom lurked his uncle Peter des Roches. Hubert had always tried to keep on good terms with the barons, even if they disliked him. Now, however, too much efficiency and disregard for custom, together with the fact that the two Peters were not only foreigners but brought in others, angered the baronage.

The treasurer turned the Wardrobe (which previously dealt only with the king's personal expenses) into a department that oversaw treasury, exchequer and taxation, and appointed sheriffs. More controversially, Poitevin, Flemish and Breton troops were imported from France to garrison royal castles, on Peter des Roches's advice. 'Poor and greedy', says the chronicler, 'these men did their hardest to cow the native English and the nobles, whom they called traitors and betrayers of their king. Naïvely, he believed their lies, putting them in charge of the shires and the young nobility of both sexes, who were degraded by ignoble marriages . . . wherever he went he was surrounded by foreigners.'[6] One reason why Poitevins were so disliked was that instead of Norman French they spoke an incomprehensible, partly Occitan, dialect.

Peter des Roches was playing a deep game. He wanted the magnates to rise in revolt so that he could crush them and build the monarchy envisaged by King John. Just as he hoped, several rebelled, led by the old marshal's son Richard, Earl of Pembroke. However, contrary to Peter's expectations, his Poitevins failed to win the ensuing war, even though Earl Richard was killed in Ireland. Henry was so alarmed that he went to pray at Walsingham. Finally, the saintly Archbishop of Canterbury, Edmund of Abingdon, denounced Peter des Roches and his nephew for giving the king bad advice that was endangering the kingdom. Unless Henry got rid of them, he would excommunicate the king. In April 1234 Henry dismissed his ministers and expelled the Poitevin troops.

The personal rule of Henry III, 1234–58

For the next quarter of a century, Henry governed by himself. The reforms of Hubert de Burgh and Peter de Rivaux stayed, the king keeping control of central government and the sheriffs. Even Peter de Rivaux was reinstated, in a different capacity. But there was no attempt to challenge the magnates' liberties – Henry wanted peace and stability no less than Hubert de Burgh. In 1237, and again in 1253, he reissued Magna Carta.[7]

In January 1236 the twenty-eight-year-old king married Eleanor, one of the daughters of Raymond Berenguer IV, Count of Provence, and his wife Beatrice of Savoy (a beauty whom Matthew Paris compared to Homer's Niobe). His choice was dictated by foreign policy – her sister had married Louis IX – but the match turned out to be one of the happiest in English royal history. A brunette, Eleanor was intelligent and well educated, writing verse that has not survived, perhaps taught by her father who was a considerable Provencal poet.

Only twelve, if 'very fair to behold', she must have been terrified when at Westminster, five days after her wedding to a man she had never seen, 'with unheard of and incomparable solemnity Eleanor wore the crown and was crowned queen'.[8] She grew into a handsome, strong-minded woman who overruled her husband more than once, although she shared his tastes and was a patron of the arts in her own right.[9] Her only weakness was a love of luxury. The couple were devoted to each other and to their children. When in 1246 it looked as if their seven-year-old, eldest son Edward was dying, she stayed by the boy's bedside for three weeks. They had another son, Edmund, who also grew to adulthood, together with two daughters, one of whom died aged three, to her parents' deep distress.

The queen brought her uncles to England, William, Bishop elect of Valence, and his brother Peter of Savoy, to both of whom Henry took a liking. Although the magnates loathed William, the king tried to bully the Winchester monks into electing him as their bishop, but failed; and he left England – to be poisoned in Italy. More tactful, if so formidable that fellow Savoyards called him 'Little Charlemagne', Peter stayed on. In 1241 the king made him Earl of Richmond, the same year that he secured the election of a third uncle, Boniface, an arrogant man whom Matthew Paris says was more distinguished for birth than brains, as Archbishop of Canterbury. These were only the most notable of the Provencals and Savoyards brought in by the queen, many of whom she married to heiresses. The English hated them no less than they did the Poitevins.

A few years earlier Henry had given the earldom of Leicester to his protégé Simon de Montfort, whose Anglo-Norman family had been deprived of it by John. In 1238 Simon secretly married the king's sister, the widowed Countess of Pembroke – according to Henry, Simon had seduced her. As the king was still childless, there were implications for the succession. His hot-tempered brother Richard, Earl of Cornwall became so angry that he threatened to revolt, supported by the Londoners and the bishops, the latter protesting that the lady had taken a vow of perpetual chastity. Richard calmed down on being paid the huge sum of 16,000 marks – nearly £12,000 – for his crusading expenses. The next year, Henry fell out with Simon, who also went on Crusade.

In 1235 Matthew Paris followed Roger of Wendover as chronicler at St Albans Abbey, which he remained until his death in 1259. He wrote so readably that great men sent to St Albans to borrow his books, and in 1236 the king ordered Matthew to write Edward the Confessor's life, *Le Estoire de Seint Aedward le Rei*, summoning him to court. Despite having little respect for Henry, whom he met many times, Matthew's account of the reign is invaluable.[10]

The end of the Angevin Empire

In February 1242 Henry summoned the magnates to London, to raise funds for another French campaign. 'Everybody knew that the count of La Marche, who was pestering the king to come over at once with all the cash he could bring, did not think much of English soldiers and had no respect for the fighting qualities and courage of our kingdom's knighthood', Matthew tells us. 'He regarded the king as a fool and was only interested in laying hands on his money.'[11] When Henry told his magnates he had accepted the count's invitation, they told him his plan was unworkable; that previously he had made their lives a misery by extracting huge sums which he squandered, and that they refused to be robbed again. Pleading, Henry found enough money for his expedition, which sailed in May.

The opportunity he thought he saw in Poitou was provided by his termagant mother Isabella. In 1220 she had married Hugh of Lusignan, Count of La Marche, the son of her former betrothed, despite his being affianced to her daughter – 'one of the most extraordinary marriages in history'.[12] In 1241, while visiting the court of Louis IX, Isabella was insulted by being told to stand when Louis's mother and other great ladies were seated. Furious, she persuaded the Poitevin barons to rebel, bullying her husband into leading them. They were joined by Count Raymond of Toulouse and various Pyrenean lords, troubadours singing songs that accused the English king of failing to free the people south of the Loire.

Louis invaded Poitou a month before the English landed, capturing castles and cowing its barons. When Henry confronted the French army at Taillebourg in July, he realized he was heavily outnumbered and reproached Hugh of Lusignan for not bringing the Poitevin knights he had promised in his letters. 'I promised no such thing', replied the count. 'Blame it on your mother, my wife. By the throne of God, she's got us into this mess without my knowing anything about it.'[13] Barely escaping capture, Henry fled, never drawing rein until he reached Saintes and finally taking refuge at Bordeaux – 'since we could no longer linger among these perfidious Poitevins who have no shame'.[14] He stayed there until the following autumn and, as the English magnates had expected, 'spent his treasure to no purpose'.

Taillebourg ended the Angevin dream of reconquest. It was a disaster mainly thanks to Isabella, who fled to Fontevrault where she stayed until her death, lucky not to be lynched: French and Poitevins gathered outside the abbey walls, yelling that she was a wicked Jezebel. King Louis fastened his grip on Poitou, Count Hugh losing his independence. Henry returned to England a beaten man, as his father had done thirty years before.

Foreign favourites

On his return, even more southern Frenchmen surrounded the king, partly because of his brother Richard's marriage to the queen's sister, Sanchia of Provence ('Cynthia' in English), who brought a fresh influx of her fellow countrymen. At the same time, after Louis IX's conquest of Poitou, Henry's Lusignan half-brothers fled to England, where William became Earl of Pembroke and Aymer Bishop elect of Winchester, while Guy was given so much money that he needed packhorses to carry it. (Matthew Paris jeered that as a result Henry was reduced to 'robbing or begging in order to eat'.) What caused deep offence was the Lusignans' arrogance and that of their agents.[15] But the king protected them, so they appeared to be above the law.

Henry wanted his wife to share his fascination with the Confessor, one reason why he commissioned Matthew Paris's biography which was dedicated to her. Spending tens of millions in today's money, he rebuilt Edward's church at Westminster Abbey in an English version of the new Gothic style, reburying him in a tomb adorned with mosaics of marble, glass and gold by Cosmati craftsmen from Rome, surrounded by a Cosmati pavement, the only example of such work outside Italy. (Their wonderful pavement in front of the High Altar was restored in 2012.) Painted in green, carmine or indigo, the entire building was designed as an extended shrine.

Learning from Matthew Paris's book that Edward had worn the plainest clothes, Henry began to dress simply. There was a statue of Edward in every palace chapel, while a likeness of him was painted on the throne and scenes from his life painted in the royal bedchambers. The cult had a political as well as a spiritual function, proclaiming Henry's right to represent the pre-Conquest kings of England. Even before work began at Westminster, he built a great hall at Winchester, where many of the old kings lay buried.

Foreign affairs

In 1252, 'unwilling to recall that he had twice presented Gascony by charter to Earl Richard, he [Henry] gave it to his eldest son Edward, mainly because of the queen's insistence', Matthew Paris tells us sardonically. 'When he heard, Earl Richard was enraged and left court.'[16] After a surprisingly successful campaign pacifying Gascony, which had been in revolt after Simon de Montfort's harsh viceroyalty, in 1254 Henry and Eleanor visited Louis IX at Paris. The visit turned into a family party as the two queens were sisters, and Louis was transformed into a firm friend. Henry was so thrilled by the new Sainte-Chapelle (built to house a relic of the True Cross) that Parisians joked he wanted to take it home with him in a cart.

Henry's piety was unruffled by papal tax gatherers syphoning off 5 per cent of the English Church's income. In 1240 the rectors of Berkshire, 'each and every one', complained in a collective letter to Pope Gregory IX that they had no obligation to finance his war on the Emperor – Frederick II might be excommunicated but he was not a heretic. They were expressing resentment that was felt all over England.

But the king did not want to upset Rome. After Frederick died, Henry reached an agreement with Alexander IV in 1255 by which the pope absolved him from his oath to go on Crusade, and recognized his younger son Edmund as King of Sicily in place of the late Emperor's bastard son Manfred. In return, Henry paid over £90,000, with gold that he had been hoarding for his Crusade. Alexander wrote eloquently of 'the royal family of England, whom we regard with special affection', and how Edmund would be 'received [in Sicily] like the morning star'.[17]

Two years later, Richard of Cornwall was crowned King of the Romans at Aachen – Holy Roman Emperor elect. He paid huge sums for the privilege, his brother telling him that such an honour exalted the whole English nation. Henry was so euphoric that he issued a beautiful gold coin worth 20 silver pence, showing the King of England on his own throne with crown, orb and sceptre. Because the gold content was undervalued, it quickly disappeared from circulation, but the six surviving examples are a monument to Henry's flamboyant heyday.

There remained the small problem of replacing the warlike King Manfred with ten-year-old Edmund. (When Richard of Cornwall had been offered Sicily before Henry accepted it for Edmund, he told Pope Alexander's nuncio, 'You might as well try and sell me the moon as a bargain, saying, "Go up there and grab it."'[18]) Optimistically, the pope invaded Manfred's territory and, after his troops were defeated, sent Henry a bill in 1257 for nearly £100,000 – although the king had already paid huge sums. Fearful of being excommunicated if he did not settle it, Henry summoned the magnates to a 'parliament' (which meant a discussion) at Westminster Abbey, parading Edmund in Apulian dress and explaining his predicament. The bishops offered just over £52,000 if the lower clergy would agree, but the barons refused outright.

The barons' war 1258–65

Henry was thought to have squandered 950,000 marks (over £600,000) in a decade. For years he had been extorting loans from Londoners and Jews, besides extracting every sort of fine and feudal due, and shortly before the pope presented his bill the barons had declined to pay another 'aid' on the grounds that they were not summoned in the way laid down by Magna Carta. Not only was the king's credit exhausted, but he had antagonized the barons by favouring the Lusignans, whose arrogance infuriated them; when Simon de Montfort came back to England and had a spectacular row with William of Valence, they applauded him. The parliament met at Westminster early in April 1258 to discuss the Sicilian business, which gave them a chance to take action.[19]

On 30 April Simon de Montfort, with the Earls of Norfolk

and Gloucester and others, entered Westminster Hall in armour, surrounding Henry. 'What's this, my lords?' gasped the king. 'Am I your prisoner?' 'No, my lord,' answered Roger Bigod. 'But make those wretched, unbearable Poitevins, and all the other foreigners, get out of your sight and ours.'[20] Henry and his heir the Lord Edward were forced to swear on the Gospels that they would introduce a new system of government. A committee of twenty-four, twelve chosen by the king and twelve by the magnates, was to discuss reforms. Somewhat tactlessly, among his twelve members Henry nominated all four Lusignan half-brothers.

What Henry's supporters called the 'Mad Parliament of Oxford' met in June 1258. The magnates ordered the knights on their estates to accompany them, armed, on the pretext of preparing for a campaign in Wales. 'They were frightened civil war would break out if there was any disagreement, and that the king and his Poitevin brethren might bring in foreign troops', Matthew tells us. 'So they put a guard on all the sea ports.'[21] It was the first time that knights had attended a parliament in such numbers and, from the magnates' point of view, it gave them ideas above their station. Moreover, these minor landowners had a lot to worry about as it was a rainy summer, which meant a bad harvest and famine.

A 'petition of the barons of England' was presented. As a result, a new council of fifteen was elected by four of the twenty-four, to appoint all great officials, sheriffs and royal castellans, while it was agreed that parliament should meet three times a year to monitor government. A justiciar was appointed for the first time since 1234, with the chancellor and the treasurer under the council's control. The petition was strongly supported by the knights, as it included their grievances about sheriffs who pocketed illegal fines and 'powerful people of the realm' who bought bonds from Jewish bankers and then foreclosed. Everybody knew that the noble bond sharks included 'Poitevins'.[22]

Reluctantly, the king swore to observe the 'Provisions of

Oxford'. Among them was an act resuming all the lands he had
granted to his Poitevin half-brothers. 'They and their henchmen take the opportunity to behave insolently, aggressively
and haughtily to Englishmen, robbing them of their goods and
treating them with utter contempt' says the act.[23] By the end of
June the Lusignans had been chased out of England.

In October another parliament at Westminster redefined
the office of sheriff and its duties, nineteen knights becoming
sheriffs of their counties. Proclamations were then issued by the
council of fifteen, which promised to redress wrongs and were
read aloud in every shire court, in Latin, French and English
– the first royal documents in the native language since the
Conquest. They stated the king's wish that swift justice should
be done throughout his realm for poor as well as rich, and made
the sheriffs salaried servants of the Crown.

Stubbs writes of Henry's 'feminine quality of irresolute perti-
nacity which it would be a mockery to call elasticity',[24] but now
he showed real political sense. Realizing that his brother-in-law
Louis IX might be persuaded to intervene, in November 1259
he went to Paris where he agreed to abandon the lost lands,
Louis acknowledging his lordship of Gascony as a French vassal;
in future, each English king was to pay homage for the duchy on
succeeding to his throne. Henry stayed in France for months,
forging a close bond with the French royal family – he was a pall-
bearer at the funeral of Louis's eldest son – while postponing a
new parliament and letting the reformers quarrel with each other.

Simon de Montfort

Unexpectedly, Simon de Montfort, who had fallen out with
Gloucester and gone abroad, returned to England in January
1260 and insisted on a parliament being held in the king's
absence. It met the next month, confirming the Provisions. The
council decided that Henry must be under surveillance between
parliaments and, besides appointing sheriffs and castellans who

were sympathetic to their ideas, set up a committee to oversee his finances. The king complained angrily that they were taking all his powers away.

Simon was an alarming opponent, a gigantic personality, austere, pious, with unusual histrionic gifts and a brilliant brain – the friend of intellectuals such as the mathematician Bishop Grosseteste and the Franciscan don Adam Marsh, who was his confessor. In 1241 he had so impressed the barons of the Holy Land that they petitioned their absentee king, the emperor Frederick, to appoint him *bailli* (regent) of the kingdom of Jerusalem, while as Lieutenant of Gascony he had been dreaded by its unruly nobles. He despised Henry, saying he should be locked up in the same way as a famously inept French monarch of long ago, Charles the Simple. 'I'm horribly frightened of thunder and lightning but, by God's head, I'm more frightened of you than all the thunder and lightning in the world', the king once told him.[25] What inspired Simon to support the 'commune of England' was what he had seen in Palestine, where barons shared power with their king.

The situation deteriorated. Llewelyn ap Gruffydd, Prince of Wales, attacked the Marcher lords, while it was rumoured that the Lusignans were invading the West Country and the Lord Edward would seize the throne. Both rumours were false, but the baronial council put London on a defence footing. Henry returned in April 1260, his mercenaries occupying the Tower, and was reconciled with Edward after keeping him at a distance for some days – worried lest affection might blind his judgement. (He said that if he saw his son he could not resist embracing him.) He hoped to have Simon tried as a traitor at a parliament held in July, but Louis intervened on the earl's behalf. Once again, Simon left England.

The king's absence in France had widened the rift between magnates and knights, and Henry began to regain control. In April a bull arrived from Pope Alexander IV, absolving him from his oath to obey the Provisions, while another bull threatening to excommunicate anyone who tried to reduce his authority was read at Paul's Cross. Henry replaced the justiciar and the chancellor, installed royalist castellans and ordered a general eyre (an investigation by judges) to examine the reforms. He even allowed the Lusignan William de Valence to return.

There was a violent reaction by the knights, which Simon returned to lead. In August Henry issued a proclamation, complaining that he had been slandered and defending his right to replace officials. In September, when three knights from each shire were summoned to an assembly at Windsor, he told them he wanted peace, and in November he outwitted the earl by promising reforms. Neither side made progress during 1262, despite Simon reappearing at the autumn parliament and Henry being forced to confirm the Provisions shortly after Christmas. In spring 1263 he refused to confirm them again, so at Whitsun Simon once more returned to England. He led an armed rising that ended in stalemate after the Lord Edward reoccupied Windsor Castle. Richard of Cornwall – the 'King of Germany' – negotiated a truce.

A wish for reform remained strong, however, especially among clerics – who warmly supported Simon. So did the Londoners, who in July stoned the queen's barge as she was being rowed up the Thames from the Tower to Windsor: the mayor had to rescue her. When Simon was trapped by royal troops in Southwark in December 1263 and feared for his life, he was saved by Londoners who let him into the City. After months of sporadic civil war, in desperation both sides asked King Louis to arbitrate, swearing to accept his decision. In January 1264 at the 'Mise' (Trial) of Amiens, Louis found in favour of his brother-in-law, who was present, annulling the Provisions of Oxford while stipulating that he must not take revenge. Simon and a number of barons refused to accept the verdict, however, and when Henry held an assembly at Oxford in March they demanded the Provisions, then rose in revolt.

Since both the King of France and the pope had decided

against them, their cause had lost its legitimacy. Supported by the upper nobility, Henry secured the Midlands, capturing Northampton in April. He then marched south, where he was joined by a contingent from the Cinque Ports. En route, during an ambush, the king's favourite cook was killed by an arrow, and in a rare moment of savagery Henry had 300 captured archers beheaded in his presence.

On 14 May 1264, at Offham Hill near Lewes in Sussex, Simon de Montfort's 600 men-at-arms and 4,400 foot soldiers, who had occupied the summit during the night, routed twice as many royal troops. The king had been so confident that he displayed the banner of the 'Dragon', ordering his men to give no quarter. However, the Lord Edward weakened his father's front by an undisciplined charge against the Londoners on the right. According to William Rishanger, he 'thirsted for their blood because of the way they had insulted his mother, and chased them for four miles'.[26] Beaten back after trying to attack uphill, the rest of the royal army disintegrated, fleeing down to Lewes. Simon killed or captured nearly 3,000, mainly foot soldiers. His prisoners included the king, Edward and Richard of Cornwall.

In June a parliament established a council of nine, chosen by three electors (the Bishop of Chichester, the new Earl of Gloucester and Simon) to direct the king, who could no longer appoint officers of state or household officers without their approval. These measures were confirmed by Simon's Great Parliament at the start of 1265, which was broader based than any previous assembly, with two knights elected by the shire court of every county and two burgesses from every city or borough. Threatened with deposition, Henry agreed to everything demanded by the 'Steward of England', as Simon styled himself.

Simon's defeat

Few barons had attended the parliament, as Simon was jeopardizing their interests by relying on knights and burgesses. They also knew that Henry III was a puppet, a prisoner of the earl. The North and the West never acknowledged Simon's government, while Queen Eleanor was raising troops in France and the Marcher lords were his enemies. His position improved at the end of 1264 when he forced the Marchers to accept his authority, but just after Easter 1265 his most powerful ally, the Earl of Gloucester, quarrelled with him – arguing that, as a foreigner, Simon had no right to rule England. In response, Simon marched westward, to seize Gloucester's castles in Glamorgan and obtain reinforcements from Llewelyn. He brought the Lord Edward with him.

At the end of May 1265 Edward made a dramatic escape from Hereford, using an exceptionally fast horse to outdistance the gaolers who had taken him out for exercise, and reached the Mortimers. Joined by Gloucester's men, he rode south with the Marchers to confront Simon in a complex campaign of manoeuvres and skirmishes. Surprising and destroying a large body of troops under Simon's son at Kenilworth, Edward then trapped Simon himself with his army (unwillingly accompanied by King Henry) on 4 August, encircling them in a bend of the River Avon near Evesham.

'God have mercy on our souls because our bodies are theirs', groaned Earl Simon. During a thunderstorm Edward's troops killed or captured over 3,000 of the earl's men after they failed to break out. Simon was among the dead. His followers had wanted the king to die with them. Without a surcoat, his face hidden by a close-fitting helmet, he was unrecognizable, and after being wounded in the neck only just saved his life by shouting, 'I am Henry, the old king of England – for the love of God, don't hit me!'[27] The earl's body was castrated by one of the victors, Sir William Maltravers, who chopped off Simon's head and limbs and nailed his genitalia to his face. The so-called 'baronial party' died with him.

Simon de Montfort had been a hero to many. The poor blessed him for making the law more accessible; the knights were grateful for their summons to parliament and rescue from overbearing magnates. 'A mighty man, prudent, far seeing', commented William Rishanger (Matthew Paris's successor at St Albans), saying how often the earl was in church, how he always asked monks and friars to pray for him, how he was a close friend of the holy Bishop of Lincoln, Robert Grosseteste. 'Once he swore [to observe the Provisions of Oxford] Simon stood firm as a strong pillar, and neither bribes nor flattery could make him join other barons in betraying his oath to reform the kingdom.' It is odd to find so warm a tribute from the pedestrian Rishanger.[28] This flattering view persisted: the Victorians regarded Simon as founder of the House of Commons.

In contrast, the Osney canon Thomas Wykes saw him as a criminal who plundered the realm and despised fellow barons as 'fickle and unstable – he never stopped calling them unreliable wretches'.[29] To him, they were nonentities, wax in his terrible hands. What makes Wykes plausible is his objectivity. He was as horrified by Henry letting London Jews be massacred in 1263 as he was by Simon taking a share of their stolen goods. Even the earl's admirer Stubbs writes that 'If Simon had lived longer the prospect of a throne might have opened before him, and he might have become a destroyer rather than a saviour.'[30]

In a parliament at Winchester in September, Henry confiscated 254 estates, which shows how many knights fought against him. Some held out in Kenilworth Castle, so in October 1266 he issued the Dictum of Kenilworth, allowing rebels to buy back their lands for a few years' rent. (It also threatened to excommunicate anyone who venerated Simon as a saint.) The Kenilworth garrison surrendered in December, but even then a small band went on holding out on the Isle of Ely. When the Earl of Gloucester occupied London in April 1267, demanding fairer treatment of the 'dispossessed', he was joined by a few irreconcilables. But Gloucester submitted in June, the Ely men in July.

Henry's triumph

At a parliament held at Marlborough in November, forgetting the humiliations of nearly a decade (and what amounted to an attempt to murder him at Evesham), the king granted the demands of the Mad Parliament nine years before, redressing the knights' grievances. There were no reprisals, a magnanimity for which he seldom receives credit. The dispossessed recovered their estates, while after paying fines the Londoners were regranted their privileges. Peace was made with Llewelyn ap Gruffydd, recognized as Prince of Wales.

Henry's victory had been inevitable as the barons did not want to be ruled by knights. By 1268 his regime was so secure that the Lord Edward felt confident enough to take a vow to go on Crusade. During the two years before he sailed, he was the last of the strong personalities who dominated Henry – no King of England ever enjoyed a happier relationship with his heir. In October 1269 at Westminster Abbey, with Prince Edmund and Richard of Cornwall, father and son carried on their shoulders the relics of Edward the Confessor to his new shrine in the apse behind the altar, although the new abbey church was only partially built. It was the realization of Henry's dream.

He died at Westminster in November 1272 after the longest reign England had ever known. As an Angevin he left instructions for his heart to be interred at Fontevrault, but as heir of the pre-Conquest kings he was buried at Westminster Abbey in coronation robes and wrapped in cloth of gold, interred in the tomb he had designed near the shrine of his 'friend' the Confessor. The funeral displayed all the elegant pomp that was his lasting gift to the English monarchy.

Retrospect

There was no Angevin demon in Henry III. Modern historians have a soft spot for him, a recent biographer discerning 'a lack of foresight and a basic goodness of heart'.[31] The best verdict is still Maurice Powicke's. 'When all is said and done, Henry remains a decent man . . . The simplicity which could by turns amuse and madden those who had to do with him maintained him in the end. He got through all his troubles and left England more prosperous, more united, more peaceful, more beautiful than it was when he was a child.'[32]

PART 2

Plantagenet Britain?

6

The Hammer – Edward I

the tall, lithe, sinewy creature described by his contemporaries, fine and attractive, clear and emphatic in speech, uncertain in temper, reasonable in counsel

Sir Maurice Powicke[1]

King of all Britain

In March 1304 Edward I held a parliament at St Andrew's 'where he proclaimed his peace'.[2] It was attended by 129 major Scottish landowners, who had been summoned by Edward as King of England, including most of their earls, barons, bishops and abbots, among them the Earl of Carrick – Robert the Bruce.[3] Scotland no longer existed as a separate kingdom.

Until recently Edward I ranked with Alfred the Great in the national myth. There was plenty of the family demon about him when angry, but with his superb physique and dynamism he seemed more like a daemon from Greek mythology – half-way between man and god. We think of him as conqueror of

Wales and 'Hammer of the Scots', forgetting his role as law-giver, for he was very much the heir of his great-grandfather, Henry II. The Jacobean jurist, Sir Edward Coke, called him 'The English Justinian', and if Edward cannot take all the credit for the law's progress during his reign, he certainly drove it. Unfortunately, he rarely comes alive in the chronicles because there was no one of Matthew Paris's calibre to guess at what was in his mind.

Early years

Born in 1239, as a young man Edward seemed so unstable that Matthew Paris dreaded how he might turn out. Having been close to the Lusignans, he joined the reformers and Simon de Montfort, then rallied to his father – whoever wrote the Song of Lewes in 1264 jeered that he changed his loyalties as the fabulous Pard did its spots. But when a former supporter of Simon, Sir Adam Gurdon, one of the 'dispossessed' who had taken to highway robbery, ambushed the prince in a Hampshire forest, Edward not only worsted Gurdon in single combat, but turned him into a loyal supporter. In any case, outwitting and destroying de Montfort was no small achievement.

Crusader

In the summer of 1270 Edward crossed to France, then sailed from Aigues-Mortes to join the Eighth Crusade at the siege of Tunis, where he learned that its leader, his uncle Louis IX, had just died. He sailed on to Palestine, landing at the capital, Acre, in May 1271 with less than a thousand troops. The kingdom of Jerusalem, now a mere strip of land along the coast, was reeling from the attacks of Sultan Baibars of Egypt, a Kipchak Turk who sometimes skinned prisoners alive. All that Edward could do was to lead a few raids.

Nevertheless, in June 1272 Baibars tried to murder him, using a Muslim whom the English trusted. Coming to his tent late at night when he was alone, the man stabbed him with a poisoned dagger, and, although Edward killed his assailant, he nearly died. The story of his wife sucking the venom from his wound is improbable – more likely, the flesh around it was cut away – but he made a complete recovery.

When Edward left Acre for Sicily in September 1272, the kingdom of Jerusalem was no more secure than when he arrived, but he had gained enormous prestige. He also made useful friends – Archbishop Tebaldo Visconti, a pilgrim to the Holy Land, and Fra' Joseph de Chauncy, Prior of the Knights Hospitaller of England, whom he made his treasurer. He had learned, too, how impregnable castles supplied from the sea could protect exposed territory.

In Sicily, news came of the deaths of his five-year-old son John and of King Henry. When the Sicilian king, Charles of Anjou, marvelled that Edward mourned his child so little and his father so much, he answered that he could beget another son but fathers were irreplaceable. At Orvieto he was greeted magnificently by his friend Visconti, now Pope Gregory X. He also received a warm welcome in Savoy from his mother's kindred, staying at the count's new castle of St Georges d'Esperance and meeting its architect, James of St George. In France, the Count of Chalons-sur-Marne tried to seize him during a tournament, hoping to extract a rich ransom – instead, Edward captured the count. At Paris he paid neatly phrased homage to St Louis's son, Philip III, 'for all the lands I ought to hold from you'.[4]

Landing at Dover on 2 August 1274, Edward and Eleanor were crowned at Westminster a fortnight later. As Stubbs says, 'He had all the powers of Henry II without his vices and he had too that sympathy with the people whom he ruled.'[5] The ceremony was attended by the King of Scots, Alexander III, who paid homage.

The start of the reign

By now central government was increasingly sophisticated, with the Exchequer for revenue, the Chancery for law and administration, and the Wardrobe for the executive. Edward found the right man to manage these departments, a young chancery clerk from Shropshire, Robert Burnell, who understood what he wanted. When appointed chancellor (in place of justiciar), Burnell established the Chancery court at London so that it no longer accompanied the king on progress. Ignoring Burnell's greed and scandalous private life, Edward got the best out of him, even if eventually it cost the Crown over eighty manors.

The upheavals of the 1260s had resulted in a dramatic rise in murder, robbery, rape and arson. Edward's solution was a team of judges who prosecuted on the slightest evidence of wrongdoing. Accompanied by the judges of King's Bench, he spent the winter on progress through the Midlands and southern England, finding so much proof of extortion, bribery, embezzlement and wrongful imprisonment that he dismissed nineteen sheriffs. Equipped with a list of forty questions supplied by him, commissioners investigated abuses in each hundred, especially of Crown rights and revenues by local landowners, and of extortion by bailiffs (sheriffs' officials). Tagged by countless parchment slips with the seals of those who made depositions, their reports – the Hundred Rolls – became known as the 'ragman rolls'.

During the next thirteen years, the 'period of statutes', Edward clarified and improved the legal code. It is wrong to compare him to Justinian, as he had no intention of creating a new, all-embracing body of law, but simply wanted to make the machinery work by codifying what had grown up haphazardly. He succeeded. 'For ages after Edward's day king and parliament left private law and private procedure, criminal law and criminal procedure, pretty much to themselves.'[6] The future of Common Law (the unenacted law of the land as opposed to statutes) became assured, resulting in a new class of lay lawyers.

The man

When Edward's skeleton at Westminster Abbey was examined in 1774, it measured 6 ft 2 in. (Most contemporaries were 5 ft 6 in.) A painting on a wall of the abbey, dating from just after his death, shows a handsome, athletic man with a clean-shaven, hawk-like profile.

'Elegantly built, enormously tall, he towered head and shoulders above ordinary men', says the Dominican Nicholas Trivet, who often saw him. 'His hair, in boyhood between silver and yellow, became darker during his youth, turning swan white when he grew old. His forehead, like the rest of his face, was broad while he had a drooping left eye that gave a certain look of his father. He spoke with a slight lisp, but was always eloquent in arguing or persuading. His arms, as long as the rest of his body, were muscular and ideally suited for swordsmanship. His girth was widest round the chest. His long legs helped him keep a firm seat when riding the most mettlesome horse.'[7]

High spirited, Edward was only saddened by the death of those he loved. His greatest fault was a temper he sometimes regretted. As a young man, he ordered his attendants to put out the eyes and crop the ears of a youth who had angered him. During his daughter Elizabeth's wedding to the Count of Hainault, he snatched the coronet off her head and threw it in the fire, while more than once he struck courtiers or servants. A dean of St Paul's who tried to rebuke him dropped dead from fright. Yet he could be merciful. 'Forgiveness?' he once said. 'Why, I'd give that to a dog if he asked me for it.' He knew how to be gracious and had a sense of fun, losing a war horse on a bet with his laundress and buying it back.

Edward was deeply in love with his wife Eleanor, to whom he had been betrothed when he was fifteen and she about twelve. If she resembled the sculpture at Lincoln Cathedral, she must indeed have been beautiful. Over a dozen children were born to them, and he never took mistresses. Like their uncle Louis,

Eleanor's father had been a crusader hero, King Ferdinand III
'*el Santo*', who regained much of Spain from the Moors.
(Ironically, she was descended from Mohammed, one of her
forebears having married a daughter of a Caliph of Cordoba.)
She was also half-French, inheriting the county of Abbeville from
her mother. Like her husband, she loved Arthurian romances,
employing scribes to copy them; and when they were on Crusade
she commissioned as a present for him a French translation of
Vegetius's treaty on war, *De Re Militari*. Eleanor's avaricious
streak – she bought up loans from Jewish moneylenders – did
not affect their relations.

Family ties meant much to the king, because of a happy child-
hood. When his mother died in 1291, he wrote to a cousin that
since his father's death she had been closer to him than any other
human being.[8] He admired his uncle Louis IX deeply, although
nobody was more different, and stayed on friendly terms with
Louis's son, Philip III – a bond between ruling families unique
in thirteenth-century Europe.

While giving alms as lavishly as his father and annually touching hundreds of sufferers for the King's Evil (scrofula), Edward
was less pious. Nor did he have Henry III's cult of St Edward.
When he had the Painted Chamber at Westminster redecorated,
it was with scenes from the life of Judas Maccabeus instead of the
Confessor's. His favourite saint was Thomas Becket, to whose
shrine he once sent a wax image of a sick gyrfalcon, praying for
the bird's cure.

As a young man he loved tournaments – according to some,
he was the best lance in Christendom. His pleasures were not
those of the mind, and while he enjoyed tales of King Arthur
and the music of Welsh harpers he was less well read than Henry
III, except in law. His Latin was poor even by thirteenth-century
standards, but he wrote French and some Spanish, and spoke
English. If he had idle moods (hunting, hawking, playing chess)
that hint at boredom, never for a moment did he lose his love
of power.

King Arthur

On his way home from Palestine, Edward commissioned Rustichello da Pisa (who later helped Marco Polo with his *Travels*) to write the *Romance of King Arthur*, a compendium of Arthurian tales. In 1278 he and Eleanor went to Glastonbury Abbey when the supposed bodies of Arthur and Guinevere, found in the previous century, had been rediscovered, and moved them to a worthier tomb before the high altar, helping personally to carry Arthur's coffin. It was probably Edward who ordered the construction of the Round Table still displayed in the Great Hall of Winchester Castle.

Enlisting the Arthurian cult in his campaign to rule all Britain, in 1284 he staged a Round Table tournament in north Wales, portraying his conquest of the Welsh as an adventure of the sort undertaken by Arthur's knights. Champions from all over Europe came to the joust, where he was presented with Arthur's crown, discovered just in time. He held another Round Table tournament at Falkirk in 1302, to show that subduing Scots was an Arthurian duty.

Pillars of the realm

The earls could not help being dwarfed by the king's huge shadow. Two were Plantagenets, his brother Edmund 'Crouchback' of Lancaster and his cousin Richard of Cornwall – both mediocrities who never caused trouble. Another two were uncles, Aymer de Valence, Earl of Pembroke, Henry III's Lusignan half-brother, and John de Warenne, Earl of Surrey, who had married Henry's half-sister. The king treated his impeccably loyal nephew John of Brittany, later Earl of Richmond, almost as a son, and he took a prominent part in the Gascon and Scottish campaigns.

Among those unrelated to the king, Gilbert de Clare, the immensely rich Earl of Gloucester, red-headed, stupid and unreliable, who had fought on de Montfort's side at Lewes, was less of a nuisance than might have been expected despite a tendency to quarrel with everybody. He married Edward's daughter, Joan of Acre. However, Roger Bigod of Norfolk, the Earl Marshal, and Humphrey de Bohun, Earl of Hereford and hereditary constable, neither of whom had blood ties with the king, were less inclined to obey. Edward had no trouble from William Beauchamp, Earl of Warwick, a fine soldier who rescued him when he was trapped by Welsh rebels at Conwy in 1295. The magnate he most trusted was Henry de Lacy, Earl of Lincoln, whom he left as Protector of England when away on the Scottish campaigns.

From the mid-1260s until Edward's death his greatest friend was the Savoyard Othon de Grandson, who accompanied him on Crusade. The king's right-hand man, Othon took a prominent part in the Welsh wars, helped to govern Gascony and fought the Scots. His family home at Grandson near Lausanne may have inspired Edward's castles in Wales.

The first great statutes

In 1275 the king presided over the enactment of the First Statute of Westminster, which strictly speaking was a code rather than a statute. Fifty-one clauses in Norman French, it overhauled and corrected the entire legal system, making justice available to everyone, rich or poor. Hitherto, only the person dispossessed had been able to sue someone who stole his or her land, but now heirs might sue. Abuse of wardship, unfair demands for feudal dues, coroners' duties, all received attention. The statute was not just an expression of the royal will, but reflected Magna Carta. Three years later, the Statute of Gloucester (or *Quo Warranto*) put right abuses uncovered by the Ragman Rolls. In future, disputes in the hundred courts over ownership of land were to be investigated by the travelling judges, to ensure that great men had not stolen the property of lesser, while plaintiffs could recover costs. It made local government fairer, defining and limiting the magnates' power to administer law in their own courts.

The barons were angry at being asked to show by what right they held their land, '*Quo Warranto*'. 'Look, my lords, this is my right', shouted the Earl of Surrey, brandishing an old sword. 'My ancestors came with William the Bastard and won my lands by the sword, and I'll use the same sword to keep them!'[9] A less formidable ruler than Edward might have faced a serious revolt and, well aware of it, he weakened the magnates by securing control of as many earldoms as possible. Royal marriages helped, while Cornwall and Norfolk were escheated to the Crown after their holders died without heirs of the body.

Another Becket?

Having made Robert Burnell Bishop of Bath and Wells, the king wanted him as Archbishop of Canterbury when the see fell vacant in 1278, but, learning that Burnell kept a mistress by whom he had sons and daughters, the pope would not allow it. Instead, a zealous Franciscan friar from Sussex was appointed, John Pecham, who denounced the custom of giving benefices to bureaucrats. He also promised to excommunicate judges who refused to arrest men under the bishops' ban, and Crown lawyers who interfered in canon law cases or infringed clerical freedoms listed in Magna Carta, posting copies of the Great Charter on church doors. When parliament met in 1279, the king ordered Pecham to withdraw his threats and remove the charter from church doors. Reluctantly, the archbishop complied. Pointedly, the king issued the Statute of Mortmain, forbidding bequests of land to the Church without royal permission.

Pecham grumbled for the rest of his life, but was too frightened of Edward to disobey.

Conquering Wales

Medieval Englishmen thought of Welshmen in much the same way nineteenth-century Americans would think of the Sioux. Apart from the principality of Gwynedd (Snowdonia and Anglesey), Wales was a mosaic of lordships, divided between native chieftains, the Crown and Marchers. The Marchers were English barons, usually with large estates in England, who had occupied the fertile south and east, and brought in settlers.

While accepting Edward's suzerainty, Llewelyn ap Gruffydd of Gwynedd, Prince of Wales, regarded himself as an independent sovereign and overlord of the Welsh chieftains in the south. Several times Edward ordered him to come to court and pay homage as his grandfather had done, but Llewelyn declined. In 1275 Llewelyn's brother Dafydd fled to England after plotting to depose him, and was given sanctuary. When Simon de Montfort's daughter Eleanor, to whom Llewelyn had been betrothed for ten years, sailed to Wales for their wedding, her ship was intercepted and she was taken to Windsor. The king refused to release her until the prince paid homage. At the end of 1276 Edward appointed commanders for north Wales, west Wales and the central Marches. Allying with disaffected Welsh chieftains, they quickly overran the new lands acquired by Llewelyn.[10]

The king understood Welsh tactics very well – to raid, then hide among trackless hills, hardy mountain ponies giving them mobility. Living in rough bothies, they could move their families and flocks at a moment's notice, luring enemies into harsh country where bad weather and lack of provisions took a severe toll. 'Grievous is war there, and hard to endure', says a chronicler. 'When it is summer elsewhere, it is winter in Wales.'[11] Their weapons were spears, javelins and long knives, while men of the south used bows that could send an arrow through a church door. If unable to face a charge by mailed knights, they were lethally effective in ambushes.

Edward did not intend to conquer Wales, however, merely to tame Llewelyn. In July 1277 he assembled an army 16,000 strong (with 9,000 mercenaries from south Wales) at Worcester, where munitions and food were stockpiled, and marched up to Flint. He brought woodmen and miners to build roads through the woods and mountains, to dig earthworks and erect stockades, as well as masons and labourers to construct castles. Thirty Cinque Port ships with supplies were stationed on the River Dee.

From his headquarters at Flint, Edward invaded Gwynedd and Powys, destroying crops and livestock, capturing enemy strongholds. By 29 July he was at Deganwy on the River Conwy's west bank, sending troops over to Anglesey, who burned the harvest on which the prince's people relied to feed them in winter. His area commanders had already wrecked much of Llewelyn's regime – and what was left disintegrated. Early in November 1277 at the treaty of Conwy, Llewelyn formally surrendered half his territory, agreeing to pay an indemnity of £50,000. When he did homage for his 'fief', the king not only remitted the indemnity but let him marry Eleanor de Montfort, giving a wedding banquet at Worcester in their honour.

Having hoped to replace his brother as Prince of Wales, Dafydd was furious. Eventually, knowing that his fellow countrymen resented the arrival of new settlers and the replacement of the code of Hywel Dda with English law, on Easter Sunday 1282 Dafydd 'went playing the fox'.[12] He and his men got into Hawarden Castle near Flint by bearing palms in token of peace, then slaughtered the garrison to show that he too hated Englishmen. Other castles fell, and even if they did not fall, the Welsh who lived around them rose, defeating the Earl of Gloucester at Llandeilo in June and massacring settlers. Realizing this was a revolt by the whole nation, Llewelyn assumed leadership. Trying to lessen the English campaign's impact by broadening the front, he moved down to Powys.

Llewelyn rushed back to Gwynedd, however, when a

shipborne force under Luke de Tany occupied Anglesey in October, building a bridge of boats across the Menai Strait to attack western Snowdonia. Meanwhile, the king established his headquarters at Rhuddlan, subduing the Perfyddwlad (Flint and Denbighshire) and eastern Gwynedd. At the same time, Marchers cowed the Welsh in their area, burning churches and slaughtering men, women and children – including babies at the breast. Yet Edward was so alarmed that secretly he offered Llewelyn an English earldom in exchange for Gwynedd.

In October the Welsh were encouraged by the death of Roger Mortimer, a Marcher lord who had been one of the king's principal commanders. In November it seemed they might win. Ambushed on the way back from a raid, Luke de Tany was drowned with many troops (including twenty knights) when the pontoon bridge collapsed into the sea as they retreated. The English counteroffensive had stalled, and Llewelyn finally rejected peace offers.

This only hardened Edward's determination. He did not see the struggle as conquest – he was punishing rebellion. To avoid being starved out of Snowdonia, Llewelyn returned to Powys, where on 11 December 1282 during a skirmish at a bridge over the River Irfon near Builth, he was run through with a lance by a knight who did not recognize him. His head was displayed on a stake at London, crowned with an ivy wreath. After the death of 'Llewelyn the Last', who despite his volatility had been a superb leader, the spirit went out of the Welsh.

The war was not over, as his successor, his brother Prince Dafydd, knew he could expect no mercy. Ignoring the winter weather, Edward marched into Snowdonia in January 1283, taking the enemy's remaining castles. When Castell-y-Bere, the last stronghold in Welsh hands, fell in April, Dafydd fled into the mountains. Betrayed by a fellow countryman, he was caught hiding in a marsh and taken in chains to the king at Rhuddlan, then tried at Shrewsbury in September by a 'parliament' of barons. It condemned him to be drawn on a hurdle to a gallows,

half-hanged, then cut down alive for castration, disembowelment and quartering – the first to suffer this ghastly penalty.

The Welsh had never stood a chance, overwhelmed by sheer
numbers. Mustering so many men was a remarkable achievement by Edward's bureaucracy.[13] Munitions as well as men were
assembled in huge quantities, crossbow bolts ordered by tens of
thousands. The king's tactics may sometimes be questioned, but
not his logistics.

In spring 1284 Edward issued the Statutes of Wales, replacing Welsh cantreds with English shires and hundreds in regions
annexed by the Crown such as Gwynedd, although Marcher
lordships retained their autonomy. English criminal law was
introduced, but this time the Welsh kept some of Hywel Dda's
code for civil matters. New towns were founded in freshly conquered areas, five defended by huge castles where settlers could
take refuge. Because of thirteenth-century land hunger there
was no shortage of 'Saxon' immigrants, who were encouraged
to settle by the king.

The biggest of eight new castles was Caernarfon, with its
polygonal towers; almost a town. Edward's architect was James
of Savoy, whose work he had seen when returning from the Holy
Land. Operating from Harlech, which he had designed and
where he was castellan, James constructed all eight. Intended to
hold down a conquered country, they were within close reach of
the sea, so that troops and supplies could be rushed in by ship.

In 1294, when Edward was preparing for war with France,
there was a dangerous revolt in north Wales, led by Madog ap
Llewelyn, a member of the old ruling family, who called himself
Prince of Wales. Still only half-built, Caernarfon was captured,
but at Harlech forty men held off Madog's entire army. The
size of the force Edward sent to deal with the rising, twice as
big as in 1277 and formed of troops needed in Gascony, shows
his alarm. He took charge of operations in December, but his
baggage train was ambushed and he found himself besieged in
Conwy – sharing his one barrel of wine with his men. Madog

was decisively defeated in March, however, all resistance petering out by summer.

Finance

Where finance was concerned, Edward was thoroughly unscrupulous. Having sucked dry the Jews (who were outside the law), he confiscated their property and in 1290 expelled the entire community from England – about 2,000 souls. He had paid for the Welsh wars by borrowing from the Riccardi of Lucca, who were allowed to collect customs duties on wool. Owing to commitments elsewhere, the Riccardi could not help with his request for a big loan in 1294, so Edward took the wool duties away from them and seized their other English assets (such as security for loans), which ruined them.

Later, he persuaded the Frescobaldi at Florence to lend him large sums, again in return for wool duties, but insolvency loomed. The only hope was taxing his subjects, but he had to secure their consent. 'After 1215 the next great halting place in the history of the national assembly is the year 1295', wrote Maitland, referring to the Model Parliament at Westminster in which earls, barons and knights agreed to give a twelfth of their movable goods to pay for war with France, burgesses agreeing on an eighth.[14] Yet it is anachronistic to think of Edward as founding parliamentary government – he soon reverted to sporadic bursts of arbitrary taxation.

At the same time, he did his best to stimulate the economy, issuing a new coinage in 1279 and introducing a Statute of Merchants in 1285 that ordered debtors to pay bills on pain of imprisonment or distraint. Aware that Winchelsea, with a bigger fleet than any other Cinque Port, was vanishing under the sea, Edward began building a town and haven in 1283 to replace it, employing an architect who had built fortified towns (bastides) for him in Gascony. Laid out on a grid pattern, it was given seventy huge cellars to encourage the wine trade with Bordeaux.

The deaths of Eleanor of Castile and Robert Burnell

In autumn 1290 Eleanor of Castile fell gravely ill near Lincoln and Edward hurried north to be with her, but she died before he arrived. Heartbroken, he rode with her corpse to Westminster, and later had a stone cross (originally wooden) erected at each halting place. A contemporary translator of Langtoft's chronicle comments. 'On fell things he thought and wax[ed] heavy as lead . . . His solace was all [be]reft that she from him was gone.'[15]

Robert Burnell died in 1292. Three years later his place was taken by Walter Langton, Keeper of the Wardrobe, who became treasurer and Bishop of Lichfield. Even greedier than Burnell, he aroused widespread dislike. Later he was charged with adultery and murder – helping his mistress to strangle her husband – besides being accused of 'intercourse with the devil' whose backside he was said to have kissed; but he was acquitted. The king ignored these peccadilloes, regarding Walter as his eyes and ears.

Gascony

Another blow was Philip IV's abandonment of the family entente. Guyenne (Gascony) had been Edward's patrimony when he was a boy. He knew it well, having spent 1254–6 there, besides visiting it on his way back from the Crusades. As a French-speaking Englishman, with southern blood from his mother and grandmother, he felt at home there. He visited again from 1286 to 1289, overhauling the region's administration, improving its legal system, building bastides and exacting homage from its noblemen – many of whom had fought for him in Wales.

The sphinx-like Philip 'the Handsome', who succeeded his father as king in 1285, was the most formidable man in Europe; he later bridled the papacy and destroyed the Templars. His forebears had conquered most of the Plantagenet lands and he wanted Gascony too, despite Edward paying homage for it. In

1293 mercantile rivalry erupted in a pirate war, during which Gascon sailors sacked La Rochelle and a Cinque Ports fleet routed a Norman flotilla. Philip saw his chance. Marching into the Agenais and Perigord, he seized Bordeaux, then summoned the English king to Paris for trial as a contumacious vassal.

Still believing in the family entente, Edward sent his brother Edmund of Lancaster, who brokered a peace deal. To show good faith, Gascony's border strongholds were temporarily surrendered to Philip, who was allowed to station small, token forces in important towns, while Edward would marry Philip's sister Margaret on the understanding that the duchy was to be inherited by their children. The French king promised to return Gascony within forty days and cancel Edward's summons to Paris.

However, Philip then occupied towns all over the duchy. War followed, sieges and skirmishes rather than battles, and a campaign at sea, Edward building thirty galleys, each with sixty oars a side. But his army had to be diverted to crush the Welsh rising of 1294 so that most of Gascony stayed in enemy hands. Edward's next move was an alliance with the Count of Flanders and the Rhineland princes, whereupon Philip withdrew most of his troops to guard his northern frontier. When the Germans did not cooperate, Edward abandoned his plan of attacking from the north and in 1297 agreed a truce with Philip, who five years later – after a terrible defeat by the Flemish at Courtrai – returned Gascony to him.

In 1299 Edward married Philip's half-sister, Margaret of France. Peter Langtoft says he had hoped to marry her elder sister Blanche, sending envoys to Paris to learn if she was pretty and had a good figure. They reported that 'in body, in face, in leg, in hand, in foot, no fairer creature could found in the whole world'.[16] Sadly, Blanche preferred to marry the Duke of Austria, who was expected to become emperor. But Edward's second marriage was unusually happy, despite his bride being forty years younger than him. He doted on 'the lady Margaret in whose least finger there is more goodness and beauty, whoever sees her, than in the fair Idoine whom Amadas loved'.[17] When she went down with measles, he warned the doctor not to let her travel before she was fully cured or 'by God's thigh, you'll pay for it',[18] while he was always giving her presents despite her extravagance. Margaret returned his affection, seeing him as a father figure, and nursed him devotedly during his last years. They had two sons and a daughter.

Civil war?

The king grew increasingly autocratic, seizing woolsacks, sheepskins and hides awaiting export, which he released only on payment of a fine. Confiscating all coined money in cathedral or abbey treasuries, he demanded that the clergy pay half their annual income or be outlawed. When the new Archbishop of Canterbury, Robert Winchelsey, obtained a bull forbidding clergy to pay taxes without papal approval, Edward again threatened them with outlawry, and they paid.

Throughout the Gascon campaign, his attitude towards his subjects was, 'I am castle for you and wall and house, while you are barbican and gate', and they were in duty bound to help him.[19] But the lords refused to accept any obligation to fight beyond the seas. When in February 1297, at a council of the baronage in Salisbury, he ordered Roger Bigod, Earl of Norfolk, to cross to Gascony while he himself led a force to Flanders, Bigod declined. 'By God, earl, you shall either go or hang!', shouted the king. 'By God, O king', Bigod shouted back, 'I shall neither go nor hang!'[20] The council broke up and, joined by Humphrey Bohun, Earl of Hereford and thirty other magnates, Bigod assembled 1,500 men-at-arms at Montgomery before marching to London. There the two leaders declared in July that they would not serve in Gascony or Flanders and would resist attempts to seize their goods. Angrily, Edward took away Bigod's office as Earl Marshal of England and Bohun's as constable.

A week later, during a public reconciliation with Archbishop Winchelsey on a platform outside Westminster Hall, Edward tried persuasion. Admitting his subjects might not be entirely happy at the way he ruled, he told the crowd that taxes were needed to defend them. 'And now I am going to risk my life for you. I beg you, if I return, receive me as you have now and I will restore all I have taken. If I don't return, crown my son as your king.'[21] He then repeated his demands for money. Despite the tears that greeted the speech, the earls produced a document of remonstrance against high taxes. Even so, Edward extracted funds for his expedition, levying a tax on the clergy which they had not agreed. In August, when he joined his invasion fleet at Portsmouth, the earls went to the Exchequer to prevent further taxes being collected and drew up another remonstrance, *De Tallagio*. Civil war seemed inevitable, but the opposition lacked a Simon de Montfort.

An unexpected disaster came to the king's rescue while he was in Flanders, when the Scots destroyed an English army at Stirling Bridge. The north country faced invasion and the magnates rallied to Edward. As soon as he returned from Flanders, he made sure of their loyalty by promising to confirm both Magna Carta and the Forest Charter.

Scotland

The king had neither time nor resources to waste on Ireland, where English settlers and native Irish went on fighting without respite, although in 1292 the Anglo-Irish lords granted him a subsidy while he used troops supplied by them in Wales and in Gascony. Crushing Madog and thwarting Philip were demanding enough.

Alexander III, King of Scots had died in 1286 after a fall from his horse. His heir was his baby granddaughter Margaret, the Fair Maid of Norway, and for the moment Scotland was governed by six guardians, who in 1290 announced her betrothal to

Edward's eldest son. But Margaret died the same year. Relations between England and Scotland were friendly, the two previous kings having married English princesses, so it seemed reasonable for the Scots to ask Edward to arbitrate on the 'Great Cause' and decide who should inherit the throne.

Although one Scots chronicler thought Edward had already announced his intention of subjugating Scotland, it is unlikely.[22] What he wanted at this stage was to be overlord in fact and not just name. Amiably enough, at Norham in Northumberland he met the Scots magnates, who recognized him as sovereign lord while their country's throne was vacant. The two main candidates, both descended from David I, were John Balliol, a great English baron with a Scots wife of royal blood, and Robert Bruce, Lord of Annandale. Edward decided in favour of Balliol, who was crowned King of Scots at Scone on St Andrew's Day 1292.

Edward's conditions were unworkable. John had to pay homage as his vassal (in the way he himself did to Philip IV for Gascony), supply troops to fight his enemies and let the Scots appeal to him from their own courts in disputed cases. In 1293 Balliol obeyed a summons to Westminster to attend an appeal by Macduff of Fife against impeachment by the Scottish parliament and, although he refused to discuss Macduff's case, his attendance angered the Scots. Two years later Scotland was infuriated when, as feudal overlord, Edward ordered King John and twenty of his lords to come to London and serve in Gascony. The Scots responded by giving John twelve advisers, who turned him into a puppet king. Not only did they ally with Philip IV (the start of the Auld Alliance), but in 1296 they made Balliol withdraw his homage to the King of England.

Edward ordered John to meet him at Berwick, storming the city when he failed to appear and massacring 12,000 men and women. Shortly afterwards, the Earl of Surrey routed a Scots army at Dunbar with a single charge. In despair, Balliol begged Edward's forgiveness, submitting to ceremonial 'degradation' at

Montrose in July, during which the Lion of Scotland was torn from his surcoat – earning him the name 'Toom Tabard' (Empty Coat). Then he was sent to the Tower of London.

In August Edward held a Scottish parliament amid the ruins of Berwick, where the Scottish lords swore fealty to him and were allowed to keep their lands on condition they attended the parliament of England at Bury St Edmunds in November. Edward went home with the Stone of Scone and the Black Rood of St Margaret, entrusting the country to three Englishmen – Surrey as guardian of the land, Walter of Amersham as chancellor and Hugh de Cressingham as treasurer. Edward had united the British isles, claimed an Austin canon at Bridlington Priory in Yorkshire, Peter Langtoft, writing joyfully that it had been prophesied by Merlin. This may have been the king's view, but it was not that of the Scots,[23] especially after Cressingham began levying heavy taxes.

In May 1297 William Wallace, a man of knightly family said by an English chronicler to be already a blood-stained brigand,[24] murdered the English sheriff of Lanark. Raising a small army with Andrew Moray, he waited for the Earl of Surrey and Hugh de Cressingham, who marched north in September with 15,000 troops to put him down. When Hugh led the English vanguard across Stirling Bridge over the Forth near Cambuskenneth, they were cut off by Wallace's 5,000 men and annihilated. (An English source says Wallace had the skin flayed from Cressingham's body, 'head to heel', to make a sword belt.) Surrey fled with what was left of the royal army.

Seizing Berwick, Wallace ravaged Northumberland and Cumberland, burning and killing, while all Scotland rose in revolt. English troops withdrew, only a few castles holding out, although closely besieged. Garrisons who surrendered to Wallace after being promised their lives were massacred. Calling himself Guardian of the Realm, he tried to re-establish law and order in Balliol's name, but the Scots magnates were afraid to join him.

Although nearly sixty, which was advanced old age, Edward

was still vigorous, a commander who slept on the bare ground like his men. Although about to attack King Philip, he hurried home from Flanders, and in July 1298 he confronted Wallace at Falkirk in Stirlingshire with 2,500 men-at-arms and 16,000 foot soldiers. These included archers and a big contingent of Welshmen skilled at pursuing a defeated enemy over rough country. Wallace, with about 10,000 pike-men and as few as 200 horse, adopted defensive tactics, positioning his infantry in 'schiltrons' (hedgehog-like rings), which proved disastrous. After routing the enemy's mounted troops, Edward used his archers to shoot down the pike-men at close range and his men-at-arms finished off the survivors. While English casualties were very low, 5,000 Scots were killed or wounded, although Wallace escaped into the moors and forests.

His place was taken by two joint-guardians, Robert Bruce, Earl of Carrick (not to be confused with his grandson) and John Comyn, Lord of Badenoch, who fought back with raids and ambushes, avoiding pitched battles. Edward won, however, because of superior resources and merciless determination. He did not see himself as an invader, but as a king asserting his rights over rebels.

Problems at home

Walter Langton at the Exchequer and John Droxford, Keeper of the Wardrobe, raised as much cash as they could from Crown revenues but it was insufficient. When the subsidy for which Edward asked the Lincoln parliament of 1301 was reluctantly agreed, a bill of complaint demanded that Magna Carta be more strictly interpreted and the Forest Laws become fairer. There was also a plea for Langton's dismissal, which the king angrily rejected. Even so, his subjects supported the Scottish war and there were no more clashes of this sort.

The clergy were another matter. Aware that Archbishop Winchelsey had encouraged the trouble at Lincoln, Edward grew even angrier when he produced a letter from Pope Boniface claiming that Scotland had always been a papal fief and ordering Edward to restore Balliol. Unctuously, Winchelsey told the king to obey 'in the name of Mount Zion and Jerusalem', to which Edward retorted, 'For Zion's sake I will not be silent and for Jerusalem's sake I will not be at rest, but with all my strength I shall defend my right.'[25] Finally, a new pope, Clement V, who as a Gascon was well disposed towards Edward, endorsed his Scottish policy and allowed a further tax on English clergy, calling the archbishop to Rome on a matter of discipline so that he was effectively in exile.

Edward would not tolerate independent minded prelates. In 1304, after giving a post to a papal instead of a royal nominee, Archbishop Corbridge of York emerged from an interview with the king so shaken that he took to his bed and died. When Bishop Bek of Durham, who had accompanied Edward to the Holy Land and been invaluable in dealing with the Scots, refused to accept his judgement on a dispute, the king confiscated his estates.

The monks of Westminster were a nuisance in their own way. In 1303 they helped an Oxfordshire merchant, Richard Puddlicott, and his gang to dig a tunnel into the crypt that held the royal treasure, stealing plate, jewels and coins worth £100,000. The gang were caught and hanged after the objects appeared on the London market. Although spared the death penalty, ten monks went to the Tower.

The final conquest of Scotland

Edward was perfectly sincere when he explained in a letter to the pope that English monarchs took precedence over Scottish monarchs as descendants of the eldest son of the Trojan Brutus, Britain's first king, whereas Scottish monarchs only descended from a second son. This was clearly stated by Geoffrey of Monmouth in his *Historia Regum Britanniae* whose veracity was only questioned by a few lunatic intellectuals. No doubt Edward treated with contempt a counter-claim by the Scots that their pedigree outdid descent from Brutus because they descended from Pharaoh's daughter, Scotia, through her son Erk.

Edward sometimes took part in the campaigns that followed Falkirk. In May 1303 he began a final conquest of Scotland, a military progress in strength through Perth, Brechin and Aberdeen up to the Moray Firth. In January 1304, led by the guardian of the realm John Comyn, the Scottish nobility surrendered en bloc, on the understanding their country's laws and liberties would be as in King Alexander's time. A parliament was held at St Andrew's where, instead of threatening the assembly, Edward was at his most diplomatic. Scots who submitted were regranted their lands, while a joint Anglo-Scots committee was to meet at Westminster and plan a new form of government for Scotland. Pope Boniface VIII ordered the Scottish bishops to end their quarrel with Edward. Until now they had opposed him, their envoys trying to persuade Rome of their cause's justice, but Boniface needed England's support against Philip of France. Prelates such as Wishart of Glasgow, who for years had striven for independence, attended the St Andrew's parliament.

Edward intended to rule Scotland in the way he did Ireland. There would be a Scottish parliament, but statutes made in England would be enforced by the king's lieutenant as they were across the Irish Sea. Petitions (like Irish and Gascon petitions) would be heard by the English parliament. John of Brittany was lieutenant and the Earl of Atholl was justiciar north of the Forth, while Robert Bruce, Earl of Carrick, was sheriff of Ayr and Lanark.

In July the last opposition ended with the fall of Stirling Castle, besieged since April. A crossbow bolt had gone through Edward's clothes while riding round the walls and a stone from a mangonel frightened his horse into throwing him. Undeterred, he had ordered his son to strip the lead off the roofs of local churches, to use as counterweights for his trebuchets – siege machines that hurled boulders and Greek fire. When the castle surrendered, he controlled the whole country apart from the trackless Highlands.[26]

Sir William Wallace was caught near Glasgow in August 1305, betrayed by a fellow Scot. A giant, taller than Edward, his appearance was ideally suited for a show trial at Westminster Hall, during which he was made to wear a laurel crown and not allowed to reply to such charges as making English captives of both sexes strip naked and sing before they were tortured to death. Hanged, drawn and quartered three weeks after his capture, as savagely as possible, his quarters were sent for display in Scotland while his head was set up over London Bridge.

Edward's dream was wrecked by Robert the Bruce, Earl of Carrick (grandson of John Balliol's competitor for the Scots crown), whom the king had failed to reward adequately. In February 1306, before the high altar of the Franciscan church at Dumfries, Robert knifed John Comyn of Badenoch, the former Guardian of Scotland who might have stopped him from claiming the throne. Then he had himself crowned King of Scots at Scone on 25 March by his mistress Isabel, Countess of Buchan, sister to the Earl of Fife – the hereditary enthroner. At first, his cause seemed hopeless, the English calling him 'Hob in the Moors'.

Any nobleman who supported Bruce was executed horribly if he was caught by Edward, while rank and file troops taken prisoner were hanged or beheaded on the spot. Nor did ladies escape. Robert's sister Mary Bruce and the Countess of Buchan, who had crowned him, were imprisoned in wooden cages hung from towers, although they were fed regularly and provided with privies.

The heir

Bruce's decision to claim the throne of Scotland was based on the calculation that Edward could not live long, and on a low opinion of his heir – whom Bruce must have met at the siege of Stirling. The Anglo-Scots regime had no chance of surviving without a strong man.

In 1301 the seventeen-year-old Prince Edward had been proclaimed Prince of Wales at Caernarfon. The king did his best to train the youth, who accompanied him on the Scottish campaigns. When he was knighted at Whitsun 1306, his father gave a Feast of the Swans at Westminster, when two swans with gilded feathers were brought in, escorted by trumpeters. The king, who had come to the palace in a litter, rose and swore by God and the swans never to rest until he had defeated the crowned traitor and the perjured nation (Bruce and the Scots), after which he would go on Crusade. Then his son rose too, swearing never to sleep twice in the same place before avenging his father's wrongs.

The king had no illusions about his successor. In 1305, when the treasurer Langton complained that Prince Edward had hunted unlawfully in his woods, using abusive language, the king forbade the prince to come within 30 miles of court and stopped his allowance; for six months the young man and his household starved, until the queen intervened. Early in 1307 he asked Langton to ask his father to make his friend Piers Gaveston Count of Ponthieu. Summoning him, the king shouted, 'Why do you want to give land away when you never get hold of any for yourself, you misbegotten son of a whore? As there's a God, if it wasn't that I might wreck the kingdom, you'd never inherit anything from me!' Grabbing Edward's hair with both hands, he tore out as much as he could until he was exhausted, then threw him out of the room.[27]

The last campaign

By his mid-sixties Edward was slowing down. Referring to his return from campaigning in Scotland towards the end of the reign, the chronicler Langtoft chides him for 'long morning's

sleep, delight in luxury and surfeit in the evenings'.[28] He suffered from insomnia, stating in a statute of 1306 that he could
not sleep, 'tossed about by the waves of various thoughts' in
worrying over what was best for his subjects.[29] Nonetheless,
he insisted on going to Scotland that autumn after Aymer de
Valence's victory over Bruce at Methven. However, he collapsed
at Lanercost Priory in Cumberland where, joined by Queen
Margaret, he was forced to spend the winter – glass windows
being fitted to their apartments. Despite difficulty in walking, in
March 1307 he managed to hold a parliament at Carlisle.

On 3 July, despite suffering from dysentery, King Edward set
out to crush the Scots, riding at the head of his troops instead
of in a litter. Had the king lived another year, Bruce would have
been a dead man – but he could only cover 2 miles a day, and
died in his servants' arms at a hamlet in the marshes near Burgh-
by-Sands, not far from the Solway Firth, on 7 July. There is a
story that on his deathbed he ordered his son to have the flesh
boiled off his bones and buried, and then to carry the bones into
battle against the Scots.

Retrospect

Edward III died on the edge of an abyss.[30] Scotland still refused
to accept his rule, Wales only did so under compulsion and
Gascony remained at risk, while tax demands had alienated
barons and clergy without raising enough money – by 1307 he
was £200,000 in debt. Even so, he almost succeeded in unifying
Britain and was unrivalled as a lawmaker. It is not easy to warm
to a ruler who added hanging, drawing and quartering to the
penal code, yet England never had a greater man on the throne.

7

The Changeling – Edward II

One of the best examples of the brutal and brainless athlete
established on a throne

Thomas Frederick Tout[1]

The Battle of Old Byland, 1322

In August 1322 Edward II invaded Scotland to avenge
Bannockburn, to find Robert the Bruce had withdrawn behind
the Forth, taking everything edible with him. Starving, the
English king and his troops retreated with their loot – a single,
lame cow. Recuperating at Rievaulx Abbey in North Yorkshire,
he suddenly learned that Robert was at the top of Sutton
Bank, a few miles away. The Earl of Richmond confronted the
Scots on high ground above the abbey, at Old Byland, but the
English were so frightened that they ran 'like hares chased by
greyhounds' and the earl was captured.[2] Leaving behind his jewels, Edward fled to Bridlington from where a boat took him to
safety. A contemporary comments that the king had always been

'chicken hearted and prone to disaster in war, having already run in terror before them [the Scots] in Scotland'.[3]

A defeat on English soil, Old Byland was even more humiliating than Bannockburn and confirmed what the king's subjects had suspected: he was not up to his job. It also fuelled a suspicion that he was a changeling, not even a Plantagenet.

'a perverted weakling'

Winston Churchill's cruel verdict on Edward II derived from the Victorians. 'He is the first king since the Conquest who was not a man of business', thundered Stubbs, 'his tastes at the best are those of the athlete and the artisan; vulgar pomp, heartless extravagance, lavish improvidence, selfish indolence . . . there is nothing in Edward, miserable as his fate is, that invites or deserves sympathy.'[4] Tout was kinder. 'It was not so much the king's vices as his idleness and incompetence which his subjects complained of', he argued. 'If he did not like work, he was not very vicious; he stuck loyally to his friends and was fairly harmless, being nobody's enemy so much as his own.' Yet in essence Tout agreed with Stubbs.[5]

Modern scholarship has unearthed nothing that might temper the Victorian view. Edward was incapable of facing the world without a strong man at his side, invariably someone whom everybody else detested. Reliance on unsuitable favourites caused constant crises, while his later years resembled a dress rehearsal for the Wars of the Roses. In his most recent biographer's words, Edward was 'a lamentable character, his reign a shambles'.[6]

Early years

Edward was born in Caernarfon Castle on 25 April 1284, the youngest of fourteen, including four elder brothers who died young. He thus became heir to the throne when a few months old. Growing up in the shadow of a terrifying father did little for his self-confidence. When he was thirteen, the king gave him a companion of his own age, whom it was hoped might be a good influence. This was a clever, athletic boy of knightly family from Béarn called Piers de Gabaston – anglicized to 'Gaveston'.

Edward II was in Scotland when his father died. Within weeks he withdrew the army, after reinforcing the Perth and Stirling garrisons, and appointing Aymer de Valence as guardian. Then he sent a message for Piers to come to him at once. In October he buried his father at Westminster Abbey in a massive tomb of grey Purbeck marble that lacked any inscription until the sixteenth century when words in Latin were carved on it:

Edward the First, Hammer of the Scots. Keep Troth

There was no effigy. The omission has been explained as a tribute to the late king's austere dignity or an attempt to copy St Louis's sepulchre at Saint-Denis. But the suspicion remains that Edward wanted to forget a nightmarish parent. He settled another grudge by sending Bishop Langton, the treasurer with whom he had quarrelled, to the Tower.

What we know about Edward comes from chroniclers who did not admire him. They include two secular priests, Adam of Murimuth and Geoffrey le Baker, and a Benedictine, Robert of Reading, who loathed him. Another Benedictine, John Trokelowe of St Albans, took a kinder view. The best source is the *Life*, wrongly attributed to a monk of Malmesbury, written by an unidentified, well-informed, baronial bureaucrat, who tried to be fair despite a bias in favour of the magnates.[7]

Gaveston

Less than a month after Edward's accession, Piers Gaveston was made Earl of Cornwall, a gift to a squire of an earldom intended by the late king for one of his younger sons. This outraged the magnates. In November Piers married the king's niece, sister of the Earl of Gloucester, who was England's richest magnate. Encouraged by Edward, he then arranged a tournament at Wallingford, hiring champion jousters from all over England to fight for him, so that the other team, including several earls and barons, were quickly knocked out of their saddles. Had he behaved deferentially, the magnates might have accepted him, but he treated no one as an equal except the king. On 20 December, before leaving for his wedding in France, Edward appointed the new earl guardian of the kingdom.

Wedding and coronation

The king's marriage to the twelve-year-old Isabella of France at Boulogne on 25 January 1308 was attended by her father Philip IV, who was no less alarming than Edward I. When his son-in-law asked what dowry he proposed to give his daughter, Philip replied that it had been given when he returned Gascony. But Isabella was welcome in England, for re-establishing the link between the two dynasties and making less likely another war across the Channel.

Met by Gaveston at Dover on 7 February, Edward embraced him again and again, giving him all his wedding presents. Since Archbishop Winchelsey was in exile, Edward and his child bride were crowned by the Bishop of Winchester at Westminster on 25 February. He swore his coronation oaths in French because of his poor Latin, making a new promise, to maintain laws chosen by the community of the realm.

Piers carried the crown, annoying the magnates still further. At the coronation banquet he dressed in purple sewn with pearls, as if to belittle other lords in cloth of gold. He had been entrusted with organizing the banquet, which was badly cooked and badly served. 'Seeing the king prefer sitting next to Piers rather than the queen, made her two uncles so angry that they went home to France', says a London chronicler, who adds, 'As a result, rumours circulated that the king was more in love with this artful and malevolent man than his bride, that truly elegant lady, who is a most beautiful woman.'[8]

The man

Tall and well built, Edward had a weak little face hiding behind a beard. Naturally indolent, his priority was enjoying himself. What his nobles disliked so much were his amusements and his friends. He preferred farm work to jousting – thatching, digging and hedging, shoeing horses, besides rowing and running races. Another pastime was play acting – the third-rate Bishop of Worcester, Walter Reynolds, owed his promotion to Canterbury to thespian skills. 'Instead of lords and ladies, whose company he avoided, he mixed with harlots, singers and jesters, with carters, diggers and ditchers, with rowers, sailors and boatmen, and went in for heavy drinking', says the chronicler Ranulph Higden, adding that the king was dangerously indiscreet and petty minded, losing his temper with those around him for the least fault.[9] His liking for low society may have been due to mental derangement.[10]

Tout's description of Edward as brutal and brainless has been questioned, but the more one learns the apter it seems. His brutality showed in a cruel streak, his lack of brains in an absence of any understanding of business or politics, and an inability to read the Latin needed for administration. Uninterested in beautiful things other than jewels, his one talent was a flair for verse in Norman French, rarely displayed. Low self-esteem and a paralysing lack of confidence explains his dependence on strong-minded favourites.

Despite having four children by his queen and another by a mistress, he has gone down to history as a homosexual, largely because of Christopher Marlowe's play *Edward the Second*, which is based on an imaginative reading of Holinshed's Chronicles. Most modern historians disagree with this assessment.[11] When the author of the *Vita* compared the king's affection for Piers to that of David for Jonathan, he was not thinking of sodomy. A more plausible reason for Gaveston's dominance is the power of a strong mind over a weak one and the support he gave to a man who suffered from panic attacks – not unlike the reassurance given by an understanding male nurse to a mental defective.

Among his few personal tastes, other than 'peasant amusements', was a fondness for two small palaces. One was King's Langley in Hertfordshire, given to him by his father in 1302, where he later founded a Dominican priory. The other was Burstwick near Hull, which after belonging briefly to Gaveston became the king's main residence in the North. 'Langley and Burstwick stood to Edward II as Osborne and Balmoral to Queen Victoria', comments Tout.[12]

Conventionally pious, he did not inherit the family cult of the Confessor, but showed a marked devotion to St Thomas, making pilgrimages to Canterbury. He also often visited the abbey of St Albans, to which he gave timber for new choir stalls.

The Ordainers

The leaders of what became an opposition were mediocrities. 'Five earldoms and close kinship with the two greatest monarchs in the west gave neither dignity, policy, patriotism nor common sense to that most impossible of all medieval politicians, earl Thomas of Lancaster', says Tout, who adds he was 'sulky, vindictive, self-seeking, brutal and vicious'.[13] John de Warenne, Earl of Surrey, was a disreputable nonentity, while the bookish Thomas Beauchamp, Earl of Warwick was treacherous. On the other hand, Aylmer de Valence, Earl of Pembroke, was impeccably honourable as well as eminently sane. So too was the aged Henry de Lacy, Earl of Lincoln, who had been among the late king's most trusted ministers.

Gaveston's worst sin was depriving them of their role as the monarch's advisers. Jointly, they took an oath to make him leave the country and surrender his earldom, arriving in London for the parliament of spring 1308 with armed retainers. Their spokesman was Lincoln, who had tried to make Piers behave sensibly but had been rebuffed. Complaining that the favourite was squandering the Crown's revenues, he insisted on his banishment. Edward dared not refuse. Giving up his earldom, Piers went to Ireland as lieutenant. Archbishop Winchelsey, who had returned to England more pugnacious than ever, announced he would excommunicate him should he dare to come back.

Even so, Edward secured Gaveston's return next year, by promising parliament to satisfy grievances such as failure to hear petitions and to improve the currency, disarming Lincoln, Hereford and Warwick with flattery. Philip IV, who had paid two of the earls to plot against Piers after complaints from Queen Isabella, withdrew his opposition when she was given the county of Ponthieu, while in exchange for more rigorous persecution of the Templars, the pope blocked Winchelsey's threat of excommunication. In July 1309 Gaveston rejoined the king, who met him when he landed at Chester, regranting his earldom and estates.

He made himself more disliked than ever, giving his fellow earls nicknames that circulated widely. Lancaster was the 'Churl', the 'Rangy Pig' or the 'Fiddler', Warwick the 'Black Dog of Arden' (from foaming at the mouth when in a rage), Pembroke 'Joseph the Jew' and Lincoln 'Burst Belly', while Gloucester, the only one who tolerated him, was 'Whoreson' – an unkind allusion to the dowager countess's hasty second marriage. Nobody saw Edward without Gaveston's approval and he had a stranglehold on patronage. People suspected he was a warlock – there were rumours of his mother having been burned as a witch.

In the autumn he had a Lancaster retainer sacked from the royal household. 'Watch out, Piers', warns the *Vita*. 'The earl of Lancaster will pay you back.'[14] At Christmas the earls refused to come to court if he was present, telling Edward that while Piers was in the royal chamber they did not feel safe. They attended parliament in March 1310 on condition he stayed away. When it met, they declared the realm had fallen into a perilous condition since the late king's death and could only be saved by an elected council. The king reluctantly agreed to the election of 'Ordainers', who included Archbishop Winchelsey and Lancaster with some of Edward I's old ministers. Then, on Gaveston's advice, Edward tried to distract them with a campaign in Scotland.

In September 1311 the Ordainers demanded that the king 'live of his own' and observe the charters, and that royal gifts and appointments to high office should be controlled by a twice yearly parliament. His household was purged of unpopular officials, while foreign merchants collecting the customs were arrested – a measure aimed at the royal banker, Amerigo de Frescobaldi, who was ruined. What hurt Edward most was the ordinance against Gaveston, accused of estranging the king from his natural advisers, unlawfully accepting estates and protecting criminals. He was exiled as a public enemy.

The end of Gaveston

In November Gaveston left for Flanders, but the Ordainers went too far by insisting that his friends and hangers-on leave court as well. Defiantly, Edward recalled him, and he was back in January with his lands restored. In response, the earls made Lancaster their leader and entrusted Pembroke with catching Piers, while Winchelsey prepared another excommunication. Unaware of this, Edward spent most of April with Gaveston in Newcastle until they learned Lancaster was coming with an army. Leaving Piers, who had fallen ill, at Scarborough Castle, the king went off to find troops.

Pembroke besieged the castle and on 19 May, without a proper garrison or provisions, Piers surrendered on condition he be kept safe until parliament met, after which he could go back into the castle if satisfactory terms had not been agreed. Pembroke took his captive south, leaving him at Deddington rectory in Oxfordshire while he visited his wife at their manor nearby. Early on the morning of 10 June the Earl of Warwick's men surrounded the house and seized Piers, dragging him off to Warwick Castle, first on foot at the end of a rope and then on a broken-down nag.

Ten days later, he was handed over to Lancaster before whom he grovelled, begging for mercy. 'Pick him up! Pick him up!', cried the earl. 'In God's name, take him away!' He was led off to Blacklow Hill 2 miles off, where a Welshman ran him through with a sword and another Welshman hacked his head off, Lancaster watching from a distance. According to the *Vita*, all England rejoiced at the news, with one exception. 'By God's soul, he behaved like a fool', cried Edward. 'If he'd taken my advice, the earls would never have got hold of him. I always told him to keep clear of them as I knew something like this would happen. Just what did he think he was doing with the Earl of Warwick, who hated Piers, as everybody knows? I was sure he could never escape if the earl caught him.'[15]

Civil war seemed unavoidable. The earls wanted the ordinances; the king wanted revenge. But while the earls controlled northern England and had captured all Edward's ready money, at Newcastle, Warwick and Lancaster shrank from a confrontation. Penniless, Edward listened to Pembroke and Gloucester, who advised against armed conflict. Philip of France and Pope Clement sent envoys to mediate. Meanwhile, parliament refused to grant supplies, so the king borrowed money from London merchants.

In November 1312 the queen gave birth to her first child, the future Edward III. 'To some extent this soothed the king's grief at Piers's death, by providing the realm with an heir', says the *Vita*, warning readers that without one there would be war for the throne when the king died.[16] It brought the father unaccustomed self-confidence. He began listening to his wife's advice, and his pardon to the earls in October 1313 stated he did so at the intercession of his dearest companion, Isabella, Queen of England.

Scotland

Living up to his name of 'Hob in the Moors', the Bruce was using hit-and-run tactics, avoiding pitched battles and demolishing castles, not only those he captured but his own, which meant there were fewer strongpoints. Small English garrisons could no longer hold down wide areas, and town after town fell to Robert. Since 1311 he had been raiding over the border into Northumberland and Cumberland, whose inhabitants grew so desperate that they paid him protection money. He even attacked Durham. Early in 1314 Edinburgh and Roxburgh fell. Other than Berwick, the only major Scottish fortress retained by the English was Stirling, besieged by Robert's brother. Its constable sent word to Edward that he must surrender if relief did not reach him by midsummer. Near to tears when he heard he had lost Edinburgh, the king was determined to save Berwick. If he did, winning a significant victory, he could afford to ignore the Ordainers.

Early in June, sending Pembroke ahead to reconnoitre, Edward marched out from Berwick with 2,000 men-at-arms and 10,000 foot. Protesting that the campaign had not been approved by a parliament and that they had no wish to infringe the Ordinances, Lancaster, Warwick and Warenne stayed away but sent troops. Edward marched at breakneck speed, with very short halts for sleep and meals. The Scots had wrecked the road by digging pits along it, so the English army was exhausted by the time it came in sight of Stirling on the afternoon of Sunday 23 June.

Robert was waiting, with half as many infantry and only 500 men-at-arms. When two English scouting parties attacked as soon as they arrived, he routed them, personally killing one of their commanders. Even so, despite spending the night on wet marshland, Edward's troops expected to win overwhelmingly next day because of their numbers and weaponry. But the king made a fatal mistake in naming Gloucester as constable (commander-in-chief) in place of Hereford, the hereditary constable, causing a dispute that deprived the English of coherent leadership. Overwrought, Edward also rejected Gloucester's advice to let his tired troops recuperate, accusing the earl of treachery.

Next morning, instead of staying on the defensive when the English moved up to attack, the Scots' four schiltrons of pikemen crossed the Bannockburn and advanced over the marshy ground towards their surprised enemy. It should have been simple enough to drive off the scanty Scottish cavalry so the archers could shoot the pike-men down, as at Falkland; but Edward lacked a battle plan and had no control over his army. Instead Gloucester led a chaotic charge that became bogged down in the marshy soil, he himself being unhorsed and killed with many men-at-arms and infantry.

Before the English archers on the right flank could do much damage the Scottish horse rode up and cut them down. Bruce's pike-men then routed the remaining English infantry. When Edward had a horse killed under him, his household warned it was no longer safe to stay, so he fled towards Stirling Castle. Seeing the royal standard leave the field, what was left of his army broke and ran. A thousand Englishmen died in the battle, many more being killed or taken prisoner during a pursuit that went on for 50 miles. Casualties included 22 barons and 68 knights – even the privy seal was captured with its keeper. The Scots lost 500 pike-men and two knights.

Anxious to make terms with Bruce and save their lives, the garrison of Stirling Castle refused to let the king enter, so he galloped to Dunbar, finding a ship to Berwick from where he sailed to York. He had suffered the worst defeat seen in Britain since the Norman Conquest. Knowing his father had destroyed a Scottish army of the same sort at Falkirk, all England realized his inadequacy. For over a decade the Scots plundered and slew as far south as Yorkshire. Carlisle nearly fell to King Robert in 1315 and Berwick went two years later. There was trouble in

Wales, where Llewelyn Bren ('Llewelyn of the Woods') raised Glamorgan and Gwent in 1316, burning English castles.

The immediate result was the triumph of the Ordainers. Three months after Bannockburn the king reluctantly confirmed the Ordinances in a parliament at York, dismissing his chancellor, treasurer and sheriffs, who were replaced by men chosen by the earls.

In February 1315 Edward interred the still unburied corpse of Piers Gaveston at the Dominican friary he had built at King's Langley, with a service led by the new Archbishop of Canterbury, Walter Reynolds, who was assisted by many bishops and abbots. Edward had hoped to make the earls attend the burial, which was why it had not taken place before. Piers's biographer stresses that the ceremony shows how much Bannockburn demoralized the king.[17]

Queen Isabella emerges

Gaveston had not been followed by 'an unending stream of catamites', whatever one popular historian suggests.[18] Queen Isabella took his place and began to play an important role in political life. Very beautiful, she had the same thick, blonde hair and large, unblinking, pale blue eyes as her father Philip IV, who was the most handsome man in Europe. She also inherited his intelligence and cruelty, and gift for hiding what he thought behind a smiling mask. She was fond of music and books, and her household included minstrels and instrumentalists, while she owned a library of illuminated Arthurian romances. She also enjoyed hunting and hawking. Noticeably more pious than the king, she was genuinely charitable, not only feeding the poor but arranging for the adoption of a small boy who had been orphaned in the Scottish wars. A less attractive quality was avarice.

In 1313 Isabella and Edward visited Paris, where she persuaded her father to confirm Edward as Duke of Guyenne. Next year she paid another visit, securing further concessions. During her stay Philip was told his daughters-in-law were unfaithful, a charge resulting in their imprisonment and their lovers being broken on the wheel – Isabella was rumoured to have been his informant. Her father died a few months after Bannockburn, supposedly summoned to hell by the Templar Grand Master, whom he had just burned at the stake.

Isabella did her best to make her husband resist the Ordainers. At this time he was devoted to her, rewarding a knight who brought the news of their second son's birth with £100. She attended the royal council meetings and in 1316, when the bishopric of Durham fell vacant, prevailed on Edward to appoint her candidate Louis de Beaumont, in the teeth of Lancaster's opposition.

The Earl of Lancaster fails

The Ordainers' leader, Edward's Plantagenet cousin, the Earl of Lancaster, had risen in public esteem for refusing to serve on the Bannockburn campaign. Three years older than the king, a man who was in every way unlike his grandfather Henry III, Thomas of Lancaster comes down the centuries as stupid, arrogant and unscrupulous despite undeserved popularity. His programme was to replace the Crown's power by a council of magnates, and win support by reducing taxes. He had no real objectives beyond his own interests and taking revenge on personal enemies.

Everything conspired against Lancaster. The weather was hostile from 1314 to 1322, rain falling day after day so that the crops failed in what became known as the Great Famine, people being driven to cannibalism. Thousands perished when disease followed hunger, killing men and animals. Farm rents collapsed, wiping out royal and baronial revenues. Law and order broke down, with riots throughout the country.

The earl had no allies after the deaths of his wise old father-in-law Lincoln in 1311 and Warwick four years later. Even if he found supporters among lesser barons and the bishops, his fellow magnates loathed him. Having dominated the royal council since Bannockburn, he became its official head in the parliament of January 1316, cancelling all grants of Crown land to favourites over the last six years. But either from arrogance or ill health he then stayed away from parliaments, making enemies of men who should have been his friends. When Surrey tried to obtain an annulment so that he could marry his mistress, Lancaster intervened and Surrey was excommunicated. He retaliated by abducting Lancaster's wife.

Meanwhile, new courtiers found favour with Edward. Hugh Audley was given Gaveston's widow and Roger Damory, an obscure Oxfordshire knight, secured the king's niece, the twice widowed Elizabeth de Clare, who was one of the richest women in the country. William Montague obtained the coveted job of steward of Gascony. Hugh Despenser, a former minister of Edward I who had recommended himself by his cynical support for Piers, also gained advancement. Others included Lord Badlesmere, a great Kentish landowner, and John Giffard.

There was also a 'middle party' led by Pembroke, which opposed both the court and Lancaster. 'If we are to make a hero in the reign at all, earl Aymer of Pembroke has surely the best claim to that distinction', says Tout.[19] With Badlesmere, he hoped to isolate Lancaster while keeping the Ordinances, and give back the king most of his powers if he governed wisely. Isabella supported this sensible but not very strong man, whose advice offered the best hope of stability.

The Treaty of Leake

By autumn 1316 Lancaster had abandoned his attempt to rule and was sulking on his estates. He prepared for civil war as did King Edward. Each man hated and feared the other. While Thomas had no wish to risk his life in battle, and he felt little affection for his wife – they lived apart – her abduction nearly drove him into rebellion because he suspected Edward of encouraging it. When his men harried Surrey's northern lands, the king saw a pretext for crushing Lancaster by force. However, Pembroke dissuaded him, while a group of bishops restrained Earl Thomas.

Two strange incidents did not make Edward feel any more secure. At Whitsun 1317 a masked woman rode a horse into the banqueting hall at Westminster and handed a letter to him as he sat at dinner, which he ordered to be read aloud. Embarrassingly, it complained of the shabby way he treated the knights of his household. Arrested, the woman confessed to being paid by one of the knights to deliver the letter.

Then, early in 1318, a young Oxford cleric named John of Powderham, who resembled Edward, presented himself at the nearby Palace of Beaumont and announced he was the true king of England, offering to undergo trial by combat with his supplanter. He claimed he had been exchanged at birth for Edward, who was a carter's son – the reason why he did not govern properly and liked peasant pursuits. Brought before the king, he called him a changeling, repeating his offer to fight for the throne, but when put on trial at Oxford he broke down, telling the court he had acted under instructions from his cat, who was the devil. He and the poor feline were hanged side by side. According to the *Vita*, this ridiculous episode was reported throughout the whole country, infuriating the queen 'beyond words'.[20]

The quarrel between the king and Lancaster simmered on, the earl claiming that, as holder of the earldom of Leicester, he should be high steward – the office held by Simon de Montfort. Finally Pembroke prevailed. In August 1318 peace between Edward and the earl was reached at Leake (in Nottinghamshire) with a treaty harking back to the barons' attempt to control Henry III sixty years before. The Ordinances, Lancaster's talisman, were reaffirmed, while five members of a council of seventeen were to supervise royal business. Badlesmere, who was acceptable to both sides, became steward of the household, and the new chamberlain was the younger Hugh Despenser.

There was general agreement that Berwick must be recovered. After capturing the town, the Scots had begun raiding further south, the people of Ripon only saving their lives by taking shelter in the minster and paying £1,000. Lancaster joined Edward's army in besieging Berwick in the summer of 1319, but was suspected of treachery. Implying he was a traitor, the *Vita* says he disgraced the royal family, but it is more likely that he merely paid the Scots protection money. When King Robert sent a force to attack Pontefract Castle, his main residence, Lancaster rushed home. He may also have heard that Edward was muttering, 'When this miserable siege is over, we'll get back to other business – I haven't forgotten what was done to my brother Piers.'[21] It was the end of the Treaty of Leake.

The rise of the Despensers

The king abandoned the siege, and it only needed a spark to set alight his feud with Lancaster – which Hugh Despenser the younger soon provided. Sir Hugh had become one of England's wealthiest men overnight after the death of his childless brother-in-law the Earl of Gloucester at Bannockburn, and inheritance of half the earl's estates by Sir Hugh's wife, yet until he was appointed chamberlain by parliament in 1318 Edward took little notice of him. From then on, however, he supervised every detail of the royal day, becoming all powerful, and by 1320 he witnessed three-quarters of the charters issued by Edward. Very different from Gaveston, he has been convincingly described as 'a war lord, a politician and an administrator'.[22]

To Queen Isabella, it seemed that Piers had come again. At this time she enjoyed so much prestige that in 1319, when she was staying near York during the siege of Berwick, the Scots diverted 10,000 troops to capture her, but the plot was discovered by a spy. 'Had the queen been taken prisoner, I think Scotland might have been able to impose peace [on its own terms]', comments the *Vita*,[23] whose author thought Lancaster had told them where to find her. Hugh must have known he could not dominate this strong, shrewd woman.

Hugh's greed verged on the manic, as did that of his father, another Sir Hugh. In 1320 they obtained the vacant marcher lordship of the Gower by persuading the king to confiscate it and then grant it to them. The Marchers were outraged, since the precedent made their own fiefs vulnerable to seizure. In any case, they were terrified of young Despenser, a violent man who had recently murdered the captive Llewelyn Bren.

In spring 1321, led by Humphrey Bohun, Earl of Hereford and Roger Mortimer of Wigmore, they mobilized. In June they attended a meeting in Yorkshire with Lancaster and other northern lords that resulted in an 'indenture' demanding the Despensers' dismissal. The protesters were joined by Pembroke, John of Brittany and Lord Badlesmere, and by such former royal favourites as Roger Damory and Hugh Audley. On her knees in tears, Queen Isabella begged her husband to get rid of the pair. When parliament met in July it was surrounded by the barons' armed retainers. Denounced as evil counsellors and enemies of the people, the Despensers were banished.

According to the *Vita*, the 'cruel and greedy father' simply went abroad (to Bordeaux), but the son took up a murderous career as a pirate, turning into a 'sea monster'. One of his exploits was capturing a great Genoese merchantman, slaughtering the entire crew and stealing its immensely valuable cargo.[24] Meanwhile, Edward plotted their return.

The end of the Ordainers

In October, ostensibly on pilgrimage to Canterbury, Queen Isabella arrived at the royal castle of Leeds in Kent, demanding to spend the night there. Suspecting she intended to seize it, the wife of its absent castellan, Lord Badlesmere, greeted her with a flight of arrows, killing six of her escort. Badlesmere made matters worse by writing a truculent letter to Isabella, saying that he fully approved of his wife's actions. Joined by a contingent from London, where the queen was very popular, the king assembled an army and besieged the castle, using stone-throwers. On learning the Earl of Lancaster refused to send help, Lady Badlesmere surrendered. She was sent to the Tower, while the garrison commander, Sir Walter Culpeper, was hanged from the battlements with a dozen of his men.

Encouraged, Edward summoned the Despensers home in December, dispatching troops to capture other baronial castles. Early in 1322 he took a small army to the Welsh border, where he routed the Marchers, seizing all their strongholds. Then he went up to northern England, to deal with Lancaster. He is often praised for the military ability he showed on the campaign, but it must have been supplied by an experienced commander at his side – the elder Despenser or John of Brittany.

Lancaster found himself outmanoeuvred. Although joined by the Earl of Hereford, he was deserted by his henchmen and Pembroke. Retreating northwards with 700 men-at-arms, he hoped to find refuge in his castle at Dunstanburgh on the Northumbrian coast, but on 16 March was intercepted at Boroughbridge in North Yorkshire by Sir Andrew Harclay from Cumberland, who brought 4,000 pike-men and archers. Trying to cross the River Ure over the bridge, Hereford was killed – stabbed up the backside with a spear by a man standing below – while his comrades' attempt to ford was repulsed by devastating arrow fire. In despair, Lancaster rode back to his lodgings in Boroughbridge, where he was arrested the next day.

Less than a week later, after a trial before King Edward in the hall of his own castle of Pontefract, during which he was forbidden to speak in his defence, the earl was led out on a donkey to a little hill nearby and beheaded as a traitor. It was not only the memory of Piers's murder that made Edward pitiless; he feared his cousin was planning to take his place. In view of the unholy regime that followed, many people venerated Lancaster as a martyr and the tomb of 'St Thomas' became a place of pilgrimage.

The 'Contrariants', the earl's leading supporters, were treated mercilessly, Badlesmere and twenty-eight knights suffering the full penalties for treason. Another eighty-six knights were imprisoned and over a hundred more received crippling fines. Two months later, a parliament repealed the Ordinances in the Statute of York, with a proviso that no restraints of this sort must ever again be placed on the king's power. Ironically, the fact that the regime used parliament to do so demonstrated parliament's increasing importance.

The Despenser tyranny

Despite the shameful defeat at Old Byland in August that year, the Despensers ruled the kingdom, since Edward confirmed all their decisions. Pembroke's death in 1324 removed the one man who might have restrained them. 'Weak as he had often been in action, doubtful as were some of his subtle changes of front, with him disappeared the best influence that had ever been exerted on the court and council of Edward II.'[25] The elder Hugh was created Earl of Winchester, securing many estates confiscated in the Midlands and southern England.

The *Vita* comments, 'the son's wickedness outweighed the father's harshness'.[26] The younger Hugh did as he pleased, knowing the king would back him. Creating a fiefdom for himself in south Wales and on the Marches that stretched from Milford Haven to Chepstow, as well as seizing the lands of his sisters-in-law, he bullied several wealthy widows into handing over their estates. A Glamorgan lady had her limbs broken, sending the poor woman insane, while Lancaster's widow was threatened with burning alive as a husband murderer, on the pretext she must have led him astray.

For a time, such methods worked. 'No one, however great or wise, dares to go against what the king wants', records the author of the *Vita*.[27] By September 1324 the younger Hugh had deposited almost £6,000 with Florentine bankers and over the next two years nearly another £6,000 with the Peruzzi – billions in today's money and only part of his wealth, which was mainly in land.

Yet there were dangerous irreconcilables, such as Sir Roger Mortimer of Wigmore, an old enemy of the Despensers from the Welsh Marches who had been imprisoned in the Tower. In 1323, having drugged his guards' wine, including that of the constable, with a potion supplied by his friend Bishop Orleton, he escaped up a chimney, over a roof and down the wall, using a series of ropes, before swimming the Thames. He then fled to France.

Paradoxically, the Despensers' rule saw administrative reforms since it suited them for Edward to be rich. They had started earlier in the reign to save the royal household from control by the Ordainers, and now the Exchequer and the household offices – the Wardrobe and the Chamber – became more effi-cient. In 1323 the treasurer, Bishop Stapledon of Exeter, introduced proper tax records. All this increased the Crown's revenues. (One of the first Englishmen known to wear spec-tacles, Walter Stapledon was a complex figure, whom the *Vita* calls 'immeasurably greedy'.[28]) Sound innovations took place at grass-roots level, sheriffs being recruited from the gentlemen of their county and holding office for only a limited period, while steps were taken to standardize weights and measures.[29]

Isabella versus the Despensers

Old Byland made it plain that the attempt to conquer Scotland had failed. Andrew Harclay, created Earl of Carlisle for defeating Lancaster at Boroughbridge, was so shaken that he negotiated a secret treaty, recognizing Bruce as King Robert in return for a guarantee that his estates would be spared by the Scots. Refusing to accept the war had been lost, Edward was so angry when he learned of Harclay's treaty that he had him executed as a traitor.

Even Londoners were alarmed by Old Byland, a delegation asking the constable of the Tower if he expected the city to be attacked by Scots. They were horrified by the perils of the queen, whom Edward had left at Tynemouth Priory on the Northumbrian coast. Taking refuge in the adjoining castle, she found herself besieged on land by Scots and from the sea by a Flemish fleet. Her husband sent letters to her but made no attempt at rescue. (The younger Despenser was later accused of telling him to let Isabella be captured.) Eventually, she escaped in a fast ship, although one of her ladies fell overboard.

Nobody knows why the younger Hugh had such a hold over Edward. Writing half a century later, Froissart says the relationship was homosexual – Despenser had been 'a sodomite, even with the king'[30] – while nearer the time Robert of Reading refers to 'illicit and sinful unions', claiming that Edward refused to sleep with the queen.[31] Yet Isabella bore him a daughter in 1321 and Hugh's wife had one in 1319 and another in 1325, which added up to a total of nine Despenser children. As with Gaveston, Hugh's fascination for the king is more likely to have stemmed from sheer force of personality.

Robert of Reading's 'illicit and sinful unions' could refer to women instead of a man. A Hainault chronicle says the king was having an affair with Hugh's wife, Eleanor de Clare, but suggestions of a 'wife-swap' are unconvincing.[32] A popular modern writer even claims that the queen was raped by Hugh, for which there is not the slightest shred of evidence.[33] All that is certain is that in 1325 Isabella announced publicly that somebody had come between her and her husband.

She had spent a year living apart from Edward after her escape from the Scots in 1322, the excuse being her desire to make several long pilgrimages. Returning to court the next autumn. she found the Despensers more firmly entrenched than ever, and still more hostile. Then the pair made a series of blunders that showed how much they underestimated her.

The queen's plot

In October 1323 a Gascon noble burned to the ground a disputed bastide on the northern frontier of Guyenne. The English seneschal at Bordeaux was blamed, his refusal to appear before King Charles IV's court at Toulouse resulting in the 'War of Saint-Sardos'. In September 1324 a French army occupied the Agenais, declaring all Gascony forfeit under feudal law. Edward's brother, the Earl of Kent, only obtained a six months' truce by surrendering La Réole.

The Despensers bore a grudge against King Charles for refusing to give them refuge in 1321 and sheltering fugitives such as Mortimer. At their prompting, as soon as the Agenais was occupied Edward confiscated Isabella's estates, pretending she might be a threat during a French invasion – the real motive being that the Despensers coveted her lands. In November she was declared an enemy alien, her household being dissolved and its officials imprisoned in religious houses. Her children were placed in the care of Hugh Despenser's wife – who may have been her husband's mistress.

It looked as if Edward was going to lose Guyenne. At the papal nuncio's suggestion, he sent Isabella to plead with her brother, Charles IV, in March 1325. Told to return by midsummer, she was given back her household as a peace offering. Possessing her father King Philip's sphinx-like quality, she deceived even the younger Hugh. 'When she left, she said good bye to everyone and went off happily enough', her husband later complained.[34] The queen had reason to look pleased since events were playing into her hands, but for six months after her departure Edward and his favourites suspected nothing.

Then the French king announced that Edward's eldest son could pay homage in his place and keep the duchy. Reluctantly, the Despensers gave approval. The thirteen-year-old Prince Edward arrived in France, escorted by Bishop Stapledon, and did homage. With her son in her hands, Isabella decided to put him on the throne of England in place of her husband.

Stapledon had brought a message from Edward, commanding her to return to England as soon as the prince reached the French court. Dressed in black like a widow, she gave an answer that frightened the bishop into fleeing back across the Channel. 'In my opinion, marriage is a union of a man and a woman, loyally living their life together, and somebody has come between my husband and myself and is trying to break the bond', she said. 'I tell you, I shan't return until this intruder has been removed and now I've taken off my wedding dress I shall go on dressing as a widow does when she's in mourning until I've taken my revenge on such a Pharisee.' King Charles, who was present, said, 'If she wants to stay here, I won't make her go – she's my sister.'[35]

In response the royal council (which meant the Despensers), instructed the bishops of England to write to Isabella. The theme of their letters was 'Hugh Despenser has formally demonstrated his innocence in front of everyone and shown he has never harmed the queen, but done everything in his power to help her, and has confirmed by his sworn oath that he will always do this in future', and, less suavely, 'you want to destroy a whole people out of hatred for one man'.[36]

She took no notice, keeping her son with her, the centre of a group of English exiles who hated the Despensers. The most distinguished were the king's brother Edmund, Earl of Kent, and John of Brittany, Earl of Richmond. They also included Roger Mortimer, ten years older than herself, who became not only her political adviser but her lover despite his having a wife and twelve children. The group left France in the middle of 1326, either because King Charles was irritated by the scandal or because he would not give them troops. In Hainault, in return for offering to marry Prince Edward to the count's daughter Philippa, she obtained the money, ships and soldiers needed for an invasion.

The fall of Edward II and the Despensers

Isabella's expedition landed near Orwell in Suffolk on 24

September, bringing 2,000 men led by Mortimer. She issued a proclamation against the Despensers, whom she denounced as murderers of the Earl of Lancaster, robbers and oppressors. When she advanced inland there was no opposition. Her opponents did not dare to raise a large army for fear it might mutiny – what troops they had ran away. Edward and the younger Hugh fled to the West Country, hoping to find supporters.

The queen announced that she would punish the Londoners if they did not help her overthrow the Despensers. They responded by rioting on 15 October, the day when the industrious Bishop Stapledon, whom the king had left behind as 'guardian', unwisely rode into the City. He was chased by a mob, dragged off his horse while trying to reach sanctuary in St Paul's and beheaded with a bread knife.

At Bristol the elder Despenser attempted to bargain for his life when Isabella's army arrived, but his men let in her troops. Although she wanted to save him, he was tried at once. 'Sir Hugh, this court forbids you to answer [the charges] because you made a law that men can be condemned without replying', he was told. 'By force and against the law of the land, and taking upon yourself royal power, you counselled the king to disinherit and undo his lieges, notably my lord Thomas of Lancaster whom you put to death without cause. You are a robber and by your cruelty you have robbed this land, so that the entire people cry vengeance on you.'[37] Found guilty by a roaring mob, old Hugh was hanged in his armour with his coat of arms reversed, then cut down alive, disembowelled and quartered. His remains were fed to scavenging dogs.

Prince Edward was proclaimed Guardian of the Realm. Meanwhile, his father and the younger Hugh tried to sail for Ireland, but were driven back by a storm. Eventually, on 16 November the pair were captured at Neath Abbey in Glamorgan by Henry of Lancaster, the late Earl Thomas's brother. The king was taken to Kenilworth Castle where he was kept under guard, Henry forcing him to surrender the great seal.

Eight days later, having failed to starve himself to death, Hugh Despenser was tried at Hereford in the presence of Queen Isabella and Roger Mortimer. Among the charges were appropriating royal powers, murdering noblemen, procuring Lancaster's execution and responsibility for defeat by the Scots, as well as destroying the queen's marriage. Forbidden to plead although too weak to speak, he was condemned to die as a thief, traitor and returned exile. Naked, wearing a crown of nettles and with mocking verses carved on his skin by knives, at one point screaming inhumanly, he was dragged into the city's main square by four horses to the sound of trumpets and bagpipes. After being half-hanged on a 50 ft tall gallows, he was disembowelled in the usual way.

The deposition of Edward II

Edward refused to attend a parliament in London summoned in his name. When it met in January 1327, rejecting any possibility of Isabella rejoining him – Bishop Orleton (an old friend of Mortimer) stated that the king carried a knife in his hose to murder the queen and said he would kill her with his teeth were it taken from him. Read by Archbishop Reynolds of Canterbury, the Articles of Deposition denounced Edward for bad government, listening to men who gave evil counsel, undignified amusements, losing Scotland and squandering the realm's treasure. He had done all he could to ruin his subjects, and his cruelty and weakness demonstrated he was incorrigible.

On 12 January Edward was formally deposed, his son being proclaimed king. At Kenilworth later that month, clothed in black from head to foot, he abdicated, weeping and half-fainting when asked to resign the Crown by a delegation that came from every section of society: magnates and gentry, prelates, abbots and friars, barons of the Cinque Ports. The entire country wanted to be rid of him. In his misery, he composed some verses, beginning '*En tenps de iver me survynt damage*':

In winter woe befell me,
By cruel fortune threatened
My life now lies a ruin . . .[38]

Edward II's murder

Shortly afterwards, the ex-king was taken by night to closer confinement at Berkeley Castle in Gloucestershire, where his gaoler was an old enemy whom he had persecuted, John, Lord Berkeley. En route, he was ill-treated and mocked by his escort, who shaved off his hair and beard at the roadside with cold water from a ditch, dressed him in old clothes, put a crown of hay on his head and made him swallow rotting food. When he arrived, he was shut in a cell over a cesspit filled with stinking animal carcases.

One chronicler says Edward was taken to other prisons as well, moved about to confuse such would-be rescuers as his confessor, a Dominican friar called Thomas Dunheved, who in 1326 had been in Rome seeking the annulment of the king's marriage. He was abetted by his brother Stephen (a pardoned outlaw) with a Cistercian monk from Hailes Abbey, Gloucestershire. In July 1327 they broke into Berkeley Castle, briefly releasing the ex-king, although he was speedily recaptured.[39] In addition, Sir Rhys ap Griffith, who was an old foe of Roger Mortimer, together with other Welshmen, plotted to attack the castle and deliver the king.

Rumours of rescue doomed Edward, since Isabella and Mortimer realized their rule was growing unpopular. The ex-king was liquidated on the night of 27 September 1327, in a way designed to conceal that he had been murdered. Held down by pillows on a table, a horn funnel was rammed up his rectum, and through it a red-hot plumber's iron was inserted. His shrieks could be heard throughout the castle.[40]

In 1340 an Italian cleric named Manuel Fieschi, a papal notary who had held benefices at Salisbury and Ampleforth, and was obviously well informed about the deposition, sent a strange letter to Edward III. He said the ex-king had escaped from Berkeley, taking refuge in Ireland and then at Avignon, sheltered by Pope John XXII, before spending the rest of his life as a hermit in northern Italy where he died. Fieschi claimed he had actually spoken to Edward, who gave him details of his escape. It is difficult, however, to avoid the conclusion that Fieschi's letter was no more than an ingenious attempt to extract money.[41]

Not only do most modern historians accept that Edward II died at Berkeley Castle, but so did contemporaries. Embalmed, his body lay in the castle's chapel for three months because Queen Isabella declined a request by the monks of Westminster to bury him, for fear it might result in hostile demonstrations by Londoners. Finally, without asking permission, the aged Abbot John Thokey of Gloucester, who had been a friend of the king, sent a hearse to bring the corpse from Berkeley for interment in his own abbey. Rumours of the murder had spread all over England and, alarmed, Isabella and Mortimer attended the funeral, both in mourning.

Gloucester Abbey became a shrine, such large crowds flocking to the king's tomb near the high altar that a wooden effigy with a copper gilt crown was placed on it. Over the years, this was replaced by one of Purbeck marble whose haunting face, seen from a certain angle, gives an unmistakable impression of weakness. There were so many offerings that the abbot was able to rebuild the church.

Retrospect

However much pilgrims might venerate the dead King Edward II, in life he had been an unmitigated disaster without a single redeeming feature. He even lacked the family demon. One cannot disagree with Tout's verdict, 'a coward and a trifler',[42] or with a modern historian who calls his reign 'the nadir of the dynasty'.[43]

PART 3

Plantagenet France?

The colourful but largely forgotten father of Henry II, Geoffrey, Count of Anjou, who was called 'Plantagenet' from his broom-flower badge. The lions in the royal arms of England derive from the lions on his shield. Enamel plaque of c. 1151 at Le Mans Cathedral. *(Bridgeman)*

The first Plantagenet king, Henry II (1154–89), who gave England the Common Law, began the conquest of Ireland and reigned over western France after marrying Eleanor of Aquitaine – shown here with him. Effigies on their tombs at Fontevrault. *(Alamy)*

Saladin's great opponent, Richard I (1189–99), a military genius who rescued Crusader Palestine, saved the 'Angevin Empire' and really did deserve the name 'Lion-heart' – given to him even before he became king. Effigy on his tomb at Fontevrault. *(Alamy)*

The wolfish, half-crazy King John (1199–1216), who lost the Angevin Empire and whose barons forced him into granting Magna Carta. 'Foul though it is, Hell itself is defouled by the presence of John', wrote Matthew Paris. Effigy of 1230-40 at Worcester Cathedral. *(TopFoto)*

A 'thriftless, shiftless king', the amiable but disastrously inept Henry III (1216–72), who rebuilt Westminster Abbey and whose conflict with Simon de Montfort saw the beginnings of England's Parliamentary system. Effigy at Westminster Abbey, cast in 1291. *(Alamy)*

Edward I (1272–1307) the terrible Hammer of the Scots and tamer of the Welsh, a great law giver – the 'English Justinian' - who added hanging, drawing and quartering to the penal code. Wall painting at Westminster Abbey believed to be a portrait. (*Alamy*)

The abysmal Edward II (1307–27), dominated by greedy favourites and routed by the Scots, a ruler so weak and incapable that his subjects thought he must be a changeling. Effigy at Gloucester Cathedral, commissioned by his son Edward III during the 1330s. *(Alamy)*

The magnificent Edward III (1327–77), whose admiring subjects compared him to King Arthur. Despite his great victory at Crécy, he failed to make himself King of France. Effigy at Westminster Abbey, commissioned in the 1380s and modelled on a death mask. *(Alamy)*

The effete, narcissistic Richard II (1377–99), who when a boy defused the Peasants' Revolt, but whose increasingly tyrannical rule eventually cost him his crown and his life. Portrait from the 1390s at Westminster Abbey – no doubt as the king liked to see himself. *(Alamy)*

Henry IV (1399–1413), who usurped the throne, murdering his predecessor. His rule saw many rebellions, including Owain Glyndŵr's valiant attempt to regain Welsh independence. Effigy of 1437 at Canterbury Cathedral – his face deformed by a mysterious disease. *(Alamy)*

Henry V (with the small, forked beard he grew in later life) whose questionable right to the English throne prompted him to claim the French throne as well – an appeal to God to give judgement in a trial by battle. Statue on a screen of 1425 at York Minster. *(© Chapter of York: Reproduced by kind permission)*

Although the fatal incapacity of Henry VI (1422–61, 1470–71) led to of the Wars of the Roses, he became late medieval England's most popular saint. This idealised image from a Tudor rood-screen at Ludham in Norfolk shows him transformed in folk memory. *(Alamy)*

The genial, murderous Edward IV (1461–70, 1471–83), who never lost a battle and ordered the killing of his predecessor, his brother and his brother-in-law. The most handsome man of his day, eventually womanising ruined his health. Window of 1482 at Canterbury Cathedral. *(Alamy)*

The elder of the 'Princes in the Tower', Edward V (9 April–26 June 1483), who was deposed by his uncle after reigning for only eleven weeks and whose mysterious disappearance the following month caused a rebellion. Window of 1482 at Canterbury Cathedral. *(Alamy)*

RICARDVS · III · ANG · REX ·

Richard III (1483–85), who destroyed himself, the Yorkist party and the Plantagenet dynasty by taking the throne, but who has become a cult figure in modern times. A sixteenth century copy of a lost contemporary portrait. *(Alamy)*

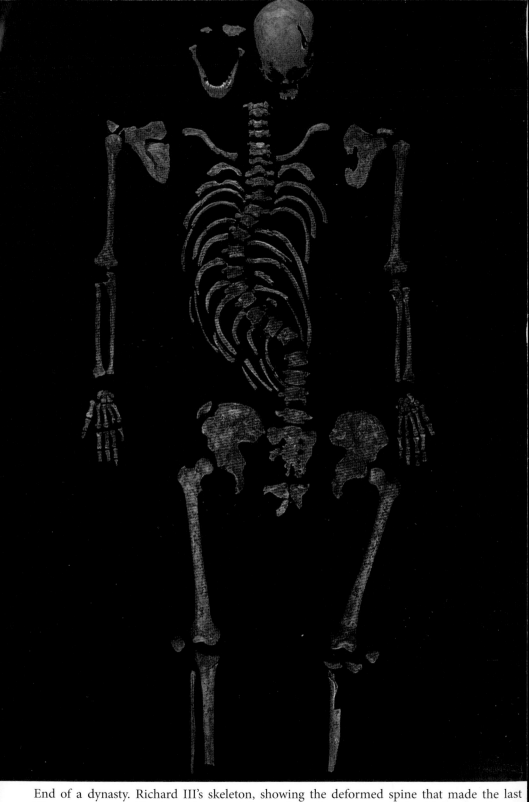

End of a dynasty. Richard III's skeleton, showing the deformed spine that made the last Plantagenet a crookback. Following defeat and death at Bosworth, his body was thrown without a shroud or a coffin into a hole in the ground at Grey Friars' church, Leicester. *(Getty)*

8

The Paladin – Edward III

And in all battles and assemblies, with a passing glory and
worship he had ever the victory

The Brut or The Chronicles of England[1]

The Battle of Les Espagnols-sur-Mer, 1350

'The king stood at his ship's prow, clad in a jacket of black velvet
with a black beaver hat on his head that suited him very well,
and (so I heard from men who were with him that day) in excellent spirits', Froissart tells us, describing Edward III at the battle
fought off Winchelsea on 29 August. He made his trumpeters
play a German dance Sir John Chandos had brought back from
Germany, ordering Chandos to sing with the minstrels and
laughing heartily. Occasionally he glanced up at the look-out in
the crow's nest.

When the enemy was sighted, Edward said, 'I see a boat coming and I think it is a Spanish ship of war!' Then he added, 'I see
two, three, four!' When the entire Castilian fleet came in view, he

cried cheerfully, 'I can see so many, God help me, I can't count them!' Sending for wine, the king and his knights drank before putting on their helmets. Although heavily outnumbered, they proceeded to win a crushing victory. The weather was fine and clear, the battle being watched from the shore by a large crowd which included the queen.[2]

That is how Edward III saw himself, and how his subjects saw him – brave and chivalrous, undismayed by danger, always in good spirits. In the national myth, he is the victor of Crécy and founder of the Order of the Garter.

But Stubbs attributed any admiration for him to Froissart's hero worship. 'The glory and the growth of the nation were dearly bought, by blood, treasure, and agony of many sorts' he complains, referring to Edward's 'foolish policy and selfish designs'.[3] However, his latest (2011) biographer Mark Ormrod calls him 'Edward the Great', praising his revolutionary battle tactics, the growth of parliamentary power during his reign, and a new partnership between Crown and ruling class.[4]

The puppet king

Edward was fourteen when Archbishop Reynolds crowned him at Westminster on 1 February 1326, the crown padded to fit his small head. It was a lavish coronation, to demonstrate support for the boy who was replacing his father on the throne. Henry, Earl of Lancaster played a prominent role in the ceremony as the coup owed much to outrage at his brother's murder. For the same reason he was made the king's guardian. In reality, if nominally ruled by a council of twelve magnates, the country was governed by Roger Mortimer and Isabella, who pretended that everything had Lancaster's approval.

When Edward came of age the queen was reluctant to relinquish power. Nor would Mortimer let her, good fortune having turned his head. Isabella shared his greed, not only regaining her dowry lands, but acquiring estates seized by the Despensers, so that her annual income amounted to over £13,000. Roger took the Despensers' vast lordship in south Wales, retaining the lands they had stolen, while securing even more in the Principality where he was justiciar. In 1328 he was created Earl of March (the Marches of Wales) and, whether at his castles of Wigmore or Ludlow or at the royal palaces, lived regally, staging lavish tournaments and escorted by a retinue of Welshmen.

The English did not see why they should be ruled by 'an adulterous Frenchwoman and her paramour' whom they blamed for the murder at Berkeley. A disastrous campaign against the Scots led by Mortimer, ending in another flight by English troops, made their regime still more unpopular. So too did the 'Shameful Peace' of Northampton in March 1329 that recognized Robert the Bruce as King of Scots. Edward had to be bullied into signing it, while the Westminster monks would not return the Stone of Scone.

Lancaster refused to attend parliament, announcing that he wanted to give the council proper powers by removing Edward from Mortimer's control. He was feebly supported by the late king's lacklustre brothers, the Earls of Kent and Norfolk, and one or two bishops. Roger responded with brutal attacks on his manors in the Midlands, even burning their churches, accompanied by Isabella (who put on armour). Lancaster submitted, to save his life.

Eager to eliminate anyone else who might lead a rebellion, Mortimer employed two agents provocateurs, a pair of rogue Dominican friars, to destroy Edmund of Kent. They did so by tricking the earl into thinking Edward II was still alive, conjuring up a 'demon' who put the royal brothers in touch. After concocting a plot to restore Edward, Kent was arrested at Winchester in March 1330 and sentenced to death, waiting five hours on the scaffold until a condemned criminal agreed to behead him – no one else would do it.

The fall of Mortimer and Isabella, 1330

'The king began to grow in body and mind, which undermined the authority of the queen, his mother, and vexed the earl of March, whose guidance the queen always followed.'[5] His court was packed with Mortimer's spies, but Edward built up a circle of trusted friends, notably a household knight, Sir William Montague (or Montacute), who commanded a small guard of twenty men-at-arms, and the Keeper of the Privy Seal, Richard Bury, who was his secretary. Secretly, he sent Montague to Pope John XXII at Avignon, explaining that he wanted to break free.

A great council was to meet in autumn 1330 at Nottingham, Isabella and her lover installing themselves in the castle. Montague planned to arrest the pair, despite Edward's reluctance to act against his mother. Sensing danger, Mortimer questioned Montague before the council and then, impertinently, the king. He could get nothing out of them, but ordered every gate and door to be locked and barred at night, placing guards everywhere, while the queen took charge of the keys, forbidding Edward to enter the castle with more than three servants.

'Better eat the dog than let the dog eat you!' commented Montague.[6] He advised Edward, who had been infuriated by Mortimer's grilling, to frighten the constable of the castle into leaving a postern door unlocked. On the night of 19 October Montague and the king led twenty-four men through the postern (a tunnel) and reached Isabella's apartments undetected. After killing three courtiers in a scuffle – during which the chancellor Burghersh tried to escape down the garderobe (privy) but got stuck – and ignoring the queen's cries to 'Spare gentle Mortimer!', they seized her lover as he was putting on his armour behind a curtain.[7]

Six weeks later, wearing a black cloak on which was painted *'Quid gloriaris?'*, 'Where's your glory now?', Roger Mortimer was tried at Westminster, accused of murdering Edward II, attacking Lancaster in 1328, procuring the Earl of Kent's death, and estranging the late king and Isabella by telling her that if she went near him 'she would be killed with a knife'.[8] The king spared Mortimer disembowelment and quartering, but his body was left hanging for two days.

Edward treated Isabella leniently. Her estates were confiscated and for two years she was confined at Windsor, where she seems to have suffered a breakdown, but in 1332 £3,000 a year (later increased to £4,000) was settled on her, together with Castle Rising in Norfolk, near Lynn. Her son regularly visited her and she went to court when it was in London, where she had apartments at the Tower. Her life was a quiet but stately one: she enjoyed hawking, reading her library of romances, listening to her minstrels and giving alms. When she died in 1358 she was buried in her wedding gown with her husband's heart.

Edward may have consulted her on how to deal with France. Only the affection felt for Isabella by successive French kings, her father and her brothers, had saved Gascony for the Plantagenets, a link she exploited in negotiations over a long period.

The personal reign of Edward III

While welcoming Edward, the magnates wanted to bring back the Ordinances so they could control him, and, seeing themselves as his natural counsellors, were offended when he chose advisers from among the Nottingham conspirators. Four of these were given earldoms, including Montague, who became the most influential man in England. Clearly uneasy, Edward replaced sheriffs and royal castellans with people whose loyalty towards him was beyond doubt.

He had not forgotten his humiliation by the Scots and in 1332 found a means of revenge. During that summer, without English help, Edward Balliol, the son of 'Toom Tabard', led a group of dispossessed Anglo-Scottish magnates (known as the 'Disinherited') on a seemingly hopeless expedition to overthrow the Bruce monarchy. Landing in Fife, with 500 men-at-arms and 1,000 archers, on 11 August at Dupplin Moor near Scone they annihilated the eight-year-old David II's much bigger army with arrow fire, losing only thirty-three men. Balliol then had himself crowned king at Scone but, finding little support, was soon driven out.

Edward at once recognized Balliol as King of Scots and in May 1333 besieged Berwick. The Scots tried to relieve it with their usual mix of spearmen and cavalry (15,000 troops, of whom barely 1,200 were mounted) under Sir Archibald Douglas, Guardian of the Realm of Scotland. The English king was waiting for them at Halidon Hill, 3 miles north-west of the city. Having learned the lesson of Dupplin, he placed six wedges of archers on each flank of a central formation of men-at-arms, who dismounted to fight on foot. After struggling through volley upon volley of arrows, 'yelling their hideous war-cry', the remnant of the Scottish schiltrons was cut down with ease when it reached the top of the hill. The English men-at-arms remounted to pursue the survivors, killing over 4,000, including the guardian and five earls. The English lost a knight, a squire and twelve foot soldiers. The Scots had been like sheep against wolves, observed a contemporary.[9] Edward had revenged Bannockburn. He had also realized the longbow's potential.

Over the next six years Edward led four more expeditions into Scotland. In summer 1336 he took 400 men-at-arms and 400 mounted archers on a '*chevauchée*', a lengthy raid whose aim was to weaken the enemy, a tactic that became standard practice during the wars in France. He went out of his way to rescue the Countess of Atholl, besieged at Lochindorb Castle in Badenoch, then rode on to destroy Aberdeen. Wherever they passed, his troops burned crops and farms, and killed livestock – and men and women, when they could catch them.

Balliol invaded again, holding a parliament at Perth and ceding five Lowland counties to Edward, to whom he paid homage at Newcastle. Inevitably, by confiscating the lands of so many great Scottish nobles and granting them to the Disinherited,

Balliol ensured bitter resistance, and within six months he was again driven out. The Scots could rely on Philip VI, who, if he did not send troops, supplied money. But Halidon Hill had ended their brief superiority on the battlefield.

The man

Tall and handsome, Edward III looked not unlike his grandfather when young, except for his yellow hair, beard and moustaches. Although in many ways Edward I was his model (he had himself buried next to him in Westminster Abbey), he lacked his grimness. A man who loved life and adventure until his health cracked in old age, he nonetheless paid meticulous attention to business, weighing each political move. 'It is as it is' was among his mottoes. He used display to restore the monarchy's prestige, avoiding 'peasant amusements' and low company, with an unending round of feasts, pageants and tournaments.

He certainly resembled his grandfather in a happy family life. If his wife looked anything like the brown-skinned, curvaceous elder sister of whom a description survives, she must have been lovely, although her funeral effigy shows a fat, homely face. She was famous for her good nature. After the birth of an heir, Edward the 'Black Prince', she gave him four more sons together with two daughters who lived to maturity, besides several children who died young. Whether she was pretty or not, her husband adored her.

Like Henry II, Edward treated his five sons as partners in a family business, especially the three eldest. The Prince of Wales received Gascony and then Aquitaine; Lionel was made Duke of Clarence and married to the richest heiress in Ireland; and John of Gaunt succeeded his father-in-law as Duke of Lancaster, inheriting over thirty estates and castles. Unlike Henry's children, all showed impeccable loyalty.

Edward was sufficiently indulgent not to object when his daughter Isabella refused to wed the young Count of Albret,

and allowed his eldest son to marry a beautiful, slightly disreputable, Plantagenet cousin, Joan of Kent, who was the daughter
of Edward II's unlucky brother. In 1340, when only twelve, she
had made a secret marriage to Sir Thomas Holland, but while
he was away fighting in France her mother forced her to marry
Lord Salisbury's son. On his return, Thomas appealed to the
pope and the couple obtained an annulment, living together
until his death in 1360. Despite her past – she was known
ironically as the 'Virgin of Kent' – the prince married Joan the
same year.

According to the poet Thomas Hoccleve, the king went in
disguise among his subjects to find out what they thought of
him. Possessing the common touch, speaking English as well
as he spoke French – in an unusually pleasant voice – he was
familiar and polite to everybody. After his victories he became
immensely popular.

He loved building, transforming Windsor from fortress
into palace, adding a great chapel for the Order of the Garter.
He rebuilt much of Westminster, including the chapel of St
Stephen, which was given a cycle of frescoes (destroyed in the
fire of 1834) with one of himself and his family, besides refur-
bishing Clarendon and other royal hunting boxes – such as a
long forgotten castle at Hampstead Marshall in Berkshire. Like
his grandfather, Edward saw himself as the heir of King Arthur,
collecting tales of his deeds and founding a 'Round Table' at
Windsor in 1344. Venerating Glastonbury for its Arthurian
associations, in 1345 he had a search made for the body of the
shrine's founder, Joseph of Arimathea.

On progress he prayed at all England's holy places, not only
Walsingham or Canterbury, but less familiar shrines – St John's
at Beverley, St Cuthbert's at Durham and many others. He
also founded two religious houses, a Dominican nunnery in
Dartford and a Cistercian abbey near the Tower of London, St
Mary Graces. But if deeply religious and a regular almsgiver, he
was scarcely a spiritual man.

No intellectual, Edward revelled in hawking and hunting, and was fond of fishing with a rod and line. His mews were staffed by twenty falconers while his menagerie held lions and leopards. Jousting, in which he took part, was a regular feature of court life. Indoors, both he and the queen played chess and dice. Pageantry in any form was his greatest pleasure, and he enjoyed wearing dazzling jewels and a costly wardrobe.

Froissart

Edward was lucky to find a chronicler, Jean Froissart (*c*.1337–1410), who immortalized him. Born in Hainault, a French-speaking cleric, Froissart recorded with unflagging enthusiasm the battles of the Hundred Years War. Sometimes called the first war correspondent, no other fourteenth-century writer possessed such gifts for describing combat, analysing personality and using dialogue. Stubbs may argue that any admiration for the king derives from Froissart, but Froissart knew what he was writing about – he first visited Edward's court in 1361, when the king was still vigorous, and for earlier events used Jean le Bel's chronicle.

France

When Charles IV, Isabella's youngest brother, died in 1328, he left no sons and was succeeded by his cousin Philip of Valois, who descended in the male line from a brother of St Louis. Although Edward had been more closely related to Charles through his mother, he recognized Philip as King of France, paying 'simple' homage to him for Gascony. He was ready to pay full homage on the right terms, which meant regaining the Agenais. Disguised as a merchant, he visited Philip VI secretly and they agreed to go on Crusade together if they did not solve the dispute. But his attitude changed when Philip showed that he intended to conquer the duchy.

In spring 1336 a fleet assembled at Marseilles for the Crusade was moved to Normandy, the Archbishop of Rouen announcing that Philip would send troops to help the Scots. In response, a great council at Nottingham granted war taxes of a 'tenth' and a 'fifteenth'. Although by now 'Gascony' was merely the coast between the Charente and the Pyrenees, the Gascons still regarded Edward III as their natural ruler, heir to the old Dukes of Aquitaine. They were subjects whom he had a duty to protect.

In 1337, angered by Edward sheltering his brother-in-law, Robert of Artois, Philip declared that Gascony was forfeit. (After poisoning his mother-in-law, Robert had tried to kill Philip and his queen with sorcery.) Edward reacted by claiming the French crown. Next year, at Robert's suggestion his court swore to make him King of France in the 'Vow of the Heron', during a banquet at Windsor at which herons were served as a dish. Meanwhile, England feared invasion after the French fleet arrived on the Norman coast, raiders burning Portsmouth and Southampton. Tension grew as privateers seized English ships, parading their captured crew at Calais minus ears and noses. The English retaliated in kind, burning Boulogne in 1339.

Halidon Hill had shown Edward he possessed a weapon that won battles, while he acquired allies on France's northern border – the Duke of Brabant, the Counts of Guelders, Hainault, Holland, Julich and Limbourg, even Emperor Louis IV. The Count of Flanders refused to join, so Edward banned the export of English wool to Flanders until the starving Flemish replaced the count with a leader who was an anti-French merchant. Money to subsidize these new friends came from heavy taxes and levies on wool that caused considerable resentment. In addition, the king borrowed from Lombard and Florentine bankers, from merchants in the Low Countries, from English woolmen and vintners. He even pawned his crown.

Edward finally invaded France in 1339, leading a *chevauchée* into Picardy of the sort he used in Scotland, burning and slaying. Philip intercepted him with 35,000 men, but refused to give battle. Edward withdrew to Flanders after only a month, returning to England in February 1340. All he had achieved was to run up debts amounting to £300,000. He told parliament he 'needed the help of a great aid (new tax) or he would be dishonoured for ever and his lands on both sides of the sea would be in peril – he would lose his allies and have to go back in person to Brussels and stay there as a prisoner until the sums he owed had been paid in full'.[10] Fearful of French invasion, parliament agreed to a ninth on agricultural produce and a ninth on townsmen's goods, while insisting he observe the provisions of Magna Carta and the Forest Charter, end the exorbitant 'maletote' on wool and stop sheriffs from holding office for more than a year. This enabled him to equip an invasion fleet.

A French armada, including Castilian and Genoese vessels, assembled at Sluys on the Flemish coast, to intercept the king. In June 1340 he sailed from Orwell to attack it, despite Archbishop Stafford warning him he did not have enough men. Although the French fleet included so many vessels that their masts looked like a forest, Edward won a great victory. Directing his fleet from his flagship the *Thomas of Winchester*, he used wind and tide to defeat them, grouping his own ships in threes – one carrying men-at-arms flanked on each side by another with archers. Outshooting the enemy's crossbows, his longbowmen massacred the French before his men-at-arms boarded. He captured 166 vessels. The main English casualty was a cog carrying ladies of the court, which was sunk by gunfire, while the king himself was wounded by a bolt in the thigh. His campaign on land was less successful, Philip VI refusing to settle matters by a duel or a full-scale battle.

Shortage of cash forced Edward into a truce. Informed by an official in London that funds for his immediate needs were available at the Tower, he arrived there at midnight, having sailed up the Thames, so unexpectedly that the constable was away. He then sacked the chancellor, the treasurer and three senior judges, arresting leading merchants and legal officials for corruption.

He also tried to send the previous chancellor, Archbishop Stratford, to Flanders as security for his debts. Stratford, who saw himself as another Becket, compared the king to the evil Rehoboam of Scripture who had threatened to chastise his subjects with scorpions, whereupon Edward unfairly charged the primate of encouraging him to wage war without sufficient funds. In a letter to the pope, he claimed that Stratford had hoped lack of money would bring about his defeat and death, even accusing the saintly archbishop of lecherous designs on the queen. In the end Stratford escaped when parliament decided that a lord spiritual could only be tried by his peers.

Out of character, the king's behaviour can only be explained by stress. His debts amounted to five times his revenue and he had pawned his crown. His perseverance was astonishing, and so was his ability to extract taxes despite bad harvests. The victory at Sluys helped to some extent, most people realizing that it made a French invasion less likely. Even so, in 1341 he was forced to appoint ministers on the advice of his lords in parliament, just as the Ordinances had stipulated thirty years before, a concession Edward cancelled after extracting the money he needed.

When his Florentine bankers, the Bardi and Peruzzi, collapsed (from lending all over Europe rather than the king's default), he borrowed from wealthy English merchants and a single, exceptionally rich, nobleman, the Earl of Arundel. The country accepted it would have to give more towards the war effort, allowing the king to levy his hated taxes on wool. Why there was such hatred of the French in a period supposedly antedating nationalism may be hard for us to understand, yet it was there all right. Edward whipped up xenophobia to overcome the grumbles of magnates and commons.

He also adopted a cheaper strategy. The Duke of Brittany having died early in 1341, the Breton succession was disputed by his brother's daughter Jeanne, Countess of Blois, and his half-brother, John of Montfort. While Philip VI accepted Jeanne's claim, Edward recognized John as duke in return for homage to him as King of France. Edward arrived in Brittany in 1342, besieging key cities, and when he went home left behind Sir Thomas Dagworth, an Essex man who although nearly seventy was an outstanding soldier. The Breton war enabled Edward to attack Philip on several fronts at once with small armies. In 1345 his cousin Henry of Grosmont, Earl of Lancaster regained the Agenais while Dagworth ravaged Brittany. Edward prepared an invasion.

He was a master of logistics. Commissions of array no longer summoned the old feudal muster but raised troops by indenture with young, energetic nobles and gentry, who each assembled a retinue – the indentures specifying number, type, period of service and rates of pay, which came from the Exchequer. Every town supplied a fixed quota of men, similarly paid, while a substantial number of archers were criminals recruited by free pardons. Horses, weapons, armour and victuals (salted and smoked meat, dried fish, cheese, flour and beans, ale) were gathered from all over England and stockpiled. The army was shipped across the sea with munitions and supplies in an armada of requisitioned ships.

In July 1346, instead of going to Flanders as the French expected, Edward landed in Normandy with 15,000 troops and sacked Caen, killing most of its population. Among the loot was a document containing Philip VI's plan to invade England in 1339, which the king sent home to be read out at St Paul's by the Archbishop of Canterbury – to show his subjects he had saved them from the miseries he was inflicting on the French. Burning and slaying, he marched to Paris where, since he was in no position to besiege it, he torched Saint-Germain and Saint-Cloud nearby. Having panicked Philip into recalling the troops sent to deal with Lancaster and Dagworth, Edward retreated northwards.

After a lengthy pursuit the enemy caught up with him near the little town of Crécy-en-Ponthieu, early in the evening of 26 August. The English, about 2,000 men-at-arms and 7,000 archers with 1,500 Welsh knifemen, occupied rising ground, one side of which was protected by a small river and the other by woods. Edward formed them up well before the battle. His cavalry were to fight dismounted, in three divisions six men deep, his archers on the flanks. After going among them, chatting and joking, he gave orders to sit down to eat and drink until the trumpets sounded, plenty of cattle and large supplies of wine having been found nearby. One reason for confidence was his archers' ability to shoot twelve arrows a minute, with a killing range of about 150 yards against unarmoured men and about 60 yards against men in armour. At most, the enemy's crossbows shot four bolts a minute.

The French army was three times larger, 10,000 men-at-arms (many from the upper nobility), with 6,000 mercenaries and 14,000 levies. Philip wanted to wait until the next day, but his nobles insisted on fighting immediately and, in their haste to get at the enemy, rode over their own crossbow men. Until after nightfall, in charge after charge French mailed cavalry were shot down by English archers, Philip being hit in the face by an arrow and having his horse killed under him before being led away. Over 1,500 French noblemen died, with 10,000 other troops, their corpses lying in heaps, while Edward lost only a hundred men.

Crécy was followed by other victories. In September Lancaster led a *chevauchée* that culminated in the capture of Poitiers, and regained four Gascon provinces. In October a raid across the border by the young King of Scots was defeated at Neville's Cross near Durham, David II being taken prisoner and brought in triumph to the Tower of London where he spent nine years. In May 1347 Sir Thomas Dagworth routed the pro-French Bretons at La Roche-Derrien, capturing their duke.

Only a month before La Roche-Derrien, Calais surrendered after an eleven-month siege that had begun after Crécy, during which the king housed his army in a town of wooden huts. A show trial of rich burghers, pardoned at Queen Philippa's dramatic intervention, was staged to distract attention from other townsmen being evicted from their homes. They were replaced by settlers who made the port an English gateway into France for the next two centuries.

Although Edward's sole gain was Calais, the war was popular as a source of plunder and profit. In 1348 there were few women who did not own something from Caen, Calais or some other town over the seas, such as clothing, furs or cushions. French tablecloths were in everybody's houses, ladies wore French matrons' finery. The Parliament Roll records how lords and commons approved motions thanking God for their king's victories and agreeing that monies voted for him were well spent. He had finally united the magnates behind him. No one could have foreseen the calamity that stopped the war.

The Great Pestilence (later called the Black Death), which reached England in June 1348, combined bubonic and pneumonic plague with other diseases. It killed quickly and horribly, exterminating half of England's population within a few months. In September, on her way to marry the King of Castile's heir, Edward's daughter Joan was struck down at Bordeaux. 'No fellow human being can be surprised that our very souls have been in torment from the sting of this bitter grief, for we are human too', wrote her father. 'But we, who place our trust in God and our life in his hands . . . give thanks to Him that one of our family, free of all stain, whom we have loved with pure love, has gone before us to heaven.'[11]

Edward ordered public prayer, fasting and penance. Dead peasants could not work the land and, realizing they were indispensable, survivors demanded pay that threatened the entire economy. In June 1349 the king issued the Ordinance of Labourers, confirmed by parliament in 1351 – anyone asking higher wages would be imprisoned; everybody under sixty must work. Despite being proclaimed at the shire quarter-sessions by country gentlemen called justices of the peace, it had no effect. Yet the Ordinance at least showed awareness of the problem.

Ignoring the plague, Edward kept an ever more splendid court. In 1348 the Knights of the Order of the Garter, which had been founded four years before, were given magnificent robes to wear at their ceremonies in St George's Chapel. For all the story of the king picking up the beautiful Lady Salisbury's garter and declaring, *'Honi soit qui mal y pense'* (may he be ashamed who thinks evil of it) to save her from embarrassment, it had a political function. Most members, veterans of the campaigns in France, were not only successful commanders but magnates, such as Lancaster and the Earl of Warwick, which reassured the old nobility.

During Christmas 1349, Edward learned that the French had bribed the Italian mercenary who was governor of Calais to hand over the city. Terrifying the governor into turning double agent, the king and his eldest son crossed the Channel and entered Calais secretly, fighting incognito under Sir Walter Manny's command and ambushing the enemy when they came to take possession. Characteristically, Edward gave his prisoners a sumptuous dinner on New Year's Eve, presiding in person and wearing a pearl coronet.

The next year he destroyed the Castilian fleet off Winchelsea in the engagement known as Les Espagnols-sur-Mer, confirming his control of the Channel. Determined to conquer France, Edward then embarked on a series of *chevauchées*, to weaken the new Valois king, Philip's son John II. Yet for a decade after Crécy no more decisive battles were fought on land. While Edward retained Calais and what had been recovered in Gascony, he did not make any further gains.

Despite the Black Death, it was easier for him to find money for the war, presented to parliament as 'a joint stock enterprise undertaken for the defence of the realm and of his legitimate claim to the throne of France'.[12] Everyone knew of his victories from his letters to bishops and abbots, read out in parish churches, marketplaces and shire courts. Since 1345 a gifted treasurer, William Edington, Bishop of Winchester, had been centralizing royal revenue under the Exchequer so that the king's income could be properly budgeted, which enabled him to finance campaigns without asking too much in taxes. In any case, lords and commons were more inclined to finance hostilities because of the loot.

Even the magnificent new coinage introduced in 1344 served as propaganda. Gold nobles, half-nobles and quarter-nobles had an image of the king in armour, standing in a ship and bearing a shield with the arms of France and England. A jingle ran:

> Four things our noble showeth unto me,
> King, ship and sword, and power of the sea.

Accompanied by the words, 'King of France and England', so that no one could fail to understand its meaning, the image symbolized Edward's claim to the French crown, his victory at Sluys and his control of the Channel. Unlike Henry III's gold penny, the noble proved a lasting success.

The king had built a team of commanders, from very different backgrounds. Lancaster, whom he made a duke in 1351, belonged to the blood royal, while the Hainaulter Sir Walter Manny was a kinsman of the queen and Sir John Chandos's Derbyshire manor had belonged to his family since the Conquest. By contrast, Thomas Dagworth – aged nearly eighty when killed in an ambush – was of humble origin, as was his successor as Captain of Brittany, Walter Bentley, another fine soldier. (Bentley made his fortune by marrying Jeanne de Clisson, a female pirate known as the 'Lioness of Brittany'.) The team included semi-bandits like Sir Robert Knolles and his half-brother Sir Hugh Calveley, who led 'free companies' of brigands. There was even an ex-serf from Norfolk, Sir Robert Salle, personally knighted by the king. But his best general was his eldest son Edward, Prince of Wales, nicknamed the 'Black Prince' from his armour.

In 1354, in secret instructions to the Duke of Lancaster, the king revealed how aware he was of his Plantagenet inheritance. In return for peace, Lancaster must demand the duchies of

Aquitaine-Guyenne and Normandy and the county of Ponthieu, just as the king's ancestors had held them. He must also obtain Anjou, Poitou, Maine, Touraine, the Angoumois, the Limousin and all lands ruled by Henry II. The next year, Edward launched two major offensives. The attack he led in the north was let down by the defection of his ally the King of Navarre, and failed. The other offensive under the Black Prince laid waste to Languedoc, destroying whole towns.

Unexpectedly, the Black Prince then won a shattering victory. In September 1356, on a similar *chevauchée*, he was intercepted by John II near Poitiers – and, astonishingly, 6,000 Englishmen routed 20,000 Frenchmen. His father's aims now grew more attainable. John was brought to England, to be housed in the Savoy Palace at London for the next four years.

David II was still in the Tower and in 1356 Balliol surrendered his claim to the Scottish crown to Edward, who immediately led a vicious raid into Scotland, known as the 'Burnt Candlemas', although bad weather soon made him withdraw, with a great booty of loot and livestock. If he hoped to become King of Scots, it was an odd way of endearing himself to his future subjects. However, later that year he released David, whom he recognized as king while extracting a crippling indemnity.

In autumn 1359 Edward again invaded northern France, to capture Rheims (crowning place of the kings of France) for his coronation. Rheims proved impregnable and after two months spent camping before its walls in the snow, he set off on a *chevauchée* that took him to Burgundy. He then appeared before Paris, but the Dauphin refused to come out and fight, so he returned to the coast through the Beauce, inflicting terrible devastation.

Despite vast plunder, Edward then accepted that he did not have the resources to make himself King of France. He compromised. In May 1360, by the Treaty of Brétigny, John II ceded Guyenne, Poitou, the Limousin and other territories in full sovereignty to Edward, who renounced his claim to the French throne. Created Prince of Aquitaine, the Black Prince ruled the new state from Bordeaux as an independent country, installing a glittering ducal court at his capital. It seemed that his father had achieved a large part of his ambitions.

Had Edward III died soon after Brétigny, he would be remembered as our greatest king. He had united England behind him with his 'we're all in this together' approach, victory after victory and a river of loot. The loot took the sting out of taxation that came to be taken for granted by the Commons.

His reputation as a conqueror and his awesome presence, enhanced by dazzling pomp, had given him a god-like image. He increased his popularity still further by fostering a sense of nationalism. In 1362 a statute ordained that English must be spoken in the law courts, while from then on the king opened parliament in English. He encouraged his courtiers to read the poetry of Geoffrey Chaucer, who was made one of his '*varlets de chambre*' in 1367 and awarded a gallon of wine a day in 1374.

French resurgence

The Black Prince possessed all his father's magnificence and physical courage, but not his charm or political sense. Haughty and extravagant, he made himself disliked throughout his principality, even in the Gascon heartland, which was normally unshakably loyal to the Plantagenets. During an ill-judged intervention in a war for the Castilian throne, although he won a splendid victory at Nájera in 1367 he incurred huge expenses. To pay for these and for his lavish court, he levied a hearth tax that alienated local magnates as well as squires. In 1369 they appealed against it to the new French king, Charles V, who took the opportunity to 'confiscate' Aquitaine. War broke out first in northern France, however, where Edward's county of Ponthieu rose against the English and declared for Charles.

Because of ill health, Charles V employed a Breton squire, Bertrand du Guesclin, to fight the war for him. Realizing English archers and dismounted men-at-arms were unbeatable,

Bertrand used guerrilla warfare, with hit-and-run raids that cut communications, isolated strongholds and wore down morale. The Black Prince fought back ferociously, massacring the entire population of Limoges after its recapture in 1370, a crime which shocked all Aquitaine. Then his health cracked, and he returned to England as an invalid.

When Poitou went over to Charles in 1372, King Edward sailed for France in August with 14,000 troops, but his armada was blown back to port by storms. Then a Castilian fleet defeated the English at sea, making it impossible to send reinforcements to Aquitaine. The next summer John of Gaunt led a *chevauchée* from Calais to Bordeaux via the Auvergne, the sole answer the English could make to the new French tactics, but it ended with Gaunt losing half his army and all his horses. By the end of 1373 the Principality of Aquitaine had ceased to exist beyond the old frontiers of Gascony. The only other English possessions in France other than Calais were one or two seaports in Brittany and Normandy.

Alice Perrers

The authority for Edward's final years is the last great Benedictine chronicler, Thomas Walsingham (*c.*1340–1422), a Norfolk man at St Albans who continued the tradition of Matthew Paris. Aided by fellow monks, well informed by distinguished visitors, his books provide the fullest account of the reigns during which he lived. Fond of scandal, he was to be the source of much of Shakespeare's history through the medium of Holinshed.

The king had been deteriorating since Philippa's death in 1369, his progresses restricted to the home counties. After the abortive campaign of 1372, he went to pieces, drinking heavily and falling further under the spell of a greedy mistress, once a lady-in-waiting to the queen. This was Alice Perrers, thirty years younger than him, the daughter of a Berkshire thatcher and widow – previously maidservant – of a London merchant, from whom she had acquired a highly professional interest in real estate.

'A shameless, impudent harlot' is how Walsingham describes Alice. 'She was not attractive or beautiful, but compensated for these defects by her seductive voice.'[13] He tells us she hired a Dominican friar, supposedly a physician but in fact a warlock, to make wax images of herself and Edward joined together, enhancing the spell with incantations and magic herbs. After giving the king a bastard son when only fifteen (before Philippa died), followed by two daughters, Alice fastened her hold. Besides extracting cash, jewels and estates that included fifty manors,[14] she developed into a ruthless businesswoman.

With a City office in Thames Street, Alice was a curiously modern figure, as much entrepreneur as courtesan. She had close links with the chamberlain, Lord Latimer, and his disreputable financial agent, the London vintner and alderman Sir Richard Lyons, whom she joined in advancing war loans to the Crown at astronomical interest. Together, they bought up at a knock-down price royal debts that were then redeemed by the Exchequer at face value, often making her 100 per cent profit. She also dealt in pearls, amassing 200,000.

Always ready to use her influence at court for cash, brazenly flaunting her position, by Edward's command Alice attended a tournament in the City in 1375 as 'The Lady of the Sun', dressed in a golden gown. She was clearly the model for the horrible Lady Meed in Langland's *Piers Plowman* (if not for Chaucer's Wife of Bath). Everybody other than the king and John of Gaunt loathed her, attributing her domination to sorcery and love-philtres – the heresiarch John Wycliffe called her 'the Devil's Tool'.

Senility and death

Looking like an Old Testament prophet, with long white beard and hair, Edward ended as a drink-sodden dotard. His third son,

John of Gaunt, Duke of Lancaster, ruled in his name, hated for his arrogance and his friendship with Alice Perrers, that 'evil enchantress'.[15] Dissatisfaction at reverses in France and an end to the loot was fuelled by a scorching summer in 1375, during which everybody dreaded a further outbreak of plague. When the Black Prince died the following spring, the English were in despair. While he was alive they had felt safe from enemy invasion as he was a fine soldier – unlike Gaunt.

At the parliament of spring 1376, the Speaker of the Commons, Sir Peter de la Mare, complained that Edward's chamberlain Lord Latimer (a veteran of Crécy rumoured to be a multiple murderer) and his agent, the shady Richard Lyons, had profiteered from trafficking in royal debts and moving the staple – the monopoly on wool for export – from Calais. Sir Peter also accused Alice of annually stealing thousands of pounds in bullion from the king. Before granting taxes, the Commons insisted that Latimer be dismissed, Lyons imprisoned and the lady banished from court.

Gaunt, who angrily referred to the Commons as 'these ignorant knights of the hedgerow',[16] took revenge in the next parliament. Packed with his supporters and having his steward as speaker, it declared the 'Good Parliament' to have been no parliament, reinstated Latimer and Alice Perrers at court, and released Lyons from a luxurious imprisonment. Sir Peter de la Mare spent several months in a dungeon at Nottingham Castle.

Walsingham says that by early 1377 Edward sat like a statue, unable to speak or move.[17] He died at Sheen on 21 June, after a final stroke. The tale of Alice stripping the rings from his fingers before fleeing from the palace, leaving him attended by only a single priest, may be untrue but shows how much she was hated. (Most of Alice's wealth was confiscated by parliament, and she spent the next quarter of a century engaged in litigation to recover it, dying relatively poor in 1404.) In reality, Edward's three surviving sons were at his deathbed.

He was given a funeral Froissart considered to be of a sort

unseen since King Arthur's time. When his hearse, escorted by 400 torch bearers, was carried through the streets to Westminster Abbey by twenty-four knights in black, his sons walking behind, the crowd wept and sobbed. According to his instructions, he was buried by the side of the grandfather whom he had venerated. The effigy on his tomb in the abbey has a face (derived from a death mask) that, although distorted by a stroke, inspires awe.

Retrospect

Edward III's conquests did not last, despite his having spent so much blood and treasure, while he became pitiful when an old man. Yet, as Froissart says, during his prime he had been a marvellous king, and not only because of his victories; he had given his subjects peace and prosperity. Throughout his long reign there had never been the slightest hint of rebellion or civil war or rebellion, and in years to come England would remember him with nostalgia.[18] Like his grandfather, he had shown himself to be a daemon rather than a demon.

9

The Absolutist – Richard II

Richard II, there can be little doubt, not only determined to
act as though he were an absolute monarch, but had a theory
of absolute monarchy

F. W. Maitland[1]

Reburying a friend

Walsingham describes how in November 1395 Richard II went
to Colne Priory in Essex for the reburial of Robert de Vere,
killed in exile three years before – by a wild boar when hunting. The king had the coffin opened, to look at his friend's face
for a last time, holding bony hands whose fingers gleamed with
costly rings.

The story recalls Edward II and Gaveston and, although a
very different personality from his great-grandfather, Richard
was fascinated by Edward, making a pilgrimage to gaze on his
effigy at Gloucester. Hoping to have him canonized, he ordered
lists to be compiled of the miracles performed at his tomb.

In the national myth, Richard is the king of the Peasants' Revolt, the boy ruler who made them lay down their arms. (A recent exam question is said to have been 'empathize with the agony of a fourteenth century peasant', indicating modern obsession with the Revolt.) No less tragic in real life than in Shakespeare's play, he lost his kingdom through trying to possess it more completely.

Born at Bordeaux in 1367, the Black Prince's son, Richard was crowned at Westminster a month after his grandfather's death. 'The City had been decorated with so many golden, silver and silk banners, and other toys to dazzle spectators that you would have thought you were watching a Roman Emperor's Triumph', comments Walsingham.[2] His uncle John of Gaunt, Duke of Lancaster, was in the forefront, carrying the sword Curtana. During the ceremony the ten-year-old boy made a touching attempt to look dignified.

Richard's early reign was dominated by his uncle Gaunt, who had been England's real ruler for some time. Born at Ghent (Gaunt) in 1340, he married his cousin Blanche of Lancaster, the greatest heiress in the land, but after her death acquired a second wife who was the daughter of Pedro the Cruel, so that he hoped to become King of Castile. The only person of sufficient weight to challenge him in England was the Earl of March, who had married the only child and heiress of Gaunt's elder brother Lionel, Duke of Clarence. However, March was too busy trying to manage his wife's enormous Irish estates. The duke hated and feared him (his son was the young king's heir), but he died campaigning in Ireland in 1381.

Lancaster was notoriously unpopular in London, where his Palace of the Savoy, in the Strand between the City and Westminster, magnificently rebuilt and hung with wonderful tapestries, was thronged by a huge staff. He was blamed not only for the defeats in France, but for failing to stop the French from sacking seaports and the Scots from raiding the North. Londoners saw the Savoy's opulence as the fruit of corruption, chasing men in Lancaster's livery through the streets. There was a general lack of trust in the man who ran the government.

The Peasants' Revolt

First levied in 1377 at a groat (4d) per head, the poll tax was raised to 3 groats in 1381, a heavy burden on the mass of the population, who toiled in the fields, earning no more than a shilling a week. Brutally collected, it caused fury. Hedge priests fanned the flames, such as mad John Ball from Kent with his rhyme:

> When Adam delved and Eve span,
> Who was then a gentleman?

In May 1381 thousands of home counties men marched on London under the banner of St George, bringing their bows and led by Wat Tyler (who took his name from his job). Lancaster was away in the North, while the authorities were taken by surprise. En route, the 'true commons' murdered tax collectors and sacked manor houses and abbeys. When they arrived they broke into wine cellars, becoming not so much drunk as demented. One casualty was the unsavoury financier Sir Richard Lyons, who had his head sawn off in Cheapside. Having burned the Savoy to the ground, they stormed the Tower, where they beheaded the Archbishop of Canterbury and the treasurer.

Similar revolts broke out elsewhere, Froissart commenting that 'England was on the point of being lost beyond recovery'.[3] Then the fifteen-year-old Richard summoned the rebels to meet him at Smithfield and discuss their demands. Swollen headed, declaring that all laws would soon come from his own mouth, Wat Tyler demanded an end to villeinage, equality of all men, abolition of every bishopric save one and division of Church lands among layfolk. When Richard and his escort arrived at Smithfield, a knight told Wat to repeat his demands. The rebel leader pulled a dagger, threatening to stab the knight for not being sufficiently obsequious, whereupon the mayor, William Walworth, knocked Wat off his horse, someone killing him as he lay on the ground.

Wat's men drew their bows, but Richard spurred his horse towards them, crying, 'I will be your king, I will be your captain and your leader – follow me and you can have everything you want.'[4] Bewildered, they followed him into the fields outside the City, then threw down their arms and begged for pardon. Wisely, he forbade his troops to attack, allowing them to disperse, aware the Essex men had not arrived and Kent was still out of control. Within a short time, the revolt collapsed, but it was weeks before the disturbances ended. There were surprisingly few executions, although the men who had been most responsible were hanged, drawn and quartered, including John Ball.

Before his execution, one of the leaders, Jack Straw, confessed that they had planned to kill all landlords, including monks and rectors and, finally, the king. They meant to keep the friars who were their friends, however, to say Mass and christen, marry and bury them. There would have been new laws for a society without rich or learned men.

The south-east and east had seen 'a kind of tribalism almost reminiscent of the age of Bede'[5] – Straw said that Tyler would have become King of Kent. But the underlying reason for the Revolt had been the peasants' wish to exploit the labour shortage caused by the Black Death and the landlords' determination to thwart them. They were also unsettled by French raids and the threat of invasion – in Kent no men who lived within 12 miles of the sea were recruited by the rebels because it was their job to guard the shore.

The man

Richard II is the hardest Plantagenet to fathom. One historian suggests that despite a weak physique he hoped to be a great king, and that the effort unbalanced him.[6] Identifying narcissistic tendencies, another argues more plausibly that Richard was a man of only average intelligence, whose wish for absolute power doomed him. 'It was not wisdom and prudence that were the characteristics of his rule; it was chastisement and tyranny.'[7]

He has had few admirers. An exception was the architectural historian John Harvey who considered him the greatest Plantagenet because of his belief in 'Divine Kingship', 'a highly intelligent and supremely cultured man, fully abreast of the intellectual attainments of his age'.[8] In reality, the king's reading was limited to chivalric romances such as *Le Roman de la Rose* and some hagiography, the English verse of John Gower and possibly Chaucer, with a few pages from law books. The only 'science' in which he showed any interest was astrology. What impressed Harvey was Richard's building – the new Westminster Hall, with a new nave for Westminster Abbey and another for Canterbury Cathedral, but these had more to do with his grandiose concept of kingship than aesthetic sensibility. Westminster Hall was rebuilt to outdo John of Gaunt's hall at Kenilworth, while the abbey was the dynasty's mausoleum and the cathedral the Black Prince's burial place.

His pleasures were hunting, hawking and horse-breeding, and often he drank far into the night. (He never jousted, presumably because of poor health.) He owned an even more expensive wardrobe than his grandfather and loved good food, ordering his master cook to produce a book of receipts, *The Forme of Cury*. Unusually clean, he frequently visited bath-houses and had new ones built at Sheen and Eltham, besides introducing handkerchiefs.

In religion Richard was ultra-orthodox, founding a charterhouse at Coventry. (The Carthusians were admired because unlike other monks they had not relaxed their way of life.) When the Church reacted to Wycliffe's heresies, he encouraged its persecution of 'Lollards'. He also adopted his ancestors' cult of the royal saints of Anglo-Saxon England – the Wilton Diptych shows him kneeling at the feet of Edward the Confessor and Edmund of East Anglia.

From Richard's skeleton, we know he was nearly 6 ft tall, big for his time. We know, too, that he had curly fair hair. Otherwise, his appearance is elusive. Painted long afterwards, the portrait at Westminster Abbey shows him at his coronation, as a boy. The Monk of Evesham says he was pale complexioned, with a round, feminine countenance. He looks handsome in the Wilton Diptych from the last years of the reign, in which he appears in profile, clean-shaven and with delicate features including a sharp, retroussé nose. In contrast, the effigy he commissioned for his tomb in the abbey gives him a full face with an incipient double chin and small eyes, its strangeness accentuated by a tiny forked beard.

Nobody could have resembled Edward III less. Arrogant, aloof, abrupt, Richard stammered when he lost his temper with servants or courtiers, which happened all too often. A highly strung, sexless, self-obsessed exquisite with a very lofty idea of his dignity, he was not exactly gifted with charm.

He got on well with his mother – he was distraught when she died in 1387 – and liked women, but did not take mistresses. In January 1382 he married Anne of Bohemia, daughter of the Emperor Charles IV, King of Bohemia – son of the blind king killed at Crécy. The court at Prague where she grew up was French and German speaking with Slavonic undertones, and her mother was Polish. The couple became devoted to each other, but there were no children – perhaps she was barren. (The crown Richard commissioned for her is among the most superb pieces of medieval goldsmiths' art to survive.) From the start, she had a good influence. 'The land was reeking with the blood of the unhappy peasantry, when the humane intercession of the gentle Anne of Bohemia put a stop to the executions.'[9] 'Beauteous her form, her face surpassing fair' is how Richard describes Anne in her epitaph.[10] Highly intelligent, not only did she read German, Czech, Latin and French, but she even owned an English Bible.

Richard always took her with him on progress, and when the couple were apart they wrote to each other regularly.

They presided over a magnificent court. Looking back, Walsingham grumbled that Richard behaved as if his resources were inexhaustible, employing 300 men in his kitchen alone. Among the courtiers was Chaucer, who in 1389 became Clerk of the King's Works. While English was Richard's first language (although Froissart comments on his good French), there is no proof that he ever read Chaucer's verse, but it is likely since he commissioned Chaucer's friend, John Gower to write a long English poem, *Confessio Amantis*.

Richard rules for himself

Surprisingly, Richard's minority lasted until he was twenty-one, under the tutelage of Gaunt and the council. When he asserted himself, sacking the chancellor, Lord Scrope, whom he replaced by the biddable Michael de la Pole – created Earl of Suffolk in 1385 – there was strong opposition. In the parliament of 1384, Richard Fitzalan, Earl of Arundel denounced the king's extravagant court and ineffective government. Richard responded by shouting at the earl, a fire-eating veteran of the French campaigns who had been his governor, that he was a liar and could go to the devil.

During the same year a Carmelite friar informed the king that Gaunt was planning to kill him. Richard ordered the duke's immediate execution, but changed his mind when courtiers protested that the friar must be a liar. In 1385 he decided to arrest Gaunt, changing his mind again when confronted by him at Sheen. The duke rebuked his nephew for listening to evil counsellors and contemplating the murder of a loyal subject. He received an apology, which was followed by a formal reconciliation.

In autumn 1385, provoked by a French expedition that encouraged the Scots to attack across the border, Richard invaded Scotland, burning Edinburgh and some villages, together with the abbeys of Melrose and Newbattle – and falling out with Gaunt over tactics. The campaign did nothing to stop Franco-Scottish cooperation. Brief as it was, Richard took the opportunity to create his uncle Edmund of Langley Duke of York and his uncle Thomas of Woodstock Duke of Gloucester.

Many people suspected that England, her wool trade increasingly crippled by taxes and her wine trade by privateers, was losing the Hundred Years War. Her Flemish and Breton allies abandoned her. The French constantly raided the south coast, burning seaports, and in 1386 the English grew terrified when Charles VI assembled an invasion armada – luckily dispersed by bad weather. Some magnates decided the country needed stronger government.

Gaunt, who on the whole had been a moderating influence, left England in 1386 to pursue his dream of a Spanish throne. Richard was so delighted to see the back of his uncle that he gave him a golden crown. His departure left a vacuum, filled by another uncle, the Duke of Gloucester, who became the king's unrelenting enemy. That autumn, the parliament, already upset by invasion scares, grew panic-stricken at a ridiculous rumour that Richard was plotting to murder all the knights of the shire. Supported by a politically minded prelate, Bishop Thomas Arundel of Ely, Gloucester seized the opportunity to attack the chancellor.

'Your people have an ancient law which, unfortunately, had to be invoked not so long ago', they warned Richard – meaning Edward II. Should a monarch 'rashly do just what he wants, then, with the people of the realm's assent and approval it is lawful to pull him down off his throne and put some near kinsman in his place.' (Gloucester meant himself.) They insisted on the dismissal of Suffolk, who was replaced by Bishop Arundel, the royal council being taken over by Gloucester and the Earl of Arundel – the bishop's brother.[11] Their policies were war with France and evicting Richard's cronies.

The foremost crony was Robert de Vere, Earl of Essex, brought up as a ward in the royal household, who had become the king's inseparable companion – allegations of homosexuality circulated, belied by Oxford's womanizing. Despite his ancient title, he had been very poor until Richard made him Marquess of Dublin (the first English marquess) and the next year Duke of Ireland. What upset Gloucester and his allies was de Vere's monopoly of royal favour: they compared him to an otter in a pond, 'grabbing all the fish it can find'.[12]

Another crony, if not so close, was Thomas Mowbray, Earl of Nottingham, three years older than the king, who had also begun his career as a royal ward. Others included knights of the household, men from the middling gentry, for some of whom Richard displayed real affection. When Sir James Berners, a chamber knight, was blinded by lightning during a visit to Ely Cathedral in 1383, the king asked its monks to pray for him to their patroness St Etheldreda, which they did so fervently that his sight came back the next morning.[13]

The Appellants revolt

A commission was set up to reform the royal household – to purge the cronies. Richard reacted by announcing in August 1387 that he would rule in his own name, with five advisers. These were the Duke of Ireland, Chief Justice Tressilian, Archbishop Neville of York, a former lord mayor of London, Sir Nicholas Brembre, and his old tutor, Sir Simon Burley. Gathering troops, they forced a panel of judges to declare the commission unlawful.

Gloucester, with the Earls of Arundel, Warwick and Derby (Gaunt's son, otherwise known as Bolingbroke), assembled an army and were joined by Nottingham, who was jealous of the Duke of Ireland. Known as the 'Appellants', they enjoyed considerable popularity since they promised strong measures against French invasion. In December, trying to intercept them, Ireland was routed by Bolingbroke at Radcot Bridge in Oxfordshire and fled to France. Arm in arm, the five 'lords appellant' confronted a tearful king in the Tower of London's chapel, insisting on the dismissal of the 'traitors'. For a few days he no longer reigned. Gloucester wanted to take the throne, but Bolingbroke, who was senior to the duke in line of succession, would not let him, and Richard survived.

In February 1388 the 'Merciless Parliament' sent Tressilian, Brembre, Burley and other household members to the block, despite Queen Anne pleading for Burley on her knees. But the new regime under Gloucester and the Arundels lasted barely more than a year. It achieved nothing in France as Gaunt, who had come back from Castile (without a crown) and was now Lieutenant of Gascony, refused to help while the Scots defeated the Percys at Otterburn in August 1388, terrifying the north country. Further demands for subsidies to pay for the war across the Channel angered the Commons, who felt they had paid enough already. Ignoring Gloucester's fury, the council opened negotiations for peace.

Richard regains control

Richard suddenly seized control in May 1389, ordering Bishop Arundel to return the great seal and sending letters to the sheriffs. 'We have reached the age of our majority, already in our twenty-second year,' he proclaimed. 'Accordingly, we wish and desire to rule and govern our person and inheritance . . . choosing and appointing our officers and ministers.'[14] The king did not show any desire for revenge, pretending his wife had persuaded him to forgive the appellants. Gloucester and Lord Arundel were invited to rejoin the council, while he let Bishop Arundel become Archbishop of York.

At council meetings Richard needed self-control to tolerate the behaviour of Gloucester, who disagreed with whatever was decided. Made Lieutenant of Ireland to keep him out of the way, he refused to go there. In his view, the Irish were 'a nasty, beggarly people with a perfectly beastly country which is quite uninhabitable – even if we conquered all of it within a year, they'd take the whole lot back from us inside another'.[15]

For a time Richard governed with restraint, helped by Gaunt, who approved of his policy towards France, a truce being signed in June 1389. Cherbourg was sold to the French in 1393, Brest three years later. Richard also hoped to settle Gascony on Gaunt and his heirs as an independent duchy, making him Duke of Guyenne in 1390. But the Gascons, who had bad memories of the Black Prince at Bordeaux, rose in revolt, so the king abandoned the plan.

When Queen Anne died of the plague at Sheen in the summer of 1394, Richard refused to go into any room where she had been, ordering the palace's demolition. The epitaph he composed for her tomb in Westminster Abbey contains a reference to her skill at settling disputes, which hints at how much he had depended on her for support and advice:

Strife she assuaged, all swelling feuds appeased.[16]

She had been the one person the king really trusted. There was an unpleasant scene at her requiem. The Earl of Arundel, scarcely Richard's favourite subject, arrived late at Westminster Abbey after missing the procession from St Paul's and begged to be excused – there were private matters that required his attention. Seizing a cane, the king hit the earl so hard on the head that he fell down, his blood running over the pavement, and only refrained from killing him because they were in a church. Arundel spent several weeks in the Tower before being bound over for good behaviour in the huge sum of £40,000.

That autumn, the king led an expedition to Ireland. Landing at Waterford in October 1394 with 7,000 men, he defeated a group of south-eastern Gaelic chieftains, whereupon every lord in the country, Gaelic or Anglo-Irish, pretended to submit. After announcing futile measures to 'civilize' the natives (who were to learn English and wear English clothes) he left in March the following year, having achieved nothing.

At home there were religious troubles. In 1378 a group of cardinals had repudiated Urban II, returning to Avignon where they elected a rival pope – beginning the 'Great Schism'. England and the Empire recognized Rome; France and Scotland looked to Avignon. In 1395 the late Dr Wycliffe's disciples posted 'Twelve Conclusions' on the doors of Westminster Hall. Among them were Scripture's superiority to tradition, that the Host was simply bread and any man could act as a priest, that monasticism and prayers for the dead were nonsense, and that the Church must not own property. Several courtiers were Lollards, including the Earl of Salisbury and a number of knights, but secretly since the king detested heresy.

Richard kept on good terms with Gaunt. When in January 1396 the duke took as his third wife Katherine Swynford, who had been his children's governess, Richard arranged for their bastard offspring (the Beauforts) to be legitimized by parliament. Because Katherine was of comparatively humble birth, the marriage outraged great ladies, who said Lancaster had disgraced himself by marrying a concubine. His brothers of York and Gloucester grumbled, too, although York – a lightweight interested only in pleasure – soon accepted it. Gaunt gave the appearance of being grateful, but had his eye on his son's succession to the throne. He was rumoured to have commissioned a forged chronicle, placing copies in important monastery libraries. This claimed that Edmund Crouchback, the ancestor of his first wife, Blanche of Lancaster, and supposedly Edward I's younger son, had really been the eldest but was set aside because of his deformity.

The Duke of Gloucester and the opposition

In contrast, Gloucester openly criticized his nephew and wanted to depose him. A Blimp-like figure, the duke was compulsively indiscreet. Cursing the king's failure to fight 'those rare boasting Frenchmen . . . his backside has grown too fat, he's only interested in eating and drinking', he predicted that 'Matters can't go on like this. He's saddled merchants with such impossibly big taxes that they're facing ruin, and nobody knows where the money goes. But I can tell you for a fact that he's spending too much, on silly, useless things, while his subjects foot the bills. There's going to be serious trouble all over the country – people are starting to grumble, saying they won't put up with the situation for much longer.'[17]

The duke wanted Richard to be replaced by the Earl of March, who was heir presumptive. (March's mother was the heiress of the Duke of Clarence, Edward III's second son.) Meeting the earl in secret, Gloucester told him he had been appointed to see that England got a new king – Richard must spend the rest of his life in prison. Terrified, March said he would think about the idea, and was very relieved to escape to Ireland as lieutenant.

In October 1396 Richard married Charles VI's seven-year-old daughter Isabel, part of his plan to end the Hundred Years War during which, in his view, too many brave men had been killed and too many crimes committed – an opinion shared by few Englishmen. He went to Calais for the wedding, an earlier Field of Cloth of Gold. While the marriage was happy enough in its way, Richard treating the little queen as a daughter, it was resented by his subjects, and not only from xenophobia. Charles persuaded him to try and force English churchmen to submit to the pontiff at Avignon who was favoured by the French. 'Our king has become a Frenchman – he wants to destroy and dishonour us, but he won't succeed!' was the reaction of many clergy.[18]

Laymen as well as clergy were unsettled. Some London merchants asked Gloucester if Calais would be surrendered because of Richard's marriage. 'Highly likely', he answered mischievously. 'The French won't care if he has all their king's daughters, so long as they can keep hold of Calais.' He advised them to ask Richard. 'You speak up and don't be shy!' added the duke. 'There's something shabby going on.' If they came back and let him know what the king had said, he would tell them how to deal with his foolish nephew.[19]

Richard was aware of Gloucester's ravings. So were Lancaster and York, who begged him to be patient with their brother. While admitting that he was the most difficult man in England, they insisted he was harmless – everybody knew Gloucester was off his head. For the moment, they succeeded in calming the king's fear of him. Luckily, Richard was more worried about the Londoners, of whom he had grown so frightened that he began to think of moving the capital to York.

Tyranny

Increasingly detached from reality, Richard spent whole days in silence amid his courtiers, seated on his throne with his crown on his head, from dinner (at 9.00 am) until dusk. Those who caught his eye had to kneel while he was addressed as 'Majesty', a new style. He even dreamed of replacing his late wife's half-brother Wenzel the Drunkard as Holy Roman Emperor.

Suddenly the king decided that Gloucester, the Arundels and the Earl of Warwick were planning a coup. In July 1397 he arrived unexpectedly at Gloucester's castle of Pleshey, in Essex, making the duke go back with him to London on a pretext of needing his advice. Nottingham, whom Richard threatened with death if he did not help, then took Gloucester under arrest to Calais, where he was smothered in a feather bed despite begging for mercy 'as meekly as a man may'. It was announced that he had died from an apoplexy.

The next move against the Appellants was to 'appeal them of treason', with calculated irony. At Westminster in September 1397, parliament was ringed by royal archers, who at one point bent their bows and drew their arrows back to their ears, terrifying everybody – as Richard had forbidden on pain of death anyone attending to bear arms apart from his own retinue, so neither peers nor MPs were able to defend themselves. A show-trial took place.

'The pardon is revoked by the king, by the lords and by us, the faithful commons', announced Sir John Bussy, referring to the pardon in 1389. The Earl of Arundel groaned, 'Where be those faithful commons?' Even his former ally Bolingbroke accused him of proposing Richard's arrest in 1388, remaining unshaken when Arundel retorted that he was lying through his teeth. 'Ye are all liars, I am no traitor', protested the earl, but he was found guilty and beheaded on Tower Hill.[20] Warwick, another Appellant, was sentenced to life imprisonment on the Isle of Man after grovelling for mercy, while everything he possessed was confiscated, reducing his wife to beggary. Thomas Arundel was deprived of his see of Canterbury and sent into perpetual banishment.

The king rewarded those who had made his revenge possible. There were five new dukedoms, Bolingbroke becoming Duke of Hereford and Nottingham Duke of Norfolk, while Lancaster's son by Katherine Swynford, John Beaufort, was created Marquess of Dorset. There was some amusement at their elevation, Walsingham recording that people called them 'dukelings'. (When the crunch came, however, Richard would find he could rely on only three magnates – his half-brother John Holland, Duke of Exeter, his nephew Thomas Holland, Duke of Surrey and John Montague, Earl of Salisbury.)

In January 1398 another parliament at Shrewsbury posthumously pardoned the king's disgraced chancellor, Michael de la Pole, besides granting Richard the customs on wool for life. Later his enemies charged him with packing the Commons by nominating knights of the shire for the sheriffs to return: modern research shows that a large proportion of the 27 sheriffs who took office at the end of 1397 had links with the royal household, while most of the others were retainers of magnates trusted by Richard. They knew they had been selected to bring government under the Crown's control.

'Not even the greatest in England dared question anything done by the king', recalls Froissart. 'He kept a paid retinue of 2,000 archers who guarded him day and night, because he did not entirely trust his uncles, let alone the earl of Arundel's kindred.'[21] These were the Cheshire men, who wore his livery of the White Hart. A chronicler credits them with telling him, 'Dickon, sleep secure while we wake and dread nought while we live.'[22] Adam of Usk says they were 'wholly malevolent, roaming round uncontrolled and doing whatever they wanted, molesting, beating up and robbing'.[23]

Richard believed he was Christ's vicar on earth, above the law, and that his subjects were in duty bound to obey him implicitly, an idea developed by Giles of Rome in the previous century. (A copy of Giles's *De Regimini Principum* had been owned by the king's tutor Simon Burley.) Writing to the Emperor of Byzantium, Manuel Paleologus, in 1398, Richard expressed outrage at the rebelliousness of England's magnates, whom he swore to crush.[24] By then he was making sheriffs take new oaths that promised stricter obedience to him, forcing his lords to swear to uphold the recent parliament's acts to the letter. Behind this lay a conviction that he alone could make the laws, that the lives and goods of every man, woman and child in England belonged to him. He thought he was restoring the Crown's authority, incapable of seeing that he was destroying its very foundations.

Richard's views did not make him feel any more secure. At St Albans Walsingham heard a rumour that the king's slumbers were so disturbed by Arundel's ghost that he had the earl's body dug up at night and buried further away from the Tower. There were signs of a growing loss of self-control. When Lady Warwick came to plead for her husband, Richard brandished a sword, yelling that he would have killed her had she been a man – scarcely the behaviour of someone who prided himself on his dignity.

Just before the Shrewsbury parliament, Norfolk told Bolingbroke (Hereford) that the king would never forgive

Radcot Bridge and meant to destroy them as he had the other Appellants. When Bolingbroke said they had been granted pardons, Norfolk replied that Richard's word could not be trusted even if he swore on God's body – the Host. This was Bolingbroke's version, but it might have been the other way round: perhaps Bolingbroke warned Norfolk of Richard's unreliability and then, fearing he might be reported, slandered him to the king.[25]

Whatever the truth, at the end of February 1398, in the king's presence, Norfolk told Bolingbroke he was a liar, after which a court of chivalry ordered a trial by combat at Coventry in September. When the two dukes appeared on the tournament field for what promised to be the most dramatic duel in English history, Richard stopped it, not daring to risk the prestige Bolingbroke would gain should he win. He banished Bolingbroke for life and Norfolk for ten years, although both were allowed to transfer large sums of money abroad. Norfolk, once the king's boon companion, died at Venice shortly after. However, Bolingbroke received such a warm welcome from the French court on installing himself in the Hôtel de Clisson at Paris that it drew a formal protest from Richard's envoys.

'Time honoured Gaunt' (not yet sixty) died in February 1399. The king turned his death into a disaster by refusing to let Bolingbroke inherit his father's duchy of Lancaster, which was confiscated, altering his term of banishment to one for life – without an allowance.

> Think what you will, we seize into our hands.
> His plate, his goods, his money and his lands.

> (*King Richard II*, Act II, scene i)

Richard made a mortal enemy, who had to regain his inheritance or die a beggar. Such flagrant injustice caused every magnate in England to fear his own estates might be confiscated in the event of royal displeasure – not even King John had dared to flout the common law like this. Ignoring the general outrage, Richard granted former Lancastrian estates to his favourites, but kept a substantial portion for himself.

Downfall

By now he had acquired very large sums of money, not only Lancastrian and Appellant revenues, but over £130,000 from his wife's dowry.[26] It made him over-confident, and in May 1399 he took another expedition to Ireland, leaving his ineffectual uncle York as regent. Writing only five years later, Froissart claims that law and order broke down while he was away. Courts were suspended, while gangs of brigands roamed the roads and plundered farms. Rich men took refuge in London. Everyone grumbled that if things went on like this they would starve, and blamed the king for letting it happen. 'All he worries about is enjoying himself – he doesn't care what happens to anybody else so long as he gets his own way.'[27]

Disguised as a pilgrim monk, the ex-Archbishop Arundel went to Henry of Bolingbroke at Paris, urging him to go home and recover his inheritance. Supporters sent ships. Landing in Yorkshire at the end of June with Arundel and 300 men, Bolingbroke rode south. After taking an oath on the Host at Doncaster that he sought only to recover his inheritance, he was joined by the northern lords and Archbishop Scrope of York, and then by the Duke of York. Retainers from the Lancastrian estates rallied to him, making a formidable army. Instead of going to London, the rebels first captured Bristol, where they expected Richard would land on his way home from Ireland, then marched to Chester.

After the Duke of York came over to his side, Henry behaved as though he had replaced the duke as 'Keeper of the Realm', executing the regime's key henchmen. These were the Earl of Wiltshire, who was Richard's treasurer, with two members of the royal council, Sir John Bussy and Sir Henry Green, popularly considered to be the 'chief aiders and abettors of his malevolence'.[28]

Froissart thought that Londoners played a key role. Henry had become their hero, a royal prince who was untarnished by pro-French policies. Since the king's heir presumptive, the Earl of March, was only eight and not a male Plantagenet, it was easy to see Bolingbroke as a likely alternative – they knew that Edward III had wanted Lancaster or his sons to inherit the throne if Richard died without issue. The mayor was overjoyed when he received news of Henry's landing, telling the City's notables they must help him. According to Froissart, more than 500 Londoners, who by now referred to their sovereign as 'Richard of Bordeaux' instead of 'King Richard' and drank to his damnation, rode off to enrol in Bolingbroke's army.[29]

Many other Englishmen thought like the Londoners, but Henry, a subtle politician who kept even his friend Archbishop Arundel in the dark, concealed his plans until he had Richard safely in his hands. Shrewd folk guessed what he had in mind, however. Among them was a Welsh protégé of Arundel called Adam of Usk, a lawyer at the Court of Arches, who left London to join Bolingbroke despite his sympathy with March's claim.

Delayed by lack of a fleet, Richard landed in Wales on 24 July, to find England had gone over to Henry. His troops deserted him, even his Cheshire archers, while his enemies had occupied Chester, the one city that might have supported him. He took refuge at Conwy Castle in north Wales, hoping the Earl of Salisbury, whom he sent ahead, could raise a Welsh army. When he reached Conwy, however, he found that Salisbury had rallied fewer than a hundred Welshmen.

The king might have found refuge at Dublin or Bordeaux, but was sure he could outwit his enemies, confiding to a French visitor that one day he would skin them alive. Under this delusion he let himself be lured out of Conwy by Archbishop Arundel and the Earl of Northumberland, who swore on the Host he should keep the throne if he restored the duchy of Lancaster to Henry. But as soon as he emerged Richard was seized and brought to Henry at Chester. His household abandoned him. When his favourite greyhound licked his rival's face, he muttered it was a bad omen.

The king was taken to London, trying unsuccessfully to escape en route – being caught climbing out of a window. When he arrived in the City (at night, by his own request, to avoid being jeered at by the Londoners) he was put in the Tower under guard. In contrast Henry received an ecstatic welcome, partly because he announced he would abolish taxes and 'live of his own' on Crown revenues. A delegation led by Henry came to the Tower where they read out a list of charges. Panic-stricken, the king blamed four household knights for the deaths of Gloucester and Arundel and for suggesting Calais should be surrendered to the French. The four were arrested, tried in an adjoining room by the mayor and then, each tied to a horse's tail, dragged to Cheapside where their heads were hacked off on a fishmonger's slab.

'King Richard was in terrible anguish, knowing he was trapped and in danger from the Londoners', Froissart tells us. 'He thought every man in England was against him . . . he began to cry.'[30] His frightened followers told him to give the Crown to Henry. Adam of Usk, who served on the committee for deposing the king, went to see him dine at the Tower. Here he heard Richard, possibly the worse for drink, lamenting, 'My God, this is a false, treacherous country, toppling, destroying and killing so many kings, rulers, great men. It never stops being torn apart by quarrels, strife and hatred.' Then he named the men he had in mind, describing what happened to them. 'I took my leave deeply moved', says Adam, 'recalling his former splendour'.[31]

Deposition

After arguing that kingship was inalienable, Richard yielded on 29 September – his opponents having made clear that otherwise he would be killed. Entering the hall at the Tower in royal regalia, he took off his crown. 'Henry, good cousin and duke of Lancaster', he said in a loud voice. 'I give and deliver to you the crown with which I was crowned king of England and all rights belonging to it.'[32]

Next day, the king's resignation was read out before parliament, in Westminster Hall. Thirty-three articles of deposition were then recited, the first indicting him for his evil rule, after which Henry made the sign of the cross and, in English, claimed the throne. 'In the name of God, I, Henry of Lancaster, challenge this realm and the crown with all its dependencies and possessions, by right line of blood from King Henry III.'[33] He produced the ex-monarch's ring as proof of his approval. One after another, the peers gave assent. Finally, Arundel took Henry by the hand and led him to the throne, whereupon the assembly acclaimed Henry IV.

On 21 October a committee of fifty lords spiritual and temporal condemned their former sovereign to perpetual imprisonment, in 'safe and secret ward'. Eight days later, records Adam of Usk, 'The lord Richard, late king, after his deposition was carried away on the Thames in the silence of dark midnight, weeping and loudly bewailing he had ever been born. At which a certain knight who was there told him, "You may remember how you treated the earl of Arundel in just the same way, always with the utmost cruelty."'[34]

Retrospect

Henry 'had never dreamed of taking the crown and would not have done so if Richard of Bordeaux had behaved in a proper and friendly way towards him', comments Froissart. 'Even then, it was the Londoners who made him king, to put right the cruel injustice done to him and his children.'[35] But it is also true that many other Englishmen besides Londoners wanted Henry of Bolingbroke to become their king.

Richard II's inability to rule according to the laws and customs he had sworn to defend meant that even without Bolingbroke his regime would have imploded. The man who claimed to represent Edward the Confessor, quartering what was thought to be his coat of arms, destroyed himself by ignoring the 'laws of King Edward' – governing without consent. The demon was in Richard, and it destroyed him.

10

The Usurper – Henry IV

a more complex Macbeth

Bruce McFarlane[1]

The usurper

When Henry IV lay on his deathbed, his son picked up the crown from a nearby table. The dying man opened his eyes and asked, 'Why do you think you have any right to it? I had none myself, as you know very well.' Enguerrand de Monstrelet, the chronicler who told the story fifty years later, accused Henry of coming to the throne by 'strange, dishonourable means'.[2] Many contemporaries shared Monstrelet's opinion.

When Henry told parliament in 1399 that he 'challenged' the realm of England, he implied he was taking the crown by right of conquest as well as descent, which meant he was ready to fight off rival challenges.[3] These duly came, in a series of risings driven by a wish to revenge his predecessor or inability to accept him as king. 'Not since I was a youth can I recall such deep forebodings by well-balanced men about the grave disorders and troubles they fear will soon afflict this kingdom', his own confessor wrote to him in 1401, an ex-Lollard who remembered the Peasants' Revolt.[4]

'Always in deep debt, always kept on the alert by the Scots and Welsh; wavering between two opposite lines of policy with regard to France; teased by the parliament, which interfered with his household and grudged him supplies; worried by the clergy and others to whom he had promised more than he could fulfil; continually alarmed by attempts on his life, disappointed in his second marriage, bereft by treason of the aid of those whom he had trusted in his youth, and dreading to be supplanted by his own son; ever in danger of becoming the sport of the court factions which he had failed to extinguish, he seems to us a man whose life was embittered by the knowledge that he had taken on himself a task for which he was unequal.' Stubbs's epitome will never be bettered.[5]

John of Gaunt's heir

Born at Bolingbroke Castle in the Lincolnshire Wolds in 1366, it seemed Henry would one day succeed his father Gaunt as England's richest magnate. In any case, he was enormously wealthy from his marriage in 1380 to the twelve-year-old Mary de Bohun, the younger of the Earl of Hereford's two heiresses. His uncle, the Duke of Gloucester, had married her elder sister, forcing Mary into a nunnery in an attempt to secure the entire Bohun inheritance, but Gaunt abducted her, the marriage being consummated when she was fourteen.

The other drama of his early years took place during the Peasants' Revolt, when he was caught in the Tower of London by a mob who wanted to lynch John of Gaunt's son – only a kind-hearted soldier's intervention saved the boy. Some suspected he had been deliberately left in the Tower by ruthless courtiers, to eliminate a potential rival of the young king.

Aged twenty-one, Henry led the Appellants to victory, routing de Vere's army at Radcot Bridge, but hedged his bets by
trying to save the life of Richard's old tutor, Sir Simon Burley.
He also blocked Gloucester's attempt to seize the throne. His
father Lancaster possessed a better claim than Gloucester while,
despite a mutual detestation of de Vere, their dispute over the
Bohun inheritance gave him reason not to trust his uncle.

The Crusader

In autumn 1390, after sailing through the Baltic and landing
near Gdansk, the Earl of Derby (as Henry was then styled) joined
the Teutonic Knights on the Northern Crusade in Lithuania.
Travelling down the River Memel, he helped to besiege Vilnius,
the Lithuanian capital. The Lithuanians' Grand Prince had converted to Christianity, but the Crusade continued, since many
of his folk were still pagans who worshipped hares and snakes.
Having wintered at Königsberg in East Prussia where he was
entertained by the Knights' marshal, Henry went home, en
route visiting the Grand Master's court at Marienburg.

In 1392 he returned to the Baltic. Finding there was peace
between the Teutonic Knights and the Lithuanians, he went
with a household fifty strong on pilgrimage to the Holy Land,
2,000 miles away. After visiting Prague and Vienna Henry sailed
from Venice to the Knights of St John at Rhodes, from where
he took ship to Palestine. At the Holy Sepulchre he swore an
oath that one day he would go on Crusade, recover the Holy
Land for Christendom and then die in the Holy City. On the
way home, he visited Cyprus whose ruler, James I – titular King
of Jerusalem – gave him a leopard that he took back to England.

Here, Henry kept on outwardly good terms with King
Richard until the final upheaval, being made Duke of Hereford
for deserting the Appellants and his part in the Earl of Arundel's
destruction. Had he been allowed to inherit his father's patrimony, it is unlikely he would have rebelled.

First years

The new king was crowned at Westminster Abbey on 13 October by Archbishop Arundel. It was St Edward's Day, to stress his sincerity in swearing the coronation oath to defend the Confessor's laws. When Arundel anointed his head, it was swarming with lice, which some saw as an evil omen. Parliament met the next day and some of the dukes Richard had created were reduced to their old rank of earl, but did not suffer financially. However, the estates of Scrope, Bussy and Green were confiscated as most people regarded them as criminals.

At the end of 1399 a band of plotters met at Westminster Abbey, whose abbot William de Colchester remained loyal to the ex-king. They planned to kill Henry with his sons during an Epiphany tournament at Windsor and restore Richard. Not knowing where he was, they found a clerk of the chapel royal called Maudelyn, who bore a resemblance, to impersonate him. On Twelfth Night (6 January), the Earls of Huntingdon, Kent and Salisbury with 500 men-at-arms rode through the night from Kingston-upon-Thames, storming the castle at dawn. Proclaiming Richard II king again, they rushed from room to room, but failed to find their enemy – Rutland had betrayed the plot to his father, the Duke of York, and Henry had escaped with his sons a few hours before. Fleeing to the West Country, the coup's leaders were lynched, their heads sent to London in fish-baskets 'to gladden the king and the Londoners'.[6] A Te Deum was sung at St Paul's by Arundel, who led a procession through the City in thanksgiving.

After the 'Epiphany Plot' Henry's advisers told him, 'As long as Richard of Bordeaux stays alive, neither you nor your kingdom will be safe.' The king said nothing, but left the room. 'Then he visited his falconers and, taking a falcon on his glove, seemed interested only in feeding it.'[7] His predecessor was dead by 17 February, starved to death at Pontefract Castle. The body was exhibited to the public at St Paul's Cathedral, on a black cushion with all but its face wrapped in lead, before burial at King's Langley Priory – not in the tomb Richard had prepared at Westminster. Even so, rumours persisted that the ex-king was alive in Wales or in Scotland, where until 1419 a madman with a likeness to him claimed to be Richard.

In September 1400 Henry led an expedition to cow the Scots,[8] provoked by an offensive letter from Robert III addressing him as Duke of Lancaster instead of king. Its aim was to forestall a Franco-Scottish invasion, but it failed when the Scots used scorched earth tactics. Just after the king returned, Owain Glyndwr of Glyndyfrdwy in Denbighshire, a descendant of the ancient princes, quarrelled with Lord Grey of Ruthin, who was a friend of the king, sacking Ruthin before being driven off into the hills. The English dismissed the incident as a local feud, although Henry took a small force into Wales in a display of English authority.

At Christmas, the king was visited by the Emperor of the East, Manuel II Paleologus, whose empire by now consisted of little more than Constantinople. Even that was threatened by the Turks, so Manuel had embarked on a tour of western courts to beg for aid. After entertaining the emperor at Eltham (which had become the king's favourite palace), Henry gave him £2,000 he could ill afford.

In 1401 the king took action against what Walsingham calls the 'detestable ravings of the Lollards'[9]. Henceforward, by the statute *de heretico comburendo*, heresy became punishable with burning at the stake, while it was illegal to read the Bible in English. But only in the next reign would persecution drive the Lollards underground.

One night in 1401 a calthrop with three razor-sharp prongs (for maiming war horses) was discovered under the royal mattress, where it had been hidden in the hope Henry would impale himself through the straw. Early the next year an Augustinian prior was executed for failing to reveal a plot to kill him. In May eight Franciscan friars were hanged for conspiring to murder the king and raise men under the pretext that Richard II was still alive. Among their allies was a bastard of the Black Prince, Sir Roger Clarendon, who went to the gallows with them. During the friars' trial, when Henry insisted, 'I did not usurp the crown, I was elected', one of them, Dr William Frisby, told him no election could be valid while the legitimate possessor was still alive and that if he had killed Richard, then he had forfeited any right to the kingdom.

Henry's title was questioned all over Europe. In 1402–3 he received letters from the Duke of Orléans, who accused him of being a usurper and no true king.[10] He looked far from secure. Quite apart from plots by friars and abuse by Frenchmen, he was desperately short of money. In 1401, when he asked the Commons for subsidies, they impertinently asked what had happened to Richard's jewels.

The man

In Stubbs's view, 'There is scarcely one in the whole line of our kings of whose personality it is so difficult to get a definite idea.'[11] This remains true today because of inadequate sources. But some of Stubbs's insights are convincing – 'suspicious, cold-blooded and politic, undecided in action, cautious and jealous in private and public relations and, if not personally cruel, willing to sanction and profit by the cruelty of others'.[12] McFarlane adds, 'Henry, in fact, was that comparatively rare combination, the man of action who was also an intellectual.'[13]

When young, he was an impressive little man, tough, elegant, urbane and handsome, with a forked beard. Describing the malady that afflicted him in mid-life, John Capgrave – the Augustinian prior of Lynn, who may have seen him there – says he lost the 'beauty of his face', suggesting previous good looks.[14] The effigy on his tomb at Canterbury Cathedral shows a bloated countenance, indicating self-indulgence rather than disease. He had a friendly manner if a sardonic wit. In no way a xenophobe like his uncle Gloucester, when in exile at Paris during 1398–9 he attended theological disputes in the university lecture halls and made an excellent impression on Charles VI, who wanted him to marry a Valois princess.

We know little about Mary Bohun, his first wife, apart from her bearing four sons who lived to manhood and two daughters. The sons were Henry, Prince of Wales, Thomas, Duke of Clarence, John, Duke of Bedford and Humphrey, Duke of Gloucester. Mary died in 1394, giving birth to her second daughter. Her successor, whom Henry married in 1403, was Joan of Navarre, the widowed Duchess of Brittany – four years younger than himself, with nine children by her first husband, an amiable lady later accused of witchcraft. Sadly, it was 'an alliance which gave him neither strength abroad nor comfort at home'.[15]

There was a merciless streak. On campaign in Wales, realizing that a Welsh gentleman was deliberately leading the army the wrong way, Henry had him hanged, drawn and quartered on the spot. Even so, he possessed a kindly side. In 1400 he awarded Matthew Flint, tooth-drawer of London and obviously good at his job, a perpetual allowance of 6d a day to draw the teeth, without payment, of anybody who could not afford an extraction.

He did not have favourites, but got on admirably with his four sons, entrusting them with responsibility from an early age. He was also on good terms with his three Beaufort half-brothers (Gaunt's children by Katherine Swynford, who had been legitimized by Richard II), furthering their careers, if introducing legislation that barred them from succeeding to the throne. He had trusted henchmen, servants of the duchy of Lancaster who became his ministers and household officials. If he listened to anybody, it was to Archbishop Arundel.

Henry loved hunting and hawking, while he was a tiltyard champion into middle age. Indoors, he was the most literate monarch since his namesake Henry II. Not only did the cupboards built for his library at Eltham hold the *Polychronicon*

(Ralph Higden's universal history) and John Gower's *Confessio Amantis*, which was dedicated to him, but a book with a commentary in Greek if he needed help to construe it. He read and wrote English, French and Latin, unlike Edward III, who had been barely able to scrawl a few words. (On a state paper of 23 October 1403 he noted '*necessitas non habet legem*' – necessity knows no law.[16]) He invited Christine de Pizan, one of the first women to write in defence of her sex, to live at his court, but she preferred to stay in Paris. He possessed a highly developed taste in music, owning the first known recorder in England, which he himself played, as well as a harp and a metal-stringed cither (half-lute, half-mandolin). He had some knowledge of polyphony, composing sacred music. He built little, however, apart from a massive gatehouse at Lancaster Castle.

In religion, Henry was deeply pious, with a cult of St Thomas of Canterbury perhaps instilled by Arundel – unusually for a Plantagenet king, he was buried in Thomas's cathedral. He also venerated another 'St Thomas', his maternal ancestor, the Earl of Lancaster, who had been executed by Edward II, presenting St George's Chapel with a set of vestments that depicted the earl's 'martyrdom'. When an invalid, he never tired of visiting shrines, in hope of a cure.

The Percy challenge

Henry's coup owed a lot to the Percy family. In recompense, Henry, Earl of Northumberland, had been made Constable of England and Lord of Man, while his son Harry Hotspur became justiciar of north Wales. Northumberland's brother, Thomas Percy, Earl of Worcester was appointed steward of the royal household, lieutenant in south Wales and Prince Henry's governor. The two earls also administered the vast Welsh estates of the young Earl of March.

However, they were angry at Henry rewarding Ralph Neville, Earl of Westmorland (who had married his half-sister Joan

Beaufort) with lands promised to the Percys. Worse still, when Northumberland routed the Scots at Homildon Hill in 1402 and took five Scottish earls prisoner, the king refused to let them be ransomed, depriving Northumberland of large sums of money even though Henry owed him £40,000. Northumberland grew even angrier after Henry forbade him to help his son-in-law Sir Edmund Mortimer, who had been captured by the Welsh, since Sir Edmund was uncle of the Earl of March, Richard II's heir. When Hotspur suggested ransoming Mortimer, he was struck by the king, who shouted 'Traitor!'

Because of their Welsh involvement in Wales, the Percys had contacts with Owain Glyndwr, who had proclaimed himself Prince of Wales in September 1400. Owain was no mere hill chieftain but a sophisticated aristocrat. Besides speaking French, Latin and English, he had studied at the Inns of Court in London, fought under the late Earl of Arundel's command and known Richard II's court. Nevertheless, as heir of the Princes of Powys, he kept alive the old Welsh ways, employing bards and harpers at his castle of Sycherth and, familiar with his native land's literature, believed in prophecies foretelling the expulsion of the English. He was not only a born guerrilla leader, but a consummate diplomat who knew how to exploit Percy dissatisfaction.

Early in 1403 the king made the other 'Prince of Wales', his sixteen-year-old son Henry, Lieutenant of the Welsh Marches (local commander-in-chief), with headquarters at Chester. By then it looked as though Owain was winning. 'And for God's love, my liege lord, thinketh on yourself and your estate or by my troth all is lost, else but ye come yourself with haste', the Archdeacon of Hereford wrote frantically to the king on 8 July. 'And all on Friday last Caermarthen town is taken and burnt and the castle yolden by Richard Wigmore, and the castle Emlyn is yolden, and slain of town of Caermarthen more than fifty persons.'[17]

Edmund Mortimer changed sides, marrying Owain's daughter

Catrin. (An 'inferior match', sniffed the monk Walsingham.)[18] He then won over his sister's husband, Harry Hotspur, whose father Northumberland gave Henry a last, veiled warning, demanding full payment of the £40,000 he was owed. He signed his letter 'Matatyas' – by which he meant he had been a father to the king in helping him topple Richard, just as Judas Maccabeus's father Matathias had helped Judas against the tyrant Antiochus.[19]

The Percys renounced their allegiance, claiming they had supported Henry's right to be Duke of Lancaster, but not his right to the throne. Marching south with several hundred retainers, Hotspur recruited many of King Richard's Cheshire archers, and was joined by his uncle, the Earl of Worcester. Their plan was to capture the prince, who was at Shrewsbury, join forces with Owain and replace Henry IV with the Earl of March.

On his way north to fight the Scots, the king reacted quickly, reaching Shrewsbury first with 14,000 men. Undismayed, on 21 July Hotspur drew up his army of 10,000 in order of battle on a low hillside 3 miles from Shrewsbury. Fearing Glyndwr or Northumberland might arrive at any moment, the king offered terms that Hotspur was inclined to accept, but Worcester told Henry, 'You are not the rightful king and we don't trust you.'

The battle began at noon, the first time English armies went into action against each other with the longbow. Flight after flight of arrows shot downhill by the Cheshire men nearly decided the outcome at the start, 4,000 royal troops bolting. Hotspur's men-at-arms charged at the king, killing most of his Knights of the Body, but failed to find him – he had dressed two of his household in royal surcoats, who paid with their lives, while he himself took refuge among his billmen. His right wing fled after its commander Lord Stafford fell dead and on the left the Prince of Wales was wounded in the face by an arrow. Hotspur's men shouted, 'Henry Percy is king!'

Then an unknown archer sent an arrow through Hotspur. As soon as the king heard, he raised the cry 'Henry Percy is dead!' and the enemy ran, pursued for 3 miles. In all about 2,000 men were killed or wounded. The Earl of Worcester was captured, to be summarily hanged and quartered. Although Hotspur's corpse had been buried, it was dug up, salted and put on show in the Shrewsbury pillory, before his head and quarters were sent off for display in the north country.

Three weeks later, Northumberland submitted, kneeling before the king at York and claiming he had known nothing of his son's plans. Placed under house arrest, he lost his office of constable and was made to hand over his strongholds. He was soon freed and given back his castles, as the best man to defend the North against the Scots.

A Welsh Wales?

Owain Glyndwr remained on the offensive, helped by the French, who supplied cannon; Aberystwyth, Caerleon, Caerphilly, Cardiff, Harlech, Newport and Usk were all taken by the 'Welch doggis' (Friar Capgrave's term) in 1404. Charles VI signed an alliance with '*Owynis, dei gratia princeps Walliae*' against 'Henry of Lancaster', sending Owain a gold helmet of a sort worn by sovereigns. Poorly armed, mainly archers and knifemen, the Welsh did not have it all their own way, as their opponents were led by Prince Henry, who was already a brilliant commander. However, he had too few troops and Owain made steady progress, avoiding battles, capturing strongholds. Harlech Castle became his residence while he set up his administrative headquarters at Aberystwyth, appointing a chancellor. In 1404 he was crowned Prince of Wales at Machynlleth, where he held a parliament attended by bishops and abbots.

Meanwhile, the old Countess of Oxford, Robert de Vere's mother, decided that Richard II must still be alive. In spring 1404 she wrote to the Duke of Orléans, asking him to land in Essex, join Owain at Northampton and proclaim Richard king again. If ridiculous, it was the sixth attempt to topple Henry since he had come to the throne.

The king was given another fright in mid-February 1405 when Lady Despenser, governess of the little Earl of March and his brother, fled from Windsor with her charges, using specially cut keys to escape under cover of darkness. She planned to join their uncle who, with Owain, would proclaim March as king. (She had her own score to settle with Henry, her husband having been lynched after the Epiphany Plot.) Riding through the night, the king caught them at Cheltenham. Lady Despenser then accused her brother, the Duke of York, of plotting to kill the king – a piece of spiteful imagination. Even so, when the duke denied it her squire offered to prove it in trial by battle, and although the combat did not take place, York spent several weeks in the Tower.

Henry soon learned why Lady Despenser had chosen that particular moment to try and take March to Wales. Towards the end of February the envoys of Owain, Northumberland and Sir Edmund Mortimer had signed an agreement at Bangor. Owain would rule Wales with the border counties, the earl would take the north country and the eastern Midlands, and Mortimer would have southern England. The document quoted a prophecy from the *Brut of England*, that 'a dragon shall rise up in the north which shall be full fierce and shall move war against the moldewarp [a magic mole] . . . [and] this dragon shall gather again into his company a wolf that shall come out of the west that shall begin war against the moldewarp on his side . . . Then shall come a lion out of Ireland that shall fall in company with them, and then shall England tremble.' The dragon (Northumberland), the wolf (Owain) and the lion (Mortimer) would expel the moldewarp (Henry) and divide England between them.[20]

But early in May 1405 a large Welsh force was beaten near Usk, Owain's brother Tudur being killed while his son Gruffydd and his chancellor Dr Yonge were captured – 300 other Welsh prisoners were summarily beheaded on the spot. Just as the king was about to follow up the victory, he heard of danger in the north.

Archbishop Scrope's rebellion

Despite welcoming him in 1399, many north country folk besides the Percys had turned against Henry.[21] Aided by the Earl of Norfolk (Nottingham's son), at the end of May 1405 Archbishop Scrope of York gathered 8,000 armed men at the northern capital, in protest against ill treatment of the clergy and excessive taxation, and demanding a free parliament at London. In reality he was preparing to support his cousin Northumberland, who was about to rebel. Inflammatory placards were posted all over York.

Before Northumberland could arrive, the Earl of Westmorland faced down the rebels at Skipton Moor outside the city, arresting the two leaders under a false parley, after which their followers went home. Northumberland fled in despair. When Henry reached York, despite Archbishop Arundel's protests and the resignation of the Lord Chief Justice, he condemned to death Scrope as well as Norfolk, parading them through the streets of York – the archbishop being made to ride a mule facing its tail.

The primate, Thomas Arundel, fainted at the news, while men prayed at the tomb of 'St Richard of York' in the minster, where miracles were said to be worked. On the evening of the execution, Henry was smitten by 'leprosy', screaming that traitors were throwing fire at him while his face and hands were covered by big red pustules – looking 'ever fouler and fouler' according to Capgrave.[22] Whether venereal, tubercular or an embolism, the disease has not been identified. He soon made a temporary recovery.

The crisis of the reign

England already thought devilish forces were working against Henry IV: when his army was routed by bad weather in Wales in 1401, people had attributed it to 'the evil arts of Franciscan friars' who had 'forged links with demons'.[23] They also suspected

Glyndwr of being a warlock who called up evil spirits. After Scrope's killing, they decided that God had turned against the king. His forces went on losing ground in Wales, where a French force landed in 1405. The next year, Owain was joined by Northumberland and Lord Bardolf. By 1406 Wales was virtually independent, Bordeaux and Calais were threatened, English shipping went in peril of French or Castilian privateers and there were raids on the south coast.

The 'long parliament' that met in March 1406 sat for 130 days, with a first all-night sitting by the Commons. It was highly critical of the king, grumbling that he was squandering his revenue, and failing to protect the sea route to Gascony and the south coast. But at the end of April Henry fell ill again and in June he nearly died. His illness affected relations with parliament. In establishing his regime he had spent too much on rewarding those who served him to ensure their loyalty, and 'put political necessity before sound finances'.[24] Admittedly, there had been no other choice if he hoped to survive. By 1406, however, it was possible to strike a balance.

Before parliament dissolved at the end of the year, the Commons forced Henry to accept thirty-one articles. The most radical obliged him to spend two days a week with his council (purged of members whom the Commons disliked), on business and dealing with petitions, while the council would control his expenditure, particularly on the royal household. Yet far from seizing control, the Commons were rallying to the support of a broken man, whose son was too young to fill his place. Their reaction has been described as 'medieval constitutionalism at its best'.[25]

During the late summer and early autumn Henry went from shrine to shrine in a litter, seeking relics that might heal him. They included the cup of St Edmund at Bury St Edmunds, Becket's comb at Thetford, the famous collections at St Albans and Walsingham and King Oswald's bones at Bardney Abbey, a few miles from Lincoln. At Bardney he kissed the relics, after which he spent an afternoon reading in the monks' library.[26] The pilgrimage was combined with a visit to Lynn, to say goodbye to his twelve-year-old daughter Philippa, who was leaving for Denmark to marry King Eric VII.

If he never recovered his health, Henry survived the crisis years of his reign; for in 1406 the strategic situation of the English in Wales began to improve when the French went home. Prince Henry demoralized Owain's men with such atrocities as drowning prisoners, while the castles in English hands deliberately disrupted trade and food supplies to create famine. Troops from Ireland overran Anglesey, so that Welsh troops who took refuge in Snowdonia starved. One by one, Owain's strongholds fell. His defeat became obvious when Harlech surrendered in February 1409 – Sir Edmund Mortimer dying during the siege. When proclamations were posted on the doors of St Paul's announcing that King Richard was about to reclaim his kingdom, no one took any notice.

Victory

Early in 1408, accompanied by his friend Lord Bardolf, Northumberland invaded northern England in Richard II's name, but their tiny army, which consisted of Percy retainers and a few Scots, was defeated by the Sheriff of Yorkshire, Sir Thomas Rokeby, at Bramham Moor near Tadcaster on 19 February, during a snowstorm. Northumberland fell in battle while Bardolf died of his wounds, the old earl's head being stuck on a pike and displayed on London Bridge – admired for its handsome face and silver hair.[27]

Not only did Bramham Moor end the Percy threat, but the Welsh lost their sole remaining allies. Owain's last raids were beaten off in 1410, after which he vanished into his woods and caves. Moreover, the murder of the Duke of Orléans by the Duke of Burgundy the next year began a feud that fatally divided, into Armagnacs and Burgundians, a France already weakened by the insanity of Charles VI (who believed he was made of glass and might shatter).

A broken man

On the third anniversary of Scrope's execution in 1408, Henry suffered so severe a stroke that he was thought to be dead, becoming a chronic invalid who had difficulty walking. Adam of Usk says he was tormented by 'festering of the flesh [ulcers?], dehydration of the eyes and rupturing of internal organs'.[28] Sometimes he could not speak. He made his will in January 1409 (in English), and when he speaks of 'my sinful soul which has never been worthy to be man but through [God's] mercy and grace, which life I have misspent', he is saying that he is being punished for murdering a king and an archbishop.[29]

When unable to attend council meetings, his place was taken by his friend Archbishop Arundel. However, at the end of 1409 the archbishop was ousted as chancellor, and Prince Henry dominated the council, assisted by his Beaufort cousins, including the formidable Bishop Beaufort of Winchester, who replaced Arundel. The prince and his circle ran the country until late 1411. Responding to an appeal for help against the Armagnacs, they sent a small expedition to France to help the Burgundians.

Deposition?

Henry's health improved. When Bishop Beaufort or the prince suggested he relinquish the throne, he called a parliament for November 1411 and sent six knights of the prince's household to the Tower, announcing he would have no 'novelties' – a coded reference to abdication. Before the end of the year, Arundel was reinstated as chancellor, while the prince's place on the council was taken by his brother Thomas. To frighten him, Henry warned the prince that after his death Thomas might dispute the succession.[30]

Early in 1412 Armagnac agents arrived in London and, for military assistance against the Burgundians, offered Henry Aquitaine 'just as his ancestors had held it'. When he heard, he stood up excitedly. 'Don't you see how God almighty is looking after us?', he told Arundel, rubbing his hands. 'This is wonderful, the day we've been longing for! Let's go to France and get back all our ancient lands.'[31] He wanted to lead an army in person. Knowing a man so frail could not possibly take the field, his subjects nonetheless admired his pluck. But Prince Henry opposed any alliance with the Armagnacs. He was justified when they and the Burgundians were reconciled, and a small force under Thomas secured nothing except huge bribes to go home.

When Prince Henry arrived in London with an army of retainers, he protested at his exclusion from the council. Withdrawing to Coventry, he issued an open letter on 17 June. First, he made a lame excuse for not leading the expedition to France, claiming the king had given him too few troops. Then he denounced 'certain children of iniquity, agents of dissension, fomenters of dissension, architects of disagreement, sowers of anger and instigators of strife', who 'with serpentine cunning are hoping to alter the succession [to the throne] . . . and suggest we are bloodthirstily longing for the crown of England and planning a violent, abominable crime by rising up against our father'. God alone knew the sheer depth of his devotion to his parent, how much he loved him, how nobody could possibly be more loyal. This extraordinary document circulated throughout the kingdom.[32]

It looks as if the prince thought he might be set aside in favour of Thomas. At the end of the month he again went to Westminster, kneeling before the king in his private chamber, insisting he had never intended to seize the crown. Then he drew his dagger, giving it to his father whom he asked to kill him. In tears, Henry threw the knife away and embraced his son. A fortnight later, however, the king created Thomas Duke of Clarence as a warning to the prince. At the same time Henry made Thomas Lieutenant of Gascony and gave him command of a new expedition to France.

In September Prince Henry complained to his father that he had been falsely accused of embezzling the Calais garrison's wages, and demanded that his accusers should face trial. The king agreed, on condition that the trial was by parliament. Nothing more was heard of the matter.

A parliament had been called for early in 1413, but on 21 February Henry fainted while praying at Edward the Confessor's shrine in Westminster Abbey and was put to bed in the abbot's lodging at the west end of the abbey. Regaining consciousness, he asked where he was and, informed he was in the abbey's Jerusalem Chamber, replied, 'I know I shall die in this chamber, according to the prophecy told of me, that I should die in the Holy Land.'[33]

Henry remained there until his death on 20 March. His confessor John Till asked him to show repentance for killing Richard II and Archbishop Scrope, and for usurping the throne, but he answered that he had received papal absolution, while his sons 'would not permit the throne to go out of our lineage'.[34] After the customary funeral ceremonies that went on for two months, he was interred in the Trinity chapel at Canterbury Cathedral, as near to Becket's shrine as possible.

Retrospect

Neglected by Shakespeare, even if he named two plays after him, Henry IV occupies little space in the national myth. Nor does modern research bear out Stubbs's anachronistic view of him as our first constitutional monarch. Yet he was far from ineffective. Despite a questionable title and a crippling lack of money, not only did he finally tame the Welsh, but he saved England from partition. He also established his branch of the Plantagenet dynasty so firmly on the throne that it was strong enough to revive the Hundred Years War.

11

The 'Gleaming King' – Henry V

I am the scourge of God

The First English Life of King Henry the Fifth[1]

The gleaming king

On the afternoon of 19 January 1419 Henry V entered Rouen, which he had been besieging since July. Gloomy faced as usual, in black from head to foot, riding a black charger with black trappings that swept the ground, he was accompanied by a single squire who carried a lance with a fox's brush fastened to the tip – one of the king's badges. Through streets lined by living skeletons, littered with dead or dying men and women, he rode to the cathedral to hear Mass in thanksgiving.

The hero of Agincourt, Henry V is 'the gleaming king' in our national myth (Winston Churchill). Stubbs saw him almost as the French see Joan of Arc, calling him 'one of the greatest and purest characters in English history'.[2] Twentieth-century English historians agreed. 'Take him all round and he was, I think, the greatest man that ever ruled England' was Bruce McFarlane's opinion.[3]

Even so, if Bolingbroke had been Macbeth, then Henry of Monmouth was Macbeth's son and no less of a usurper. His claim to the throne of France was based on Edward III's claim through a female line, but if a female line descent took precedence over a junior male line descent, then by the same logic Edmund, Earl of March was Edward III's heir and rightful King of England. Henry's solution lay in reviving the Hundred Years War, as trial by combat. As he saw it, success in battle would prove that God acknowledged his title.

Henry was born in September 1386 on the Welsh border, in the gatehouse of Monmouth Castle. When Richard II banished Bolingbroke, he took charge of the boy whom he knighted on his Irish campaign. Henry developed a deep loyalty to his father's enemy, briefly rejoining him during the coup of 1399 and later reinterring his remains at Westminster. In no way Shakespeare's dissipated Prince Hal, as a very young man he was a highly effective commander-in-chief in Wales, whose siege-craft, accompanied by artificially induced famine and systematic terror, followed by conciliation, finally broke Owain. After the end of the Welsh war in 1409, his participation in the government of England was so enthusiastic that, as has been seen, he contemplated replacing his father on the throne.

Henry took an active part in persecuting Lollards. At Smithfield in 1410 he superintended the burning of a Worcestershire tailor, John Badby, who had declared that a toad or a spider were worth more than the Host because they were living things. Tied in a barrel, the tailor screamed horribly when the fire reached him, and the prince ordered the faggots to be removed, offering him a pension if he would recant. When Badby refused, Henry had him replaced in the flaming barrel. The prince's future confessor,

Friar Thomas Netter, said he saw a black spider trying to enter the dying man's mouth, so big that several people were needed to beat it off. Even so, the parliament of 1410 still contained a group of knights who were secret Lollards.

He was crowned at Westminster on Passion Sunday (9 April) by Archbishop Arundel, a blizzard blowing outside that some believed to be an ill omen. A chronicler across the Channel was told that many in the abbey thought the Earl of March should have been crowned instead and there would be civil war.[4] During the anointing the king looked gloomy, while he ate and drank nothing during the banquet – it was said he did not eat for three days. It may have been bad digestion, but some suspected it might be conscience. However, nobody was prepared to raise March's standard, least of all the earl himself.

Henry quickly rid himself of any misgivings. His brother John, Duke of Bedford, became his second in command, another formidable if very different personality, a big, hook-nosed, young man with an unusually gracious manner. Clarence, now heir to the throne, proved impeccably loyal, as did Gloucester. His Beaufort uncles were useful, too, the Earl of Dorset capable of dealing with any military emergency. However, Thomas Dorset's immensely rich younger brother Bishop Henry Beaufort – Henry's former tutor – was a domineering figure, who needed careful handling. Luckily, he was devoted to his nephew.

The king appointed Bishop Beaufort as chancellor, Arundel conveniently suffering a stroke. The Earl of Arundel was made treasurer. Self-confidence showed in his reburying Richard II at Westminster Abbey and restoring the sons of the earls involved in the Epiphany Plot of 1400 – Huntingdon, Oxford and Salisbury – to their family estates. His rival, the Earl of March, now twenty-one, was released after being confined since 1399 and given back the Mortimer lands in England, Wales and Ireland. He was even allowed to marry a cousin who was also a descendant of Edward II since he was no danger, an amiable mediocrity with a weakness for gambling. Nevertheless, Henry saddled Edmund with a marriage fine so big that it forced him to mortgage several of his estates, 'an abuse of the crown's feudal rights without parallel since the reign of King John'.[5]

Early dangers

In September 1413 Sir John Oldcastle, who had served under Henry in the Welsh wars, was arrested for heresy. Having insisted that the Host was only bread and bishops were tools of the Devil, he was sentenced to death and imprisoned in the Tower. Escaping, he plotted with fellow Lollards to kill the king and his brothers at Eltham on Twelfth Night, after a Lollard army assembled in St Giles's Fields and took over London.

'Along the footpaths and highways and at crossroads, you could see crowds of men hurrying to the meeting place, from every county in the kingdom, recruited by the promise of big rewards', writes Walsingham. 'If the king had not acted so shrewdly that night, up to 50,000 servants and apprentices, with some of their masters, would have risen.'[6] Walsingham's reaction shows the fear aroused. In reality, only 300 Lollards went to St Giles's Fields, and they were nearly all killed or captured by royal troops. Seventy were condemned to death within two days, but Oldcastle escaped to lurk on the Welsh border. Parliament passed savage new measures to ensure the Lollards would never again be a threat.

From the moment Henry became king, he prepared for war with France, stockpiling munitions. The army he assembled consisted partly of men who enlisted and were paid wages by him, partly of indentured men raised by magnates. Before invading, he tried to divide the Burgundians and Armagnacs, but lost patience when an Armagnac ambassador, Archbishop Guillaume Boisratier, told him he did not even have a right to the crown of England, which belonged to Richard II's heirs. Declaring war in July 1415, he called on God to witness how Charles

VI refused to do him 'justice'. The invasion fleet assembled at Southampton.

On 1 August the Earl of March reported a plot. Its leader was his brother-in-law, Richard of Conisburgh, Earl of Cambridge, who was supported by Lord Scrope and Sir Thomas Grey of Heaton. They planned to take March into Wales, proclaim him king and issue a proclamation denouncing 'Henry of Lancaster, usurper'. Northumberland's outlawed heir would raise the North, while Owain's followers rose in Wales and Sir John Oldcastle's on the Welsh border. The king reacted swiftly, arresting, trying and executing the three ringleaders, claiming untruthfully that they had been bribed by the French.

The Southampton plotters' motives are obscure. They had a low opinion of the capabilities of March, whom Grey called 'but a hog' and would have been a mere figurehead had he become king.[7] That all three were in financial straits can only be part of the reason – if penniless, the Earl of Cambridge was heir to his child-less brother, the enormously rich Duke of York. Scrope, whom Henry had considered a close friend, may have joined to avenge his uncle, the martyred archbishop. The most likely explanation, however, is that all three genuinely believed the king was a usurper.

Had they succeeded, they would have found supporters. The French astrologer Jean Fusoris, who accompanied Archbishop Boisratier's embassy, heard that many Englishmen would have preferred the Earl of March. The next year a canon of Wells Cathedral, John Bruton, was charged with telling one of his tenants that, like his father before him, the king possessed no right to the throne. Scrope and his accomplices had been right, said the canon, adding that he was ready to give £6,000 to help depose Henry V.

The man

Bruce McFarlane considered Henry V 'a paragon and a hero, a Bayard and a Solomon in one . . . a faithful exponent of the chivalric ideal'.[8] This has not been every historian's opinion, however. In the 1960s E. F. Jacob thought the traditional picture owed too much to biased Tudor historiography, and that in the last analysis Henry was an adventurer and not a statesman.[9]

The popular image of Henry is the National Gallery portrait (a sixteenth-century copy) of a prim young man with a high-coloured, clean-shaven face, long nose, full-lipped mouth and hazel eyes beneath brown hair cut in pudding basin style. This was how he appeared on coming to the throne – Jean Fusoris, who met him in 1415, says he looked more like a bishop than a warrior. But a miniature of St George in the *Bedford Book of Hours*, painted a few years later and modelled on the king, shows him with a small forked beard like that worn by Richard II. His effigy on a stone screen at York Minster from about 1425 also shows a forked beard, with thick, elaborately curled hair over a handsome if frowning face. He was lean and slightly built, and all sources agree that he was very good-looking, with a terrifying presence.

Henry had a first-class mind, iron self-control and inflexible determination. His administration cannot be faulted nor his statecraft. Militarily, he demonstrated that he was a superb strategist and tactician, an inspiring leader on the battlefield. A man who never rejoiced even when he won a battle, he was without either optimism or pessimism. 'The fortunes of war tend to vary', he told troops who had been defeated. 'If you want to make sure of winning, keep your courage at exactly the same level, regardless of what happens.'[10]

'From the death of the king his father until the marriage of himself, he never had knowledge carnally of woman.'[11] He saw his queen Catherine of Valois as a tool for becoming King of France rather than a wife. 'I shall honour and love my brothers above all men, as long as they be to me true, faithful and obedient', he had told his father. 'But any of them fortune to conspire or rebel against me, I assure you I shall as soon execute justice upon any one of them as I shall upon the worst and most simple person.'[12] In early years, he had friends, although not in his later. However, he gave lavish rewards to men who served him well on the battlefield, such as the Earl of Salisbury.

An athlete when a boy, a runner and jumper, as an adult Henry had no taste for hunting or hawking, although he enjoyed watching wrestlers and mummers. Like his father, he took pleasure in songs and musical instruments, spending large sums on choirs and singing men, even composing motets himself. He was fond of reading, constantly adding to his library, which included histories of the Crusades, treatises on hunting, books of devotion, some Seneca and Cicero, the works of Gregory the Great and contemporary productions such as Chaucer's *Troilus and Criseyde*, Lydgate's *Life of Our Lady* and Hoccleve's *De Regimine Principum* – the last two dedicated to him. While he spoke, read and wrote French and Latin, his preferred language was English. He was the first king since the Conquest to use it for business, in terse letters and directives. Some experts see his letters on the progress of the war in France as the beginning of Standard English.

On the night his father died, Henry 'called to him a virtuous monk of holy conversation to whom he confessed himself of all his offences'.[13] Almost immediately, he founded two monasteries for austere orders, one next to the palace he rebuilt at Sheen that was for the Carthusians – where nobody was allowed to interrupt him when he was hearing Mass. Like his father, he was always visiting shrines, developing a devotion to St John of Bridlington, a Yorkshireman who had supposedly cast out evil spirits, walked on water and changed water into wine. His choice of the Carmelite friar Thomas Netter as confessor reflected his orthodoxy. Netter was a famous scourge of heretics, who when Henry came to the throne preached a sermon at St Paul's accusing him of laxity in persecuting them. Understandably, Lollards called Henry 'the prince of priests'.

Sometimes the king's religion degenerated into superstition, as when he ordered the prosecution of all sorcerers. No English monarch was more terrified of warlocks and necromancers.

First expedition to France

On 13 August 1415 the English armada entered the Seine estuary. Within days Henry's troops were besieging the port of Harfleur, isolating it with stockades so that no one could get in or out, while his ships blockaded the harbour. Harfleur had strong walls and deep moats, however, and a determined commander, Raoul de Gaucourt, who had brought in 300 experienced men-at-arms.

Battering rams could not be used so the king employed artillery, as he had learned to do in Wales. Although his primitive cannon needed to be trundled within range on huge wooden platforms and took several minutes to load and fire, their stone cannon balls, which were as big as millstones, demolished masonry and burst like shrapnel. Whole sections of the town walls came crashing down, even buildings in the centre, while fires were started by flaming arrows or cannon balls wrapped in flaming tow. Eventually enough damage was done for the English to push siege towers across the moats, capturing the barbican that defended the main gate. Starving, with no hope of relief, the defenders surrendered on 22 September.

The siege, which had lasted nearly six weeks in the heat of summer, took its toll on the English, too, and not just because of accurate shooting by the defenders' cannon and crossbows. Bad wine and cider and dirty water contributed. 'In this siege many men died of cold in nights and fruit eating, eke of stink of carrion', wrote Friar Capgrave, who says that casualties from disease (which meant dysentery and malaria) included the king's friend Bishop Courtenay of Norwich, and the Earl of Suffolk, while the Duke of Clarence and the Earls of March and Arundel were so ill that they had to be sent home.[14] In all, 2,000 Englishmen died, with 2,000 sick shipped back to England as hospital cases.

The garrison's leaders and sixty hostages were forced to kneel in shirts with halters round their necks for several hours until admitted to Henry's presence. In cloth of gold, seated on a throne, for a time he ignored them, then delivered a tirade of abuse for trying to stop him taking 'our town of Harfleur'. Finally, the king entered the town barefoot to give thanks at the main church. The Host was borne before him through the streets, to demonstrate that God was on his side. (Had he lived, he would have been outraged by the Maid of Orléans's similar claim.) Sixty knights and 200 gentlemen were ordered to present themselves at Calais for ransom, while rich bourgeois were sent to England until they bought their freedom. The 'poorer sort' of men, women and children were expelled, so their dwellings could be given to English settlers, and they were forbidden to take goods or valuables with them; these were shared out among Henry's troops. Houses were allotted as rewards, while a man who had brought two shiploads of provisions to the siege obtained 'the inn called the Peacock'. The king's uncle, the Earl of Dorset, was appointed governor.

Instead of sailing back to England, the king decided to take his battered army to Calais and show the enemy was powerless to stop him. He marched out on 6 October with supplies for eight days. Most of his archers and not just his men-at-arms were mounted. 'Marvel it was, that he with so few durst go through all the thick woods in that country', comments Capgrave.[15] It was not the forests that threatened, however, but a French army. The English did not realize this until they were attacked 2 miles from Harfleur. Then they found the bridges over the Somme demolished and fords guarded, only managing to cross waist deep near the source on 19 October. The rain beat down, while they ran out of food, living on walnuts and a little dried meat. Many suffered from dysentery, riding or marching with their breeches down, which grew worse when they plundered stocks of wine. They struggled on, archers taking care to keep their bow strings dry. Despite insisting God was on his side, Henry was desperate to avoid a confrontation with the French.

Agincourt

However, on 20 October French heralds came to Henry, announcing that their masters would intercept him and take revenge for Harfleur. He warned them to get out of his way. But four days later the Duke of York's scouts sighted the French army, 'an innumerable multitude',[16] which meant there was no chance of avoiding a battle against alarming odds. Starving and terrified, the English spent the night in fields near Maisoncelles beneath pouring rain. Apart from confessing their sins, they were ordered to stay silent, under pain of forfeiting arms and armour if gentlemen or an ear if of lesser rank (the reality behind Shakespeare's 'touch of Harry in the night').

Rain was still falling on the morning of 25 October. The English took up a position east of the village of Agincourt, halfway between Abbeville and Calais, in a huge field of new sown wheat that narrowed to about 1,000 yards where there was a small wood on each side. They had about 800 dismounted men-at-arms in the centre and a little under 5,000 archers on the flanks, who planted a line of stakes in front of them. Henry commanded the centre, the Duke of York the right and Lord Camoys the left.

After hearing three Masses and taking communion, the king mounted a grey pony and, wearing a gold-plated helmet with a diadem of pearls, rubies and sapphires, addressed his men. He told them he had come to France to recover his lawful inherit-ance, adding that the French had sworn to cut fingers from every captured English archer's right hand. 'Now it is a good time, for all England prayeth for us', he told them. 'And in remembrance that God died on the Cross for us, let every man make a cross on the earth and kiss it, and in [so] tokening that we will rather die on this earth than flee.'[17] 'Sire', they yelled back. 'We pray God will grant you a long life and victory over our enemies.'[18]

Led by Charles d'Albret, Constable of France, and Marshal Boucicault, their opponents were 9,000 dismounted men-at-arms in plate armour, who included the greatest names in France, with 3,000 crossbowmen. Because of their number, the French front was twice as wide as Henry's. The constable wanted the smaller English army, weakened by hunger and dysentery, to attack him, but had no control over his blue-blooded troops. For several hours each side stood waiting for the other's onslaught. Finally, Henry advanced to within 300 yards of the enemy so that his archers could shoot. Seeing the archers' weariness as they trudged across the field, and infuriated by being shot at, the French, who lacked any proper command structure, could no longer be restrained. A preliminary cavalry charge against the English bowmen by their mounted men-at-arms disintegrated, the horses becoming unmanageable and bolting beneath the arrows. The field was too narrow to deploy their crossbowmen.

Grasping sawn-off lances, dismounted French men-at-arms forced their way through soft soil churned into knee-deep mud towards the English, whose archers kept on shooting. Heads down to avoid arrows penetrating the eye-holes of their helmets and unable to see, their wide front narrowing into an inchoate mass when they reached the two woods, they crashed into the line of the English men-at-arms, almost knocking them over.

The attackers were so tightly packed that they could not use their lances. More and more of them were pushed off their feet into the liquid mud from which, weighed down by heavy armour, they were unable to rise – many drowned or were suffocated by the bodies on top. In contrast, the comparatively few English men-at-arms stayed on their feet, swinging pole-axes. Even unarmoured English archers had an easy advantage over the French who remained standing, before finishing off those on the ground. John Hardyng, a former squire of Hotspur's who was there, tells us 'more were dead through press than our men might have slain'.[19] Some, however, were lucky enough to be taken prisoner.

Within half an hour a second mass of the enemy lumbered forward, to die the same way. Waiting for a third French onslaught,

Henry heard shouting from the rear and, assuming he was being charged from behind – in reality, it was peasants trying to loot his baggage – ordered that the prisoners should be killed, detailing 200 archers. All except those worth valuable ransoms were, in the words of a Tudor chronicler, 'sticked with daggers, brained with pole-axes, slain with mauls [mallets]'.[20] One group was burned alive in a shed.

The remaining French men-at-arms were so demoralized that they remounted and rode off the battlefield. In four hours the English had defeated an enemy force twice as large. Among the 8,000 French dead were the constable d'Albret and three dukes, with ninety other great nobles and over 1,500 knights. The English lost only 500 men – including the Duke of York, an immensely fat man who fell down and was trampled to death. Henry had won a great victory. He saw it as confirmation that God recognized his right to the thrones of England and France.

The king reached Calais without further trouble, but had a stormy voyage to Dover, landing amid a blizzard. At London, on 23 November, he was welcomed ecstatically. Adam of Usk says 'the City wore its brightest appearance, hearts leaping for joy'.[21] Henry rode to give thanks at St Paul's, where the next day he had a requiem sung for those on both sides who had fallen at Agincourt. There was an unmistakably xenophobic atmosphere. Adam quotes a poet whose verses praising the king refer to the 'odious might of France' and 'the invidious race of French', while a huge effigy on a tower of London Bridge bore the words:

> A giant that was full grim of sight
> To teach the Frenchmen courtesy.[22]

No longer did anyone question Henry's right to be king.

In summer 1416 the King of the Romans, Sigismund of Hungary, who was the future emperor, came to England to persuade Henry to make peace. Instead, he recognized Henry's claim to the French throne. Henry also hoped that Sigismund would obtain an endorsement of his claim by the council currently meeting at Constance to end the Great Schism, but here his guest could not help him.

The diplomatic offensive distracted Henry's attention from Harfleur, which he nearly lost by leaving insufficient food. The Count of Armagnac blockaded it by land and sea, and it was about to surrender when in August the king's brother John, Duke of Bedford arrived with a fleet. After a sea-battle lasting seven hours, Bedford routed the enemy's carracks despite a hail of quicklime and flaming tow from their tall superstructures, and relieved the beleaguered port. The next year, the Earl of Huntingdon sank the remaining French warships off the Chef-de-Caux.

Henry prepared to subdue his new kingdom. Subsidies were granted by parliament, and loans obtained from City corporations and merchants, upper clergy and rich landowners by pawning everything in the royal coffers, whether jewels or plate – Bishop Beaufort lent £14,000 against the royal crown. Foodstuffs and munitions were collected, cannon, rock-throwing catapults, siege-towers, leather bridges, scaling-ladders, spades, shovels, picks, sheafs of bows, tubs full of arrows. The invasion force consisted of 12,000 men-at-arms and archers. There were miners, engineers, armourers and farriers, with gunners and masons who were not only demolition experts but quarried gun-stones. (Newly developed artillery could fire 800 lb missiles as far as 2,500 paces.) The king's brothers – Clarence, Bedford and Gloucester – and his uncle the Duke of Exeter, formerly Earl of Dorset, provided the senior commanders, together with the Earls of Salisbury, Warwick and Huntingdon.

Henry had expanded his navy to more than thirty vessels, not only the usual cogs but square-rigged nefs or 'great ships' (one of over 1,000 tons) and two-masted carracks – three captured from the Genoese. There were also nine ballingers, oared, shallow-draughted sailing barges that could sail up rivers and move troops fast along the French waterways. Transport vessels for men and horses were collected from every port in England.

He began his Norman conquest in reverse by landing on 1 August 1417 at the mouth of the Touques, between what are now Deauville and Trouville. Burgundian and Armagnac feuding ensured there was no one to oppose him. After a fortnight Caen, whose walls had been breached by his artillery, fell on 4 September. Herded into the marketplace, its inhabitants were massacred in an orgy of rape and looting, but he ordered the killing to stop when he saw a baby sucking at the breast of its headless mother. Terrified, city after city, town after town, surrendered, so that by early the next year half Normandy was in his hands.

The king recommenced in spring 1418, taking Louviers in June. When it surrendered, he hanged eight enemy gunners for firing at his tent – one source says he crucified them. Pont de l'Arche fell in July after the English crossed the Seine in what seem to have been portable Welsh coracles, cutting off Rouen downstream.

The siege of the Norman capital began at the end of July. Well fortified, with large stocks of food, it was defended by 22,000 men under veteran commanders, who outnumbered their besiegers. At first, the Rouennais were defiant. The vicar-general of Rouen excommunicated Henry from the walls, while when he hanged prisoners from gibbets in front of them, the captain of the crossbowmen, Alain Blanchard, hanged English captives from the ramparts with dead dogs tied round their necks. But by October its citizens were eating horseflesh and 12,000 useless mouths, old folk or nursing mothers, were driven out into the city's ditch. Henry refused to let them leave it. 'I put hem not there and that wot ye', he reminded the Rouennais,[23] and they died in the ditch. Envoys were told, 'Rouen is my heritage'.

When the city surrendered on 19 January 1419, after kissing each one of forty-two crosses borne by the clergy the king attended a Mass of thanksgiving at the cathedral of Saint-Maclou.

Among those excluded from the terms of surrender, the vicar-general who had excommunicated Henry spent five years in chains while the captain of the crossbowmen was hanged on the spot. The surviving inhabitants looked like funeral effigies, deaths from hunger continuing for days despite the arrival of food carts. The English quickly conquered the rest of Normandy, which saw no chance of rescue.

In May a hell-fire Dominican preacher, St Vincent Ferrer, came to Caen and in a sermon rebuked Henry for killing Christian men and women who had never done him any harm. After it, he told Vincent, 'I am the scourge of God sent to punish people for their sins'. Emerging from their meeting, Vincent assured everybody that while he had once seen Henry as the worst tyrant in Christendom, he now believed him to be the most pleasing to God of all rulers. He added, 'His quarrel is so just and true that undoubtedly God is and shall be his aid in these wars.'[24] The story conveys some idea of the impact of Henry's personality.

Meanwhile, the political situation turned upside down. In 1418 the Burgundians had captured Paris, slaughtering the Armagnacs and their count, whose surviving followers became known as Dauphinists. In September 1419 John, Duke of Burgundy was hacked to death as he knelt in homage before the new dauphin, dividing the French irreparably. John's successor, Duke Philip the Good, wanted revenge and in December allied formally with Henry, promising to help him conquer France.

In July Henry had already taken the first step towards capturing Paris, his men storming Pontoise which they sacked brutally. The little city commanded the River Oise, so its new English garrison was able to cut off the capital's food supplies. Led by Clarence, they terrorized the area around, robbing, raping, killing, seizing landowners and bourgeois for ransom. St Germain fell to them in September.

In the meantime the king isolated Dauphinist France diplomatically, allying with Emperor Sigismund and the Rhineland elector-archbishops and with the republic of Genoa. He tried

– unsuccessfully – to marry Bedford to the Queen of Naples, and Gloucester to the King of Navarre's daughter, while his ambassadors visited the King of Poland and the Teutonic Knights. The most important treaty of all came in May 1420 when at Troyes in Champagne he met Queen Isabeau, who controlled the insane Charles VI. On his way there, he took a circular route, riding within view of the walls of Paris and praying at St Denis – burial place of the French kings. Isabeau declared that the dauphin was a bastard, while Henry became 'Heir and Regent of France' and married Charles's nineteen-year-old daughter Catherine.

The king spent his honeymoon besieging Montereau on whose bridge John of Burgundy had been murdered. As at Rouen, he hanged prisoners in view of the ramparts to encourage their comrades to surrender. Next, he invested Melun on the Seine, which took eighteen weeks to capture. When it surrendered Henry wanted to hang the garrison commander, Arnaud Guillaume de Barbazan, who escaped by appealing to the laws of chivalry – as he had crossed swords with the king in the siege-mines beneath the walls, he was a brother-in-arms. Instead, Henry placed him in an iron cage, but he hanged twenty Scottish prisoners on the grounds that they were technically his subjects. He was 'much feared and dreaded by his princes, knights and captains, and indeed by people of every class', the chronicler Waurin (a veteran of Agincourt) tells us, 'as he put to death anyone who disobeyed his orders'.[25]

On 1 September, accompanied by Charles VI and the Duke of Burgundy, Henry rode into Paris, cheered by the Parisians, who were relieved they would not suffer the fate of Rouen. They were miserable enough. It was a bitterly cold winter and the price of bread had doubled – houses were pulled down for their beams to make firewood while many of the poor starved to death, wolves regularly swimming the Seine to devour corpses in the street. The English king spent the twelve days of Christmas of 1420–1 in splendour at the Louvre, in contrast to his mad old father-in-law, who, dirty and unkempt, was all but deserted at the Hôtel de Saint-Pol. Burgundian noblemen did not care for Henry's arrogance – he had Jehan de l'Isle-Adam, Marshal of France, arrested for daring to look him in the face when answering a question – but saw no alternative. Philip of Burgundy, who besides the duchy and county of Burgundy and the entire Low Countries ruled large areas of northern France, thought only of revenge on the dauphin who had murdered his father.

Before returning to England to raise money, Henry presided over a meeting at Rouen of the estates of 'our duchy of Normandy' – nobles, clergy and bourgeois. There were representatives from other conquered provinces which, with Normandy, formed a separate entity from the Lancastrian kingdom of France. Since 1417 the king had been distributing lands, castles and titles to adventurers as well as great lords, bringing in English settlers. While replacing the Norman nobility, he tried to win over bourgeois, reducing the gabelle, the hated tax on salt. The military establishment was English, however, with strategically sited garrisons in towns or castles near rivers which were patrolled by ballingers so that garrisons could be rushed in quickly. (A garrison's average strength was three men-at-arms and nine archers, all mounted.) After announcing there would be a new Anglo-Norman currency, he travelled to Calais from where he and his new queen set sail for England.

They went straight to London for Catherine's coronation. While he was away, Bedford and then Gloucester had ensured there was no trouble. Richard II's supporters abandoned the struggle, the Welsh remained cowed and the Lollards were crushed, Sir John Oldcastle having been caught in 1417 to be roasted in chains as he swung from a gibbet, promising to rise on the third day. Even so, shortly after Henry's return a kinsman of the Earl of March, Sir John Mortimer, was arrested for treason and sent to the Tower. The unspecified charge can only have been scheming to put March on the throne.

Welcomed joyfully, the royal couple went on progress through the West Country, the Midlands, East Anglia and the north country, visiting the richer towns – including Bristol, Coventry, Lynn, Nottingham and York – as it was a fundraising tour. While in Yorkshire they visited the shrine of St John of Bridlington and that of St John of Beverley – to whose intercession Henry attributed his victory at Agincourt. In March news came that on the day before Easter the English had suffered a defeat at Baugé during which the 'Regent of France', Clarence, had been killed. 'To avenge it as thoroughly as he can, the lord king is busy fleecing everyone who has any money, rich or poor, all over the kingdom, in readiness for returning to France with as many troops as possible', wrote Adam of Usk on the last page of his chronicle. 'I fear the kingdom's entire manpower and money will be wasted.'[26]

England was war weary. Even so, the king raised £38,000 from clergy, landowners, burgesses, artisans and yeomen, and despite complaining of poverty, parliament confirmed the Treaty of Troyes, granted further subsidies and gave the royal council power to act as security for debts incurred by the king. His financial dealings could be devious, as when he confiscated lands legally entailed on Lord Scrope's children. In autumn 1419 he arrested his stepmother, the queen dowager Joan of Navarre, for trying to kill him with sorcery and employing a necromancer to do so. Never brought to trial, she was imprisoned at Leeds Castle, in luxury with a large allowance. Joan was entitled to a dowry of more than £6,000, when his government's basic income was rarely over £56,000, and he wanted it.

Henry struck a godly attitude before returning to France, listening sympathetically to a group of monks who denounced relaxations in the Benedictine way of life. After consulting a Benedictine who had joined the Carthusians, the most austere religious order, he summoned 400 brethren from monasteries all over England to Westminster Abbey in May 1421 and read out a list of criticisms, urging them to reform. Among his motives may have been an awareness that support for Richard II had survived longest at several famous abbeys.

The next month he landed at Calais with 4,000 troops. Learning that Paris was threatened by raids from two Dauphinist strongholds, Dreux and Meaux, the king besieged and captured Dreux. Before marching to Meaux, he took the castle of Rougemont, whose garrison he hanged, drowning those whom he caught later.

On a bend of the Marne, Meaux was guarded on three sides by the river and on the fourth by a canal. Although a bloodstained brigand, its garrison commander, the Bastard of Vaurus, was a fine soldier. Henry invested the city in mid-October and the siege dragged on through the winter, his camp waterlogged as rain fell incessantly and the Marne burst its banks. The king went down with dysentery, a physician being sent from England to attend him. By Christmas a fifth of his army had deserted. The defenders felt so confident that they took a donkey up on to the wall, flogging it until it brayed, shouting that it was the King of England who spoke.

Henry held on, with draconian discipline, ordering a man who ran away during an ambush to be buried alive. His troops plundered the entire area for miles around the city, which even then was famous for its mustard. When a delegation of local dignitaries came to complain to him about the burning of farms, he made his only recorded joke. 'War without fire is like sausages without mustard.'[27]

From his tent he ran the entire war effort as well as affairs at home and abroad, issuing edicts and ordinances, sending a stream of letters. The supply of guns, gun-stones, saltpetre, coal and sulphur, of bows, arrows and remounts, needed watching, so a king's clerk of the ordinance was in attendance, to keep Henry in close touch with the artillery depot at Caen and the arsenal at Rouen. Like a modern staff officer, the king paid special attention to food and transport. He also found time to answer a stream of petitions, whether from England or Normandy.

He moved cannon on to an island in the river, to shorten the range, protected by earthworks. Wooden bridges brought other guns nearer the walls. A floating siege-tower, higher than the ramparts, was mounted on two barges. After several attempts at relief had failed, Meaux surrendered in May. The Bastard of Vaurus was hanged from his own execution tree, after which his head was stuck on a lance next to it with his body wrapped in his banner at the foot. A trumpeter who had mocked the king from the walls was beheaded while the donkey beaters vanished into dungeons; 250 prisoners were sent to Paris in barges, chained by the legs, many dying of starvation; 800 more were shipped to England to work as 'indentured servants' – slaves.

Henry returned to Paris, rejoining his queen, who had borne him a son. In July, however, there were public prayers for the Heir and Regent of France. Although a very sick man, the king tried to ride to the relief of a Burgundian stronghold besieged by Dauphinists, but was carried back to Vincennes in a litter. 'Because of a long period of over work, he had contracted a high fever and dysentery, which so weakened him that the doctors dared not give him medicine.'[28] Told that he was on the point of death, he appointed Gloucester Regent of England but under Bedford's authority. Bedford was to be Regent of France although only if Philip of Burgundy declined the post. Henry also instructed Bedford to concentrate on saving Normandy should the war go badly.

The king died at Vincennes in Friar Netter's arms on 20 August, aged only thirty-five. There was a moment when he feared for his salvation, screaming as if in reply to an evil spirit, 'Thou liest, thou liest, my portion is with the Lord Jesus Christ!'[29] (Significantly, he left orders in his will for 20,000 Masses to be said for the repose of his soul.) As his cortège passed through London to lie in state at St Paul's a man stood in front of every house, holding a flaming torch. 'Among Christian kings and princes before him none could be compared', wrote the octogenarian Walsingham on almost the final page of his chronicle.[30] Henry's helm, sword and shield still hang above his tomb at Westminster, in the chantry chapel for whose building he gave instructions in his will.

Retrospect

Despite his demon's energy, Henry V did not have the resources to complete his grand design. The unwinnable war he bequeathed ended in bankruptcy and humiliation for the Lancastrian monarchy, then destroyed it, since Henry's marriage to the daughter of an insane Valois gave England a king unfitted to rule. His ultimate legacy was the Wars of the Roses.

PART 4

Lancaster and York

12

The Holy Fool – Henry VI

God can send no greater curse on a country than a ruler of
limited understanding

Philippe de Commynes[1]

Coma

At Clarendon in August 1453, told that his troops had been
defeated in Gascony, Henry VI fell into a coma. Unable to
speak, understand or walk, he needed to be fed with a spoon.
When he recovered, on Christmas Day 1454, he was informed
that his queen, Margaret of Anjou, had borne a son. Astonished,
the king asked if the child's father was the Holy Ghost.

Yet Henry should not be written off as a mental defective.
Despite his oddity, his lovable personality inspired deep affection and loyalty among those who knew him well. 'He was a
simple man, without any crook or craft of untruth', wrote John
Blacman, a Carthusian monk and former royal chaplain. 'When
in the end he lost both the realms, England and France, which

he ruled before, along with all his wealth and goods, he endured it with no broken spirit, but a calm mind.'[2] Revisionist historians dismiss this as Tudor propaganda, but it has now been established that Blacman died before the Tudors came in.[3] It was no accident that Henry VI was late medieval England's most popular saint, another Edward the Confessor.[4]

The child king of France and England

Born at Windsor in October 1421, Henry was nine months old when he became king, England being ruled by the council with the Duke of Gloucester as titular Protector. In September 1423 he attended Parliament, peers pledging their loyalty while he 'shrieked and cried and sprang'.[5] At seven, he was given a tutor, Richard Beauchamp, Earl of Warwick, a paladin of the wars in Wales and France, who was renowned throughout Europe for his courtesy and was one of the best read Englishmen of his age. In 1429 the boy king was crowned at Westminster. England was at peace, well governed, even if Gloucester and Cardinal Beaufort vied for control of the council.

Across the Channel, the Duke of Bedford seemed firmly in control as regent. Normandy was an occupied country, with English colonists – troops who had bought confiscated land cheap, artisans given free houses in the towns – while the rest of Lancastrian France was garrisoned by English troops and run by Burgundian officials at Paris. The Parisians fought loyally for him against the Dauphinists, and in 1424 his victory at Vernueil appeared to confirm Anglo-Burgundian invincibility.

The first setback came in 1429 when Orléans, besieged by the English as the key to the Dauphinist heartland, was relieved by Joan of Arc. Worse still, she led an army through occupied territory to Rheims Cathedral (the traditional crowning place of French kings) for the dauphin's coronation. For a time, the English were terrified, convinced that the 'Witch of Orléans' was using sorcery, but she was captured by Burgundians who handed her over to them. Cardinal Beaufort then took care to revive their morale by ensuring that she was tried and burned at Rouen.[6]

There was no longer hope of final victory, so Bedford concentrated on holding what had been conquered. It was important Henry should be seen by his French subjects as their king and, after spending six months at Rouen, he went to Paris for his coronation at Notre-Dame on 16 December 1431. The Parisians cheered his '*joyeuse entrée*', but Beaufort, who crowned the boy, upset them by using the English Sarum rite instead of the Gallican, while they were disgusted by a parsimonious, badly cooked coronation banquet. Nor was there any lessening of heavy tax burdens.

The death of Bedford's wife, Anne of Burgundy, in November 1432 spelled disaster. Her brother, Duke Philip, changed sides a few days after Bedford himself died in 1435, recognizing Charles VII as King of France. Henry wept on receiving a letter from Philip no longer addressed to his sovereign. Yet despite losing Paris the next year, the English hung on in the north-west, beating off a Burgundian attack on Calais. There was a vociferous war party, led by the Duke of Gloucester (a veteran of Agincourt where he had been wounded 'in the hams'), while there were plenty of good commanders in the field – Lords Scales, Willoughby and Talbot, and the young Duke of York.

However, because of Henry's lack of any sense of reality where money was concerned, it became increasingly difficult to finance campaigns in France. When his minority ended, he gave away nearly 200 royal manors to knights and squires of the Body, who kept the rents for life. Characteristically, he refused to accept £2,000 in gold from Cardinal Beaufort's executors unless it went towards endowing his colleges at Eton or Cambridge. His annual revenue sank to no more than £30,000 a year when his household alone cost £24,000, and the Crown was nearly £400,000 in debt.

Only western Normandy and parts of Maine remained immune from French raids, English colonists taking refuge in towns or castles. Meanwhile, Charles VII, the despised dauphin, had matured into a formidable ruler determined to regain his lost provinces. In 1443 Henry, who loathed bloodshed and regarded it as a Christian duty to make peace with his uncle, sent the Earl of Suffolk (in practice his first minister) to Charles, seeking an end to the war. In return for a promise to surrender Maine, Suffolk secured a two-year truce and Charles's niece as a bride for Henry. The daughter of René of Anjou, titular king of Sicily, Margaret was a beautiful, intelligent and high-spirited girl of sixteen, whom Henry married in 1445 – naïvely supposing that the marriage meant lasting peace.

Collapse in France

Most Englishmen opposed the surrender of Maine, but in 1442 Humphrey of Gloucester, the war party's leader, had been discredited by the discovery that his duchess was trying to kill Henry with witchcraft – her warlocks having contacted 'demons and malign spirits' – so that he could inherit the throne. In 1447 Suffolk had Gloucester arrested on a false charge of treason, the duke dying from a stroke brought on by rage, although many people suspected murder. Meanwhile the warlike Duke of York had been replaced as Lieutenant of Lancastrian France by the more biddable Edmund Beaufort, Duke of Somerset, and made Lieutenant of Ireland to keep him out of the way.

In 1448 Maine was handed over despite the local English commanders' reluctance and the truce extended for another two years. Intent on ending the war, the king became so pleased with Suffolk that he made him a duke.

To save money, English garrisons in Normandy were reduced. Then in May 1449 Somerset broke the truce, seizing the town of Fougères as a bargaining counter in securing the release of Henry's friend Gilles de Bretagne, who had been imprisoned by the French. Charles VII responded by sending 30,000 troops, who captured Rouen in October, and Harfleur and Honfleur during the winter. Somerset held out at Caen but in April 1450 the last English relief force was annihilated by the new French cannon at Formigny, Caen falling in July. 'And this same Wednesday was it told that Shirburgh [Cherbourg] is gone and we have not now a foot of land in Normandy', John Paston was informed on 19 August.[7] By late summer 1451 Gascony had gone too.

All England felt humiliated as destitute settlers flooded back across the Channel, parading through Cheapside with their bedding and begging in the City's streets. In January 1450 Adam Moleyns, Bishop of Chichester and former privy seal, was lynched at Portsmouth for betraying Normandy. Before dying, he blamed the Duke of Suffolk. When the duke was impeached in March, Henry – whose policies were the real reason for its loss – insisted on his acquittal. Fleeing to Calais, Suffolk's ship was boarded by sailors and he was beheaded with a rusty sword over the gunwale of a boat.

Collapse in England

In June an armed mob from Kent stormed into London, led by 'Jack Cade', an Irish ex-soldier who used the name Mortimer, claiming he was the Duke of York's kinsman. They wanted to kill the king's ministers, because of whom 'his lands are lost, his merchandise is lost, his commons destroyed, the sea is lost, France is lost, himself so poor that he may not pay for his meat and drink'.[8] Taking no notice of Henry, who rode through the streets in armour telling them to go home, they robbed, raped and stole, broke open gaols and freed criminals. The treasurer, Lord Saye and Sele, was caught and beheaded. Finally the infuriated Londoners took up arms, evicting this 'multitude of riffraff' after a two day battle on London Bridge.[9] Cade was tricked by a false pardon, then hunted to his death.

Ignoring Somerset's unpopularity, Henry made him his first minister. Unabashed, the duke set about recouping himself with grants of royal land for the estates he had lost across the Channel. Owed huge sums by the government, York was enraged, while he also suspected Somerset of plotting his destruction. Assembling an armed force at Blackheath, in February 1452 he charged him with losing Normandy and planning to sell Calais, demanding that he be put on trial. However, York found himself confronted by a much bigger royal army. Peers who had supported him were forced to kneel in the snow in their shirts and beg for pardon; lesser men were executed. He was replaced as Lieutenant of Ireland by the Earl of Wiltshire and made to swear at St Paul's that he would never again take up arms.

During the summer Somerset's prestige rocketed when the Earl of Shrewsbury ('Old Talbot') recaptured Bordeaux, regaining Gascony overnight. A parliament at Reading in March 1453 agreed to everything Somerset asked for and he appeared to be in complete control. Nevertheless, he was unable to eliminate Richard, Duke of York.

York, a small, sharp-faced man, had been born in 1411, his father being the Earl of Cambridge who had plotted to kill Henry V at Southampton. Through his mother Anne Mortimer he was heir to Edward III's second son, while the Lancastrians descended only from a third son. Inheriting the lands of York, March and Ulster, a prince of the blood, he was the greatest nobleman in England and expected to be treated as such. (His pride of birth showed in using Plantagenet as his surname, the first of his family to do so since Count Geoffrey.) During his time in Ireland, the semi-regal respect given to him as viceroy heightened his resentment at exclusion from government at home.

The man

There is no good likeness of Henry VI. We only know that he was tall, slender and handsome. Sixteenth-century copies of a lost portrait show an anxious-looking man with worried eyes, who clasps his hands nervously. A portrait in a window at King's College Chapel gives the same impression of anxiety. Shabby clothes did not help – John Blacman tells us that he usually wore an ordinary burgess's gown with a rolled hood and a farmer's round-toed boots.

Awareness of his inadequacy explains why Henry relied so much on Suffolk and Somerset; yet he was very conscious of being a king and 'diligent in dealing with the business of the realm'.[10] He took special care when appointing bishops, choosing theologians instead of the usual canon lawyers, frequently men whom he had encountered as court chaplains. He also did his best to see justice was administered fairly and every year spent months on progress, hearing appeals in the provincial law courts: hundreds of documents survive with his signature, often annotated by him.[11] Because of his fragile dignity, once or twice he hanged men who had insulted it, although he much preferred to pardon them. He detested cruelty, ordering a traitor's impaled quarter to be taken down and buried.

Henry did not see his marriage in terms of sexual satisfaction or begetting a much-needed heir, but as 'a sacramental pledge of peace'.[12] Even so, he respected Margaret of Anjou as 'a woman of great wisdom'.[13] Admittedly, his sexuality seems peculiar by today's standards if not to clerics of his time. Blacman tells us approvingly that he had a horror of nudity, male or female. Riding through Bath, Henry was shocked to see men taking the waters naked, while when 'a certain great lord' brought a troupe of young ladies with bare bosoms to dance before him at Christmas, he was so outraged that he left the room.

As a young man, Henry had cronies, the closest being his tutor's son, Henry Beauchamp, whom he created Duke of Warwick and loaded with gifts, but who died in 1446 at only twenty-one. (The duke had shared his piety, reading the entire psalter every day.) Another was Gilles de Bretagne, the Duke of

Brittany's brother, who also died early – strangled in his cell by French gaolers. The king was on excellent terms with members of his household.

The next world mattered most to him. His foundations at Eton and Cambridge had a spiritual purpose, the former designed as a chantry for priests to say Mass for his soul (if seventy boys were given a free education), while sixty of the seventy fellows at King's College were to study theology – only ten would read canon law, common law, astronomy or medicine. He planned two huge complexes to which he devoted long hours, but the chapels alone were built. Even these were not completed until long after his death, and that at Eton is merely the choir of the building he had in mind.[14]

A mystic influenced by the *Devotio Moderna* – the fifteenth-century religious revival – who practised solitary prayer, Henry meditated on Christ's sufferings and the Real Presence with an intensity that no doubt induced hallucinations. On occasions of state he wore a hair shirt. Yet his library was not restricted to works of piety and included ancient chronicles that he enjoyed reading, among them a copy of Bede's *Ecclesiastical History of the English People*. His interest in the past inspired him to campaign for Alfred the Great's canonization.[15]

Apart from his breakdown in 1453 there is no recorded instance of mental collapse. As a Carthusian, Blacman was accustomed to search out qualities that suited men for his own demanding form of hermit life, one of which was sanity, and he saw Henry as sane and a natural contemplative. Understandably, the king found his calling a burden. His chamberlain, Sir Richard Tunstall, told Blacman how Henry 'complained heavily to me [about this] in his chamber at Eltham, when I was alone there with him employed together with him upon his holy books . . . There came all at once a knock at the king's door from a certain mighty duke of the realm, and the king said: "They do so interrupt me that by day and night I can hardly snatch a moment to be refreshed by reading."'[16]

Some lines from a Latin poem by Henry, translated in the next century, convey how daunting he found his role as king.

> Who meaneth to remove the rock
> Out of the slimy mud,
> Shall mire himself, and hardly scape
> The swelling of the flood.[17]

Civil war

England was unsettled by the 'Great Slump' of 1440–80, a dearth of gold and silver coin due to a shortage of bullion.[18] Farm produce sold for less, with even a fall in rabbit prices, while cloth merchants found difficulty selling their goods abroad. There was hardship everywhere, worsening with the loss of Norman and Gascon trade (the cost of wine soaring in the taverns) and from bad relations with Burgundy and the Hansa ports. In some areas violence and cowed juries were endemic since bastard feudalism – paying retainers (annuities) to local gentry – meant that every magnate had his own 'affinity' or private army.

On 17 July 1453 French cannon wiped out Old Talbot's troops at Castillon, which meant that Gascony was lost for ever. Henry's mind gave way at the news, afflicted by a mysterious malady probably inherited from his grandfather Charles VI. (Lasting too long to have been schizophrenia, it sounds as if it had more to do with amnesia than depression.) In March 1454 the council appointed York as Protector, whereupon he sent Somerset to the Tower.

Most magnates distrusted York, but he had supporters. Besides the Duke of Norfolk, the Earl of Devon and Lord Cromwell, they included his Neville kinsmen, the Earls of Salisbury (brother-in-law) and Warwick (nephew), who had their own feud with Somerset. He rewarded the Nevilles by imprisoning their enemies in the north country, Lord Egremont and the Duke of Exeter, and making Salisbury chancellor. The sworn foe of Henry's ministers and courtiers, York planned to cut the royal household drastically, taking back lands the king had granted away from the Crown. Other plans included improved defences for Calais and the Scottish border, with measures to prevent the flight of bullion, all of which were welcomed by the London business community.[19]

'Blessed be God, the king is well amended, and hath been since Christmas Day', the Pastons were informed early in January 1455. 'And he saith he is in charity with all the world.'[20] Somerset became first minister again, in no forgiving frame of mind, with spies everywhere who were said to be disguised as friars or sailors. When York and his friends learned they would not be summoned to a council of the realm at Leicester they feared the worst. Their letters to the king receiving no answer, they marched on London (where York was popular) to plead their case at the head of 3,500 armed men.

Henry and Somerset, with the Duke of Buckingham and the Earls of Devonshire, Northumberland, Pembroke and Wiltshire, had left London for Leicester on 21 May, escorted by their households who numbered about 2,000. Few bothered to bring armour. When they rode into the main street of St Albans towards 9.00 am the next day, York's followers blockaded each end and, after the king refused to surrender Somerset, killed seventy-five of the royal party, including Somerset, Northumberland and Lord Clifford who were targeted. Henry was wounded in the shoulder by an arrow before sheltering in a tanner's cottage. York lost only two dozen men.

The 'battle' of St Albans left several young noblemen with kindred to avenge. The vendetta gradually expanded into a nationwide faction fight involving the entire ruling class, since the magnates could not avoid taking sides and dragged in their 'affinities'. What made civil war inevitable was the queen's suspicion that York was aiming at the throne. Described by a contemporary as 'a great and strong laboured woman, for she spareth no pain to sue her things to an intent and conclusion',[21]

Margaret replaced Somerset as leader of the court party. Anticipating armed confrontation, she made Henry move the court to the Midlands to Kenilworth Castle (the 'Queen's Bower), Chester Castle or the cathedral priory at Coventry, from where she could call on support from duchy of Lancaster tenants.

Henry fell ill in November 1455 (although not from insanity), York securing a second protectorate, which ended when the king recovered in February. Henry's wish for peace showed in a declaration that the late Duke of Gloucester had been loyal and no traitor (contrary to the court party's insistence) and in the Earl of Warwick's appointment as Captain of Calais. He defused a quarrel between Warwick and the new Duke of Somerset during a council at Coventry in 1456, and the next year he accepted York's oath never to resort to arms, if warning him he would not be pardoned again.

'King Henry stood consistently for conciliation, mediation, compromise, reconciliation and arbitration, repeatedly seeking to settle the differences between York and Somerset and then between York and Somerset's heirs', a modern historian comments. 'He had a remarkable capacity to forgive and to start again.'[22] His approach was epitomized by the 'loveday of St Paul's' in March 1458. (A loveday meant celebrating the end of a quarrel.) At his invitation, accompanied by huge escorts, the magnates of England came to London, where the government promised to repay York and the Nevilles the sums they were owed, and Warwick was appointed lord high admiral. In response, they agreed to have requiems said for those killed at St Albans. Both factions attended a Mass of reconciliation at the cathedral, arm in arm, the Duke of York leading the queen by the hand.

But in the autumn Warwick was attacked at Westminster by the royal household, having to hack his way through to the Thames and escape on a barge. Instead of apologizing, the queen ordered his arrest, whereupon he fled to Calais. She then decided to destroy York's party by attainder, at a parliament to be held in Coventry in autumn 1459.

The Yorkist peers' only hope was to go to Kenilworth and force Henry to drop the proceedings. Salisbury marched south with 5,000 men to join York in Shropshire, defeating at Blore Heath a force sent by Margaret to intercept him and killing its commander, while Warwick sailed back from Calais with 600 veteran troops. In October the Yorkists occupied Worcester. When a royal army advanced to meet them, they prepared to fight at Ludford Bridge, but lost their nerve and fled during the night, York taking refuge in Dublin, Salisbury and Warwick at Calais.

The 'Parliament of Devils' (as Yorkists called it) met in November 1459. York was attainted for being behind Cade's revolt, for rebelling in 1452, for St Albans, for breaking oaths sworn at Coventry in 1457 and on the loveday, for Blore Heath and for Ludford Bridge. His followers were attainted with him by a majority of peers, who took an oath to defend the Prince of Wales's right to the throne. Henry knew that this ended any hope of peace, but could not overlook York questioning his son's legitimacy.

In exile York and the 'lords of Calais' ran a smear campaign, claiming Henry was simple minded and run by evil advisers – he had given away so much to them that nothing was left for him to live on. The whole country was 'out of all good governance'.[23] They also alleged that Margaret's son was a bastard, and accused her of poisoning the Earl of Devon.

In June 1460, bringing with him the Calais garrison and York's seventeen-year-old heir Edward, Earl of March, Warwick landed at Sandwich. Warmly welcomed at London despite resistance from royal troops at the Tower, he marched to the Midlands to confront the king and 5,000 supporters, who were waiting on the bank of the River Nore near Northampton, behind a deep ditch defended by cannon. Not only did the Yorkists outnumber them, but rain spoilt their gunpowder and their right wing changed sides. It was all over in half an hour, Warwick's men targeting the enemy's leaders – the Duke of Buckingham being cut down with an axe outside the royal tent. Henry was taken to London, where Warwick and Salisbury ruled in his name. When York arrived from Ireland in September he claimed the throne as heir of the Earls of March, telling the House of Lords, 'though right for a time rest and be put to silence, yet it rotteth not nor shall it perish'.[24] The lords rejected his request for Henry to be deposed, but agreed to an 'Accord' by which he would become king on Henry's death.

We can guess how the king felt about York's claim from what he said later, when a prisoner at the Tower. 'My father was king of England and wore the crown of England in peace for the whole of his reign. And his father, my grandfather, was king of the same realm. And I, as a child in the cradle, was peaceably and without any protest crowned and approved as king by the whole realm, and wore the crown for forty years, and every one of my lords did me royal homage and swore to be true to me.'[25]

As it was, many great magnates stayed loyal to him, refusing to accept the Accord and joining the queen at Hull with their retainers, so that soon she had a large army. Early in December, the Duke of York and Salisbury went north to disperse it, but were routed near Wakefield, the duke being killed, while Salisbury was taken prisoner and executed. Their heads were stuck over the gates of York, the duke's crowned with a paper crown. Margaret's army, 12,000 strong, then marched south to rescue the king, pillaging towns en route and doing grave harm to Henry's cause.

On 17 February, trying to intercept them at St Albans, Warwick's smaller force was attacked from behind at dawn, fleeing after heavy casualties, although the earl escaped. Henry, whom they had brought with them, was found sitting under an oak tree, smiling at their discomfiture. However, terrified of 'Northern men', London refused to admit the royal army and Margaret dared not antagonize the Londoners by forcing her way in. After a few days, the royal couple and their troops retreated to York.

Unless the Yorkists replaced Henry VI, they faced extermination.[26] On 28 February 1461 Warwick rode into the City with York's son Edward, Earl of March, who had just defeated a royal army on the Welsh border. Declared king on 4 March, 'Edward IV' issued a proclamation denouncing Henry's rule, listing the complaints made by Jack Cade. Wild rumours circulated – from Brussels Prospero di Camulio reported, 'They say here that the queen of England, after the king abdicated in favour of his son, gave him poison.'[27]

Towton

On 29 March, at Towton in Yorkshire, Edward attacked the royal army, which was led by the Duke of Somerset – son of the man killed at St Albans in 1455. It was Palm Sunday, and Henry spent the day in prayer at York. In a blizzard, nearly 40,000 men fought the bloodiest battle in English history, the royalists shouting, 'King Henry! King Henry!' (That so many fought to the death for him shows how strongly they believed in his cause.) During the afternoon the combat turned in favour of the Yorkists when the Duke of Norfolk's troops arrived, but Henry's army did not break until the evening. Then it was annihilated, most of its leaders dying on the battlefield, in the pursuit or on the headman's block.

While their enemies stormed into York from the south, Henry and Margaret galloped out from the north into the snowy dark with wardrobes and money-bags strapped to packhorses. They found shelter in Scotland, first at Linlithgow Palace and then at the Dominican friary in Edinburgh. Henry ordered Berwick to surrender to the Scots, while small Lancastrian garrisons occupied the castles of Alnwick, Bamburgh and Dunstanburgh.

In October 1463 he returned to England, installing himself at Bamburgh to reign over a tiny area of Northumberland. He never saw his wife and son again – Margaret had gone to France to obtain help from Louis XI, offering him Calais. In May 1464 the last Lancastrian army was defeated at Hexham and Henry, who during the battle had been in Bywell Castle nearby, was almost caught, leaving behind his cap of state. He evaded capture for over a year with the help of his carver, Sir Richard Tunstall, hiding in Lancashire and Westmorland, but in June 1465, was betrayed by a monk and captured while fording the Ribble at Bungerly Hippingstones. His sole companions were a squire and two clergymen, one of whom was a former Dean of Windsor.

Taken south, Henry was led through the City, wearing an old straw hat, his feet tied beneath his horse's belly, before disappearing into the Tower of London. In no danger while his son remained alive, he was allowed to receive visitors. One tried to behead him with a dagger, inflicting so grave a wound that he thought he had killed him and ran off. Characteristically, when Henry regained the throne he forgave the man.[28] He retreated into his world of mysticism and visions, probably happier than he had been for years.

The 'Readeption'

In 1466 the bones of Thomas of Lancaster at Pontefract were rumoured to be sweating blood again, for Edward IV had grown unpopular. In France Queen Margaret schemed implacably and in England there were numerous Lancastrian plots. Then the Earl of Warwick turned against Edward, who fled abroad. Having allied with Margaret and betrothed his younger daughter Anne to Henry's son, on 6 October 1470 Warwick announced that Henry VI had reascended the throne in the 'Readeption'. As the Cambridge don Dr Warkworth puts it, 'all his lovers were full glad, and the more part of [the] people'.[29] At the Tower, the earl found him 'not worshipfully arrayed as a prince, and not so cleanly kept as should [be]seem such a prince: they had him out and new arrayed him and did to him great reverence, and brought him to the palace of Westminster, and so he was restored to the crown'.

A week later, he was recrowned at St Paul's, since 'an overwhelming majority of the politically active wanted him back'.[30] As if Towton had never happened, new coins were struck bearing his name, while in November he presided over a parliament attended by thirty-four peers, to whom Warwick's brother Archbishop George Neville preached a sermon on the text 'Turn, O backsliding children'. Warwick was made Lieutenant of the Realm with full powers. Henry asserted himself only in appointing Sir Richard Tunstall, the companion of his wanderings, as Lord Chamberlain. The one significant gesture he made during the Readeption was to prophesy that Henry Tudor would wear the crown, and even this is questionable.[31] Apart from opening parliament, he rarely appeared in public, spending his time quietly in the Bishop of London's palace at Fulham.

In March 1471, Edward IV landed in Yorkshire, gathered an army and proclaimed himself king. Henry, who rode through the streets of London with Archbishop Neville leading him by the hand, cut a forlorn figure as he tried to persuade its citizens to fight for him. Outmanoeuvring Warwick, Edward marched into the capital on 11 April. Henry found himself a prisoner again – the Readeption was over. Two days later, Edward marched out, taking his rival with him, and on 14 April destroyed Warwick's army at Barnet, the earl being killed. On 4 May he annihilated the last Lancastrian army at Tewkesbury.

A Yorkist account says blandly that Henry died from melancholy at the news of Tewkesbury. But, writing a decade later, Warkworth records, 'the same night that King Edward came [back] to London, King Harry being inward in prison in the Tower of London was put to death, the 21st May, on a Tuesday night between eleven and twelve of the clock, being then at the Tower the duke of Gloucester, brother to King Edward, and many other'.[32] (When his skeleton was examined in 1910, the hair was found matted with blood, which suggests a blow to the head.) Put on display at St Paul's, in an open coffin so all might see his face, his corpse was rumoured to have bled on the cathedral pavement, a sign of sanctity.

> Poor key-cold figure of a holy King!
> Pale ashes of the house of Lancaster![33]

After a discreet funeral at Blackfriars, the coffin was taken by barge up the Thames for obscure burial at Chertsey Abbey.

Retrospect – 'King Henry the Saint'

Henry VI's inadequacy was a major cause of the Wars of the Roses, yet no king who lost his throne has ever been so popular. After his murder many of his subjects venerated him as a martyr, and by 1473 prayers were being said before his image on a stone screen in York Minster that portrayed the kings of England. In 1479 Edward had it removed, besides trying vainly to prevent pilgrims from flocking to Henry's grave at Chertsey.

Richard III reburied him in St George's Chapel, where his tomb attracted no fewer pilgrims than Becket's at Canterbury. He was credited with many miracles, generally of healing – the most spectacular were bringing back to life a plague victim who was being sewn into her shroud, and preventing the rope from hanging a man falsely accused of theft. In churches and cathedrals throughout the land, he was commemorated with images on rood screens, in stained glass windows and paintings, with fervent hymns and prayers composed in his honour. As Stubbs puts it, he 'left a mark on the hearts of Englishmen that was not soon effaced . . . the king who had perished for the sins of his fathers and of the nation'.[34] Before the break with Rome, as heirs of the Lancastrians the Tudors hoped to have him canonized, planning to rebury his remains in their new chapel at Westminster. Even after the rupture, the banner of 'King Henry the Saint' was carried at Henry VIII's funeral.

Catholics continued to venerate him. In 1713 Alexander Pope referred to the 'Martyr–King' in his poem *Windsor Forest*, while during the 1920s there was an unsuccessful campaign to secure his canonization.[35] Later, he became one of Evelyn Waugh's favourite saints.

13

The Self-Made King – Edward IV

It was in the hour of need that his genius showed itself, cool, rapid, subtle, utterly fearless, moving straight to its aim through clouds of treachery and intrigue, and striking hard when its aim was reached . . . His indolence and gaiety were in fact mere veils thrown over a will of steel

John Richard Green[1]

The conqueror

The reason why the Yorkists won at Towton was Edward IV's leadership. Even in a snowstorm, he stood out. A giant in 'white' (burnished) armour with a coronet on his helmet, wherever he pushed his way forward his pole-axe felled every enemy who dared to face him.

For Stubbs, Edward was 'vicious far beyond any king that England had seen since the days of John, and more cruel and bloodthirsty than any king she had ever known'.[2] But Stubbs could not forgive him for destroying a Lancastrian constitution that never existed. There were Victorians who disagreed with Stubbs, such as Green, with whom the king's contemporaries would certainly have sided. Thomas More, only five when Edward died, but friendly with men who had known him, says he was 'of heart courageous, politic in counsel, in adversity nothing abashed, in prosperity rather joyful than proud, in peace just and merciful, in war sharp and fierce, in the field bold and hardy'.[3]

Edward IV gave England the firm rule she had lacked for decades. The best-looking man of his day, with a magnetic personality, he ended by being worshipped by his subjects who overlooked his massacres as well as murders, that included his predecessor, his brother and his brother-in-law.

Youth

Edward was born on 28 April 1442 at Rouen where his father Richard, Duke of York was Lieutenant General of Lancastrian France. His mother Cicely Neville, the Earl of Westmorland's eighteenth child, was known in the north country as the Rose of Raby from her beauty. (Stories of Edward being the bastard of an archer called Blaybourne when York was away are ridiculous – if the duke was defending Pontoise at the time the boy was conceived, he could have commuted to Rouen quickly enough, on a ballinger along the Seine.) His nurse was a Norman girl, Anne of Caux, to whom he gave a large pension after he became king. He spent most of his childhood in the great castle at Ludlow, York's favourite residence.

In 1454 Edward was created Earl of March. The next year, barely thirteen, he accompanied his father to St Albans, and presumably watched the battle. When the duke and his friends fled from Ludford Bridge, instead of going to Ireland with his father, Edward went to Calais with Salisbury and York, returning with them to London in summer 1459. Had he ridden north with York in December, history might have been different – his brother the Earl of Rutland was stabbed to death after the Battle of Wakefield by Lord Clifford, who shouted, 'By God's blood, thy father slew mine and so will I and all thy kin!'[4]

March had gone to crush Henry's army in south Wales, 2,000 strong and led by Jasper Tudor, Earl of Pembroke, which was marching towards London to join Queen Margaret. On 2 February 1461 it was intercepted by Edward with a slightly larger force, on the banks of the River Lug at Mortimer's Cross near Leominster. His men were alarmed at seeing three suns in the sky (a 'sundog') but he assured them it was a good omen – 'therefore let us have a good heart and in the name of almighty God, go we against our enemies!'[5] In his first battle as a commander, he routed Jasper Tudor's men, who became bogged down advancing over marshy ground, then launched a ferocious pursuit. When sensing victory Edward always gave the order, 'Kill the gentles and spare the commons!',[6] sending captured enemy leaders to the block. Among the dozen beheaded this time was Owen Tudor, the former husband of King Henry's late mother.

Then he joined forces in the Cotswolds with Warwick, who had just escaped from defeat at St Albans. Fourteen years older, the 'Kingmaker', Richard Neville, Earl of Warwick had married the heiress of the Beauchamp Earls of Warwick (just as his father married the heiress of the Montague Earls of Salisbury) and become England's richest magnate, while the deaths of his father and his uncle York turned him into an elder statesman. If a poor soldier, prone to panic and losing the two battles where he commanded, Warwick was a redoubtable fighting seaman who when Captain of Calais rid the Channel of pirates. He was also an exceptionally wily and determined politician, his young cousin relying on his support.

Shaken by Margaret's victory at St Albans, the pair knew they were dead men without a king of their own. March therefore claimed the throne as his father's son and by right of the Accord of 1460, riding into London on 28 February. He was warmly welcomed, if observers noted that apart from Warwick there were few great lords with him – his only other ally of substance, the Duke of Norfolk, was absent, raising East Anglia. At Westminster on 4 March, although not crowned king, 'Edward IV' was invested with the Confessor's regalia.

On 13 March he rode out from the City to find and destroy Margaret, driving his army of about 16,000 men so hard that regardless of snow and bad roads it covered 180 miles in sixteen days. He then engaged an army of fellow countrymen numbering approximately 20,000 who firmly believed that Henry VI was their rightful sovereign.

The Lancastrians occupied a strong defensive position on higher ground, but the wind blew the snow into their faces so that the Yorkist archers outshot them. Forced to come down and fight at close quarters, they held their own for six hours. Even after the Duke of Norfolk arrived with Yorkist reinforcements and charged their flank, they fought on into the dusk before breaking. Thousands were killed as they tried to flee over the narrow bridge across the River Cock or drowned in the little river which was in spate. An area of snow-covered ground 6 miles long and 3 miles wide was red with blood – heralds are said to have counted 28,000 bodies, although 16,000 is a more likely figure. Edward had ordered his men to give no quarter, and magnates and gentry taken prisoner were beheaded on the battlefield.[7]

Coronation

When Edward returned to London he was greeted euphorically. Not only had he won a decisive victory, but he was strikingly different from the former sovereign – young, handsome, high spirited, commanding. Everybody expected reform and good government. There was a sense of renewal during his coronation at Westminster Abbey on 29 June 1461, and when Parliament met in November it warmly confirmed his right to the throne, the Speaker even complimenting him on his 'beauty of personage'. Henry VI was attainted as a usurper, with twelve peers and a hundred knights and squires who, whether dead or alive, became outlaws under sentence of death, losing their lands and property. Two new earls and seven new barons were created, while his brothers were made princes – George, Duke of Clarence and Richard, Duke of Gloucester – and England acquired a new royal family.

Edward knew the war was not over, as he hinted in an address to parliament when he referred to the 'horrible murder and cruel death of my lord, my father, my brother Rutland and my cousin of Salisbury, and others'.[8] The Milanese Prospero di Camulio commented, 'Anyone who reflects at all upon the queen's wretchedness and the ruin of those killed and considers the ferocity of this country, and the victors' state of mind, should indeed, it seems to me, pray to God for the dead, and not less than the living.' The canny Milanese added, 'grievances and recriminations will break out between King Edward and Warwick, King Henry and the queen will be victorious'.[9]

The new king could not feel safe, and established a widespread network of spies who regularly sent him reports. In 1462 he gave the constable, John Tiptoft, Earl of Worcester, power to proceed in cases of treason, 'summarily and plainly, without noise and show of judgment, on simple inspection of fact',[10] which was contrary to Common Law and earned Tiptoft the name Butcher of England. In their 'simple inspection', the council used the rack or 'burning in the feet'.

Yet Edward also tried conciliation, pardoning the Duke of Somerset who had been Lancastrian commander at Towton, restoring his estates and even sharing a bed with him. But 'Harry of Somerset' was the son of the duke killed at St Albans and rejoined Henry VI at Bamburgh. Warwick and his brother Lord Montague then eliminated Henry's last bastions. They did so with enthusiasm since it involved the final destruction of their arch-enemies in the North, the Percys. Resistance came to an end in 1464 when Montague routed Somerset at Hexham, executing him immediately on Edward's express orders. In reward, Montague was made Earl of Northumberland.

Warwick dominated England, to the extent that a Frenchman joked that the country had two rulers, 'M. de Warwick and someone whose name escapes me'.[11] Even the chancellor was his brother, Archbishop George Neville of York. The earl also dictated foreign policy, and from across the Channel Louis XI set out to make friends with him, rightly suspecting that King Edward intended to renew the Hundred Years War.

But a fortnight before Hexham was fought, Edward had secretly taken a step that nearly cost him his throne.

The man

Like Stubbs and Green, modern historians differ in their view of Edward IV, but no one denies he was colourful. With an overwhelming presence that matched his physique, he dominated everyone around him.

When his tomb was opened at Windsor in 1789, the skeleton was found to be 6 ft 3½ in tall – a fifteenth-century giant. No portrait conveys the yellow-haired, fair-skinned good looks noted by the chronicles, but Philippe de Commynes says he had never seen a more handsome prince when he first saw him in 1470. In an age when a nobleman spent a year's income on clothes, he dressed with eye-catching opulence, in cloth of gold, velvet brocades, silk damasks, in furs and the finest linen, and was covered in priceless rings, chains and hat badges.

His manner was unusually informal and friendly, 'so genial in his greeting that when he saw a newcomer bewildered by his regal appearance and royal pomp, he would give him courage to speak, by laying a kindly hand on his shoulder', writes the Roman scholar Domenico Mancini. 'He listened very willingly to plaintiffs or to anyone who complained to him about some injustice – charges against himself he disarmed by an excuse even though he might not put the matter right.'[12] Flatteringly, he could remember the name of every landed gentleman in the kingdom, with the name of his estate. He was equally charming to City merchants and their wives, whom he often entertained. When he asked a rich widow for a loan and she said she would give £10 he kissed her, whereupon she gave him £20.[13]

Although in no way an intellectual, he collected several hundred illuminated manuscripts, bought in Flanders, mainly histories or historical romances (which were more or less indistinguishable), including the chronicles of Froissart and Waurin. Apart from missals or primers, all were in French. Several English chroniclers dedicated their works to him, such as Capgrave and Harding, but there is no evidence he read them. Nor is there evidence of his patronizing the printer Caxton. He built more lavishly than any king since Edward III, adding to his favourite castles of Fotheringhay and Nottingham, but – except for the hall of Eltham Palace and St George's Chapel at Windsor, little of it has survived. As for relaxation, hunting ranked high, especially fallow buck or hares in the Thames Valley, while he enjoyed angling. A gentler side is revealed by a 'garden of delights' at Windsor – herbs, roses and lilies.

Apart from gluttony – he purged his belly after a meal to begin all over again – Edward's main pleasure was womanizing, which eventually ruined his health. When he married, he told his mother that his bride was sure to bear him children since she had plenty already, while 'by God's Blessed Lady I am a bachelor and have some too'.[14]

Mancini heard how the king behaved badly towards his conquests, whom he seduced by money or promises, passing them on to friends as soon as they bored him. He pursued ladies whether married or unmarried, high born or low, getting Lady Eleanor Butler into bed by promising her marriage, which later caused serious political trouble. Although Mancini says that he never forced them, Vergil tells us he tried to rape one of Warwick's kinswomen under the earl's own roof. Nonetheless, he treated Queen Elizabeth with respect and was an indulgent father to his daughters. (At least one, Elizabeth, inherited his looks.)

Edward was a good friend, especially to William Hastings, a young Warwickshire squire who had fought for him with outstanding bravery at Mortimer's Cross, doing so again on more than one occasion. William became his boon companion and trusted lieutenant, rewarded by being made a peer and Lord Chamberlain. Thomas More heard that he had been 'a loving man and passing well-beloved',[15] although the queen hated Lord Hastings for encouraging and sharing in her husband's womanizing, and as an enemy of her kindred.

When at Sheen, a favourite residence, Edward liked to hear Mass in the external chapel of the charterhouse next door. He established a friary at Greenwich, also a favourite palace, for the Observant Franciscans, one of the period's few genuinely fervent orders. A cleric who knew him well comments that despite his self-indulgence he was 'a most devout Catholic, an unsparing enemy towards all heretics, and a most loving encourager of wise and learned men, and of the clergy'. The same writer adds that the king died a sincerely religious death.[16]

Marriage and the Wydevilles

For all his piety, Edward's uncontrollable libido brought him a most unsuitable wife. Elizabeth, Lady Grey was the widow of an impecunious Lancastrian knight mortally wounded at Towton and a former lady-in-waiting to Queen Margaret. Her father, Richard Wydeville, Lord Rivers, was a very minor Lancastrian peer who had married the Duke of Bedford's widow Jacquetta of Luxembourg. Twenty-six, blonde, beautiful and tough, she resisted the king's attempts to seduce her, even when he drew a dagger, saying that if she was too humble to be his queen she was too good to be his harlot.

In despair, he married Elizabeth 'in most secret manner' early on the morning of May Day 1464 at Grafton near Stony Stratford, while supposedly hunting. The only other people at the most romantic wedding in royal history were the priest, the bride's mother, two gentlewomen and a young man to help the priest sing. Not until September did Edward reveal he had a queen – making a fool of Warwick, who had been in Paris negotiating the king's marriage to Louis XI's sister-in-law. Some of Edward's subjects were so shocked that there were rumours of witchcraft. Even so, Elizabeth was crowned at Westminster in May 1465. The Earl of Warwick did not attend the ceremony.

A grasping courtier on the make whom Warwick described contemptuously as the son of 'but a squire',[17] old Lord Rivers quickly exploited the situation. By 1466 he was treasurer of England and an earl, marrying his numerous children to the greatest catches in the country, the immensely rich Dowager Duchess of Norfolk, 'a slip of a girl of about eighty', being forced to wed his twenty-year-old son John, in what an anonymous chronicler called 'a diabolical marriage'. (She was only in her sixties.) Allying with new magnates such as Lord Herbert, the Wydevilles formed what was virtually a court party.

Warwick defects

In 1467 it became clear that Edward had turned against Warwick when he dismissed his brother Archbishop Neville from his office as Lord Chancellor. He also repudiated Warwick's pro-French foreign policy. The earl did not want to revive the Hundred Years War, fearing King Louis might finance a Lancastrian revolt, but in 1468 Edward married his sister Margaret to the new Duke of Burgundy, Charles the Bold, who was Louis's arch-enemy. Warwick realized he had lost all influence.

Humiliated at home and abroad, the 'Kingmaker' saw the Wydevilles as the Duke of York had seen the Beauforts, convinced they meant to destroy him. He tried to regain power with a series of political manoeuvres that came in three phases. First, he plotted to put Edward under strict control and rule through him, as York had done through Henry VI as Protector; then to replace him on the throne by his younger brother George, Duke of Clarence, who was the Yorkist heir presumptive; and finally to restore Henry.

The first phase began in July 1469 when, with Warwick's secret encouragement, thousands of north countrymen led by a mysterious 'Robin of Redesdale' rose in Yorkshire. Listing grievances similar to those of Jack Cade, pointing out that Henry VI had lost his throne because of bad government and courtiers such as the Wydevilles, they marched south. At the same time Clarence sailed with Warwick to Calais where the earl was still captain and married his elder daughter Isabel, then returned to England with his father-in-law. On 24 July Robin's men cut a royal army to pieces at Edgecote Heath near Banbury, Rivers being captured and beheaded. Edward, who had not accompanied the army, surrendered, but after a brief confinement and promising to govern as Warwick and his brother wished, freed himself and returned to London. No more was heard of Robin of Redesdale. This first coup had petered out by Christmas 1469, the king issuing pardons. He did not feel himself strong enough, however, to move against Warwick and Clarence.

The second phase opened in Lincolnshire in February 1470, after Lord Welles and his son Sir Robert attacked a neighbour who was Master of the Horse, and Edward announced his intention of punishing them. Encouraged by messages from Warwick and Clarence, Sir Robert started a full-scale rebellion. Lord Welles lost his nerve, however, and went to court, hoping to defuse the situation. Although he pardoned him, the king sent a message to Sir Robert, saying he would execute his father unless he surrendered. When Robert defiantly marched to attack the royal forces, Edward beheaded Lord Welles, then crushed the rebels at 'Losecoat Field' near Stamford – where they threw away their doublets to run faster.

During the battle they had shouted, 'A Clarence! A Warwick!' and on the scaffold Sir Robert confessed he had hoped to make Clarence king. Similar risings had been planned elsewhere, but collapsed after Losecoat Field, despite appeals by Clarence and Warwick, who rode through Derby and Lancashire in the hope of finding supporters. On 2 April Edward denounced his brother and the earl as 'rebels and traitors' and they fled to Calais.

Outwardly, the Yorkist regime still looked safe. The king felt confident enough to restore Henry Percy to the earldom of Northumberland, compensating Warwick's brother with the title of 'Marquess Montague' and lands in the West Country – a package that privately the new marquess spurned as a '[mag] pie's nest'. Looking back from the 1480s, Dr Warkworth comments how everybody had hoped Edward would 'bring the realm of England in great prosperity and rest'. Instead, there had been 'one battle after another and much trouble, and great loss of goods among the common people'.[18] And the Great Slump went on and on.

Warwick's third attempt against Edward started at Angers in July 1470, where he begged Queen Margaret's pardon for having fought against the House of Lancaster. He acknowledged Henry VI as king and Edward of Lancaster as Prince of Wales; Edward was then betrothed to Warwick's younger daughter, Lady Anne Neville. Surrendering his place as heir presumptive, Clarence was accepted as the prince's heir – should the prince not beget sons. Eager to overthrow an ally of Burgundy, Louis XI supplied funds, and a Lancastrian invasion force landed in Devon on 13 September. Having been decoyed up to Richmondshire by a feigned rising, which melted away as soon as he arrived, Edward was too far off to organize a defence in time.

Overthrow and recovery

Only just avoiding an attempt by Montague to arrest him at Doncaster, Edward galloped to Lynn. From there, on board a small English merchantman and two 'hulks of Holland' together with 800 Yorkists who included his brother Richard, he sailed to Flanders on 28 September, pursued by hostile Hansa ships. When they landed at Flushing he presented the English skipper with a marten fur coat in lieu of payment as he was penniless. The Duke of Burgundy gave Edward a pension but refused to see him, sending envoys to congratulate Henry VI on his restoration. Living at Bruges or The Hague, Edward heard how Warwick took control of England as Lieutenant of the Realm, with Clarence as deputy and George Neville as chancellor, and how parliament confirmed Henry's Readeption. The Neville brothers felt so confident that they dismissed their troops.

In reality, Warwick faced alarming difficulties. He was obliged to restore the confiscated estates of Lancastrian grandees, such as the Duke of Exeter and the new Duke of Somerset, upsetting those to whom they had been granted. In any case, it was clear that Exeter and Somerset hated him. Nor did they conceal their dislike of Clarence. The situation was likely to grow even worse for the earl and his son-in-law after Margaret's return.

When Louis XI declared war on Burgundy in December 1470, Duke Charles changed his mind, giving Edward £20,000 to equip an invasion force. On 11 March thirty-six little ships sailed out from Flushing with 1,200 troops on board – Yorkist exiles and hired hand-gunners. Anchoring off the Norfolk coast and learning that the Lancastrian Earl of Oxford was waiting for him, Edward sailed north, only for his fleet to be scattered by a gale. Barely escaping shipwreck, accompanied by Gloucester and Lord Hastings, he landed at Ravenspur at the mouth of the Humber (where Bolingbroke had disembarked eighty years before) and assembled about a thousand troops who had also survived the storm.

Entering York, he ordered his men to shout 'King Henry! King Henry!', swearing at the minster's high altar that he merely intended to claim his duchy of York. However, joined every day by supporters, he proclaimed himself king again at Nottingham.

Warwick, always an indecisive soldier, did not try to intercept him, waiting for Clarence to bring reinforcements, but Clarence rejoined his brother at Banbury in a public reconciliation. On 12 April Edward rode into London, to be greeted by his queen, who during his absence had given birth to their first son in the sanctuary at Westminster Abbey.

Yet Warwick could call on troops from his northern and Midland estates, from Wales (of the sort who held out for so long at Harlech), from the West Country and from Kent. Had they combined, Edward would have been doomed. Instead, Warwick advanced on London, while the Earl of Devon went down to the west with the Duke of Somerset to meet Queen Margaret, who was coming over from France with the Prince of Wales.

On the day after Edward's arrival in London, Yorkists and Lancastrians confronted each other at Barnet (then a market town called Chipping Barnet) 11 miles north of the City. The king, who had about 9,000 men, commanded his army's centre, the Duke of Gloucester the right and Lord Hastings the left. The Lancastrian force was bigger, probably 15,000, its centre under Marquess Montague with Warwick behind in reserve, the right under the Earl of Oxford and the left under the Duke of Exeter. Throughout the night Lancastrian gunners bombarded their opponents' camp, but, miscalculating the range, fired over it.

Edward attacked at 4.00 am next morning, Easter Sunday, in a thick fog that hid the opposing divisions' uneven alignment – Oxford on the Lancastrian right outflanked Lord Hastings, while the Yorkist right outflanked the Lancastrian left. As a result, the battle pivoted like a rugby scrum, swinging round at right angles, Exeter's defeat on the Lancastrian left being counterbalanced by Hastings's rout on the right.

Then Montague in the centre mistook the star and streams worn as a badge by Oxford's troops for Edward's sun and streams and turned on them, so that Edward was able to launch a decisive charge. Montague fell on the battlefield while Warwick was killed as he lumbered towards the horse-park, trying to find a mount on which to escape. (Later, the two brothers' bodies were exposed in coffins on the pavement at St Paul's.) The Duke of Exeter, knocked unconscious, was saved by a faithful servant, Oxford being the only Lancastrian leader to escape unhurt.

Landing at Weymouth with Edward of Lancaster two days before Barnet, Margaret was met by Somerset and Devon, who had raised an army about 9,000 strong, but with too few men-at-arms. As Edward guessed, they made for Wales, hoping to join forces with the Lancastrians of Wales and Lancashire. Determined to intercept them before they crossed the Severn, despite burning hot weather he drove his own 2,000 men-at-arms and 3,000 foot at a merciless pace, covering over 30 miles a day.

He caught up with Margaret's army at Tewkesbury on the evening of 3 May, attacking next morning. Her troops occupied an excellent position on a low ridge south of the town, guarded by hedges and lanes, but the king's archers and hand-gunners shot volley after volley at them until Somerset, an inexperienced commander, was provoked into charging down on the Yorkist left. Ambushed by a body of mounted men-at-arms, the duke's troops broke and ran. Regaining the ridge, Somerset accused Lord Wenlock, who led the centre, of treachery and brained him with a pole-axe. When the Yorkists advanced uphill all along the front, what was left of the Lancastrian army bolted, 2,000 being slaughtered in the pursuit, including the seventeen-year-old Edward of Lancaster. Somerset and a dozen other leaders took refuge in Tewkesbury Abbey, to be dragged out and beheaded in Tewkesbury marketplace. Margaret was captured at a nearby nunnery.

Warwick had been popular in Kent, because of his campaigns against Channel pirates, and his cousin, Thomas Neville, the Bastard of Fauconberg, helped by the mayor of Canterbury and a small force from the Calais garrison, raised 5,000 Kentishmen.

The Bastard attacked London on the day Tewkesbury was fought, bringing cannon to bombard the City. Led by Earl Rivers, the Londoners beat back their attempt to enter across London Bridge, and then used pardons to trick Fauconberg and the mayor into abandoning their men. The pair were hunted down and executed regardless of pardons, their heads being set up on London Bridge.

'From the time of Tewkesbury field', crowed a Yorkist chronicler – ignoring the Bastard's onslaught – 'King Henry's party . . . was extinct and repressed for ever, without any manner hope of again quickening.'[19] With Henry's murder the direct male line of Lancaster was extinct. So was the male Beaufort line, except for a boy who was only a Beaufort on his mother's side and a refugee in Brittany – 'the only imp now left of Henry VI's brood'.[20]

The second reign of Edward IV

Edward's entry into London after Tewkesbury resembled a Roman triumph, with Margaret of Anjou dragged along in a cart for the public to jeer, on her way to the Tower. A Yorkist future seemed assured. Not only did the king have siblings, but he had a son and heir. He felt so secure that he forgave many old enemies, thirty attainders being reversed between 1472 and 1475, besides employing former Lancastrians as ministers – such as Dr John Morton, whom he made Master of the Rolls and Bishop of Ely.

He also pardoned Sir John Fortescue, once Lord Chief Justice, who had gone into exile with Margaret, on condition he drew up a refutation of his arguments in favour of Henry VI. Before his death in 1479 Fortescue (the finest English legal mind of his age) wrote that Edward 'hath done more for us than ever did King of England, or might have done before him. The harms that hath fallen in getting of his realm be now by him turned into the good and profit of us all.'[21]

A last flicker of resistance came during the winter of 1473–4 when, supplied with ships by King Louis, the Earl of Oxford (who had been one of the Lancastrian commanders at Barnet) occupied St Michael's Mount. In whose name he did so is unclear. It was definitely not that of Henry Tudor, and his action may have been a mere gesture of defiance. He was soon starved into surrender.

Otherwise, Edward's only worry was bad blood between Clarence and Gloucester. 'These three brothers, the king and the two dukes, were possessed of such surpassing qualities that, if they had been able to live without dissension, such a threefold cord could never have been broken', commented someone who saw a lot of them.[22] But George and Richard fell out. Clarence had married Isabel Neville, the older of Warwick's heiresses, while Gloucester married Anne, the younger, despite Clarence trying to hide her in the City disguised as a kitchen maid. Both men quarrelled furiously over who should inherit the earl's vast estates.

Edward took care not to make excessive demands on parliament. In 1472 the first assembly for two years voted new taxes, but when their collection descended into chaos he resorted to 'benevolences' – forced gifts from the rich – not merely from London merchants, but from those in all the towns he visited on progress. He made sure that customs duties (which went to the royal Treasury) were collected more efficiently, raised rents on Crown lands, enforced feudal dues and economized on his household. Having long been a 'merchant king', who on his own account exported wool, cloth (dyed and undyed), tin and pewterware, he used Italian and Greek agents to engage in the lucrative Levant trade – in commodities such as alum, prized as a dye-fixer by cloth manufacturers.

The Hundred Years War again?

One reason why Edward levied benevolences was to restart the Hundred Years War. He had a grudge to settle with the French

king, who had financed Warwick in 1470. Originally, he planned
to invade Normandy and strike at Paris, flanked by a Burgundian
army on his left and a Breton army on his right. When Duke
Francis II of Brittany lost his nerve and dropped out, Edward
still believed a Burgundian alliance should be enough to defeat
Louis XI.

An English invasion force crossed to Calais at midsummer
1475, 11,000 men with cannon and a wagon train carrying supplies in case of scorched earth tactics. Philippe de Commynes
– who saw them ride by – thought they resembled a mob on
horseback, not realizing the English dismounted to fight.
However, they did not begin the campaign until July and were
hampered by heavy rain. Worse still, obsessed with trying to
found a kingdom, Duke Charles saw them as merely a means to
stop Louis intervening in his war against the Habsburgs. He had
no intention of providing Burgundian troops.

'Ah, Holy Mary, even now after I've just given you 1,400
crowns, you don't help me a bit!', Louis moaned on learning
of the invasion.[23] Nonetheless, he suspected he might be able
to buy off Edward, who was in poor shape for a long campaign.
He sent a message in which he apologized for aiding Warwick
and offered good terms. He had guessed correctly. English
envoys agreed to make peace if the money was right, and Louis
made sure it was. On condition Edward left France at once, he
would pay him 75,000 crowns down, with an annual pension of
50,000 crowns, while the Dauphin was betrothed to his daughter Elizabeth. Louis also bought Margaret of Anjou for 50,000
crowns – he wanted her to bequeath him her rights in Lorraine
and Naples.

Terrified Edward might change his mind, the French king
neutralized the English army with a week's free eating and
drinking at Amiens. There were tables in the streets laden with
wine, unlimited credit at the taverns and whores free of charge.
An orgy of drunkenness ensued, English troops lying in heaps all
over the city – while many caught the pox. The two rulers met

on 29 August 1475 to sign the treaty, on a bridge at Picquigny near Amiens. Commynes tells us that the King of England, wearing cloth of gold and a black velvet bonnet with a fleur-de-lys jewel, bowed to within 6 in of the ground, and spoke quite good French. He also noted that although still good looking, he was running to fat.

By early September, the English army was back in England. (One casualty on the way home across the Channel was the king's brother-in-law, the Duke of Exeter, who did not fit into a Yorkist world – thrown overboard on Edward's orders.) Having been told for three years that it was their duty to pay for a war, not everybody at home was pleased. In Burgundy Duke Charles was so angry that he was said to have eaten his Garter. But England could not afford to go on fighting France while, added to the profits from his business ventures, the French pension enabled Edward to rule without parliament. The Great Slump was ending and prosperity returning. Picquigny marked the start of a Yorkist golden age.

The Yorkist golden age

Nobody enjoyed ladies, feasting and hunting more than Edward IV. According to Thomas More, he boasted he had three concubines, each with a special gift – 'one the merriest, another the wisest, the third the holiest harlot in his realm, as one whom no man could get out of the church lightly to any place but it were his bed'. The merriest was Jane Shore, adds More. 'For many he had but her he loved.'24 The estranged wife of a City merchant, Jane was famous for her kindness as well as promiscuity, intervening with the king to save friends from ruin – there is a tradition that she stopped him from dissolving Eton. Mrs Shore was hated by the queen, on whom Edward nonetheless found time to father at least ten children.

Not even siblings defied the king with impunity. Angered by Edward stopping him from marrying the heiress to Burgundy,

Clarence became impossible. Early in 1477 he hanged one of his late duchess's ladies for supposedly poisoning her beer, then hanged a servant for poisoning his younger son. He also claimed the king was trying to kill him with witchcraft. In July, after two men were executed for plotting to murder Edward with sorcery, the duke pushed his way into the council when the king was absent, insisting that they were innocent. Infuriated, Edward arrested his brother and in January 1478 had him attainted for treason – among the charges were practising necromancy and spreading rumours that Edward was a bastard. Clarence died at the Tower the next month, drowned in a butt of wine.

Trouble abroad began in 1482. War broke out with Scotland, while at the end of the year Louis XI and Archduke Maximilian, Burgundy's new ruler, made peace. Throwing over Princess Elizabeth, the Dauphin was betrothed to Maximilian's daughter, while Louis stopped Edward's pension. Throughout Christmas, the king thought of nothing but vengeance, summoning parliament in January to vote money for a war. Yet he no longer had the energy for campaigning, self-indulgence having made him 'fat in the loins'.[25]

About Easter 1483 Edward fell ill. Mancini heard that it began by his catching cold during an angling party on the Thames.[26] The disease may have been pneumonia, to which his corpulent body could offer little resistance. After ten days, still only forty years old, the king died in the Palace of Westminster on 9 April 1483. Immediately after his death his body was exposed for ten hours, naked from the waist, so that it might be seen by the lords spiritual and temporal, and by the mayor and aldermen of London.

Retrospect

Modern historians stress that when Edward IV died there was barely enough money in the treasury to pay for his funeral. Yet he had been far from unsuccessful. Although his foreign policy was wrecked by the alliance between French and Burgundians, he deserves credit for realizing that England could not continue the Hundred Years War against a reunited France.[27] He never lost a battle – Towton, Barnet and Tewkesbury were no mean victories – and kept the Crown he usurped until he died in his bed.

Despite Edward's murderous streak, he was mourned by his subjects, who admired his infectious zest for life and conviviality. Pleasing everyone who crossed his path had become second nature, while his scandalous private life only enhanced his popularity. During his last summer he invited the aldermen of London to 'hunt and make merry with him' at Windsor. Nothing earned the first Yorkist king more affection than this friendliness – 'gat him either more hearts or more hearty favour among the common people'.[28]

14

The Suicide – Richard III

The story is not a long one, for the shadows begin from the moment of his accession to deepen round the last king of the great house of Anjou

William Stubbs[1]

A long-term plan?

According to Sir Thomas More, on the night Edward IV died a member of the royal household, William Mistlebrook, ran to the house of a City attorney called Richard Pottyer, who lived in Redcross Street without Cripplegate. Rapping urgently on the door, as soon as he was let in, he gave Pottyer the news of Edward's death. 'By my troth, man', said the attorney, 'Then will my master the duke of Gloucester be king!'[2]

More adds that some thought Gloucester had designs on the throne even when his brother was alive, 'whose life he looked that evil diet should shorten', but admits he cannot be sure about this. The Mistlebrook–Pottyer story is plausible, however.

Sir Thomas says he heard it from his father, who at the time was living near Redcross Street, while both William Mistlebrook and Richard Pottyer have been identified by historians. Mancini commented in 1483 that there were people aware of Richard's 'ambition and deceitfulness, who never had any doubt where his scheming would lead'.[3] It led to the dynasty's suicide.

Until a hundred years ago everybody (apart from cranks like Horace Walpole) believed that Richard had murdered the 'Princes in the Tower'. Stubbs spoke for almost all Victorians when he wrote, 'Brave, cunning, resolute, bound by no ties of love or gratitude, amenable to no instincts of mercy or kindness, Richard III yet owes the general condemnation, with which his life and reign have been visited, to the fact that he left none behind him whose duty or whose care it was to attempt his vindication.'[4] However, since the emergence in 1924 of the Fellowship of the White Boar (now the Richard III Society) he has found partisans who see him as another King Arthur. (One product of their point of view was Josephine Tey's enjoyable if misleading novel *The Daughter of Time*.)

In 2012 Richard's skeleton was found at Leicester, in a Franciscan friary demolished at the Dissolution of the Monasteries. Its spine is curved by scoliosis, which made one shoulder higher than the other. Far from being Tudor propaganda, as defenders have claimed, his nickname 'Crookback' was justified.

Youth

Richard was born on 2 October 1453 at Fotheringhay Castle in Northamptonshire, the Duke of York's seventh and youngest son. Stories of his coming into the world with hair and teeth are plainly hostile propaganda, while his scoliosis probably only developed during boyhood. After his father's death in 1460 he was sent to Flanders for safety with his brother George, returning after Edward IV's victory at Towton to be

made Duke of Gloucester. He spent 1465–8 in the Earl of
Warwick's household at Middleham Castle in Wensleydale –
which no doubt was how he acquired his attachment to the
north country.

Unlike Clarence, Richard did not intrigue with Warwick,
going into exile in Flanders with Edward and fighting for him
at Barnet and Tewkesbury. Tudor chroniclers allege that he had
a hand in killing the Lancastrian Prince of Wales, but there is
no evidence for this (even if Stubbs thought it was true). We
know from a Yorkist source, however, that he commanded the
vanguard at Tewkesbury, where he presided over the drum-head
court martials that condemned the captured Lancastrian commanders. He also hunted down the Bastard of Fauconberg. Some
chroniclers heard he was in the Tower when Henry VI died, and
a strong element of suspicion remains about his complicity.[5]

Richard's appointments as Great Chamberlain and Lord
High Admiral of England on 18 May 1471 was clearly a sign of
Edward's trust. In addition, he was given the Earl of Oxford's
estates with all Warwick's lands north of Trent. Having prised
Warwick's daughter, Anne (the widowed Lancastrian Princess
of Wales) out of the Duke of Clarence's keeping, he first placed
her in sanctuary at St Martin's, then married her at Westminster
Abbey in spring 1472 after the necessary dispensation from the
Church – they were first cousins. He also obtained control of
her mother, Warwick's widowed countess, who was confined at
Middleham for the rest of her life so that he could keep her
dowry.

Clarence refused to hand over anything and the two young
dukes argued their cases before the king at Sheen in February
1472, astonishing lawyers by their grasp of legal argument.
Eventually an act of parliament divided the Warwick inheritance
between them, Gloucester receiving the lion's share. During
the contest, 'Clarence proved the more petulant and unac-
commodating of the two', writes Charles Ross (1981) – still
Richard's best biographer – 'but both brothers showed a greed

and ruthlessness and disregard for the rights of those who could not protect themselves which shed an unpleasant light on their characters'.[6]

At Christmas 1472 Richard sent sixteen men to Bromley Priory at Stratford-le-Bow, and they abducted the Dowager Countess of Oxford – confined there by King Edward as the mother of a leading Lancastrian. The old lady was dragged through the snow to Stepney where the duke was waiting in a house owned by a member of his household. He told her she must give him her estates or be taken to Yorkshire and imprisoned in one of his castles. Lady Oxford, 'considering her great age, the great journey and the great cold which was then, of frost and snow, thought that she could not endure to be conveyed thither without great jeopardy of her life and [was] also sore fearing how she should be there entreated'. Terrified, she was brought to another house in Walbrook where she signed the deeds. 'I thank God', she cried, 'I have those lands which shall now save my life.' Her trustees were then bullied into accepting the transfer.[7] The tale hints at a certain lack of chivalry in a young man of twenty.

Richard accompanied Edward IV to France in 1475, bringing the largest armed retinue of any English nobleman. Eager to fight, he stayed away from the meeting at Picquigny between his brother and King Louis, refusing Louis's bribes. However, after seeing other magnates pocket them, he changed his mind and accepted rich presents.

Some observers thought he was behind his brother George's destruction in 1478. Even if they were wrong, he certainly profited from it. Three days before Clarence was killed, Richard's small son was created Earl of Salisbury, one of his uncle's former titles, while three days later Richard became Great Chamberlain again, an office that had been taken from him in 1472 and given to Clarence.

Richard in the North

After 1478 Gloucester was seldom at his brother's court, but in the North. Middleham and Sheriff Hutton were his favourite houses, but he owned many others, used on frequent progresses to York, Carlisle and Durham. Effectively a viceroy, he governed England down to the River Trent, anticipating the Council of the North.

Scottish privateers, operating from Leith, were a menace to English shipping. (It was not just a matter of losing cargoes; captured crew were thrown overboard.) However, fitting out ships and using Scarborough as a naval base, Richard swept the sea-lanes free of them. He must have sailed on board his patrols, since the Croyland writer mentions his 'skill in naval warfare'.[8] In 1474 one of his vessels captured a Scottish ship called the *Yellow Carvel* owned by the King of Scots and an embassy had to be sent to apologize. With a harbour guarded by an impregnable castle, the little port of Scarborough was ideal for his purpose, and later he created it a county in its own right.

Richard became a hero in the north country, acquiring a big following among the gentry and in the cities. 'The popularity which he had won before his accession, in Yorkshire, where there was no love for the house of York before, proves he was not without the gifts which gained for Edward IV the lifelong support of the nation', Stubbs admits.[9] Much was thanks to his precautions against Scottish raiders, not only as warden of the Western Marches but along the entire border.

His standing was enhanced when war broke out between England and Scotland. Scottish raids over the border had revived while James III was dangerously pro-French, and in May 1480 Gloucester was made Lieutenant General with power to raise troops throughout the North. This did not deter the Earl of Angus from sacking Bamburgh, and in retaliation the duke and the Earl of Northumberland led a raid into Scotland. In November King Edward ordered preparations for a full-scale invasion, which he intended to lead in person but called off because of ill health. Even so, during the winter of 1481–2 English ships harried the Scottish coast while English troops besieged Berwick. In June 1482 Richard burned Dumfries and other towns in Galloway.

The invasion plan was revived, this time with Gloucester as commander. The aim was to replace James III with his brother Alexander, Duke of Albany, who promised to surrender Berwick and other border lands, besides repudiating any alliance with France. In return, the English would establish him at Edinburgh. Gloucester led 20,000 men across the border, informing King Edward of his progress by a species of pony express. On 24 July he routed a Scots force at the Battle of Hutton Field. No details survive, but it must have been a very minor engagement – the Scots could not find enough troops to oppose so large an army because James III was squabbling with his barons. Berwick surrendered as soon as Richard appeared, and he occupied Edinburgh. Unexpectedly, Albany abandoned any claim to the throne of Scotland in return for recovering his duchy. A truce was negotiated, but all Richard could extract was Berwick with a vague promise that the King of Scots' son should marry Edward's daughter Cecily. After only three weeks of expensive *promenade militaire*, he evacuated Edinburgh and disbanded his army. Yet the campaign put the seal on Richard's popularity in the North. Besides occupying the capital of the hated Scots, he had knighted forty-nine northerners at Hutton Field, many of whom later served him loyally.

As a reward for regaining Berwick, when parliament met in January 1483, Edward created a palatinate for his brother, consisting of Westmorland and Cumberland, an independent principality in which the king's writ would not run. He also made him hereditary warden of the Western Marches. Edward felt that a further war with Scotland was looming, and lacked the energy to fight it in person.

The man

Dark haired, with a thin, tight-lipped face and a sharp, watchful expression, in the best portrait (an early sixteenth-century copy) one has the impression of a highly strung, wiry little creature without an ounce of spare flesh. Because of the scoliosis that twisted his spine, he stood a foot less than his five feet eight inches, but made up for it by dressing splendidly, often in cloth of gold. Constantly looking round, fidgeting with a ring or the dagger at his belt, he chewed his lower lip when thinking. It is likely that he spoke with a strong Yorkshire accent and a dry rasping cough (due to roundworm). He was oddly pale, from the pain induced by his scoliosis. Yet clearly he was impressive. In 1484 a Scots ambassador told him, 'nature never enclosed in a smaller frame such remarkable powers'.[10]

More tells us that he could be 'merry' and 'companionable', and his court was full of music and dancing, banqueting and feasting. He had a flamboyant streak, evident in the white boar that he chose as a personal emblem, worn by members of his household on doublets and bonnets or as a neck-badge. His motto was '*Loyauté me lie*' (loyalty binds me) – an ironic choice in the light of future events.

He knew how to make people like and even love him. He acquired a number of committed henchmen, the best known being Sir Richard Ratcliffe, William Catesby and his child-hood friend Francis, Viscount Lovell, whom he made his Lord Chamberlain. (Lovell was devoted to him in the same way Hastings had been to Edward IV, taking a dog for his crest in token of fidelity.) Yet he was a poor judge of character. The Duke of Buckingham, Lord Stanley and the Earl of Northumberland all had reason to be grateful to him – and all betrayed him.

We know nothing of Richard's relations with his wife, except that in the end he saw her as an encumbrance. He was an indulgent father to their sickly only son Edward of Middleham, providing him with a chariot so he could follow the hunt. He also ensured that his two bastards (born before his marriage) were well provided for: Katherine became Countess of Huntingdon while John of Gloucester was made Captain of Calais. There are hints of womanizing after he became king.

Richard preferred falconry to hunting, while he took particular pleasure in bear-baiting (during which mastiffs savaged the animal to death) and appointed a royal 'bear-herd' in 1484. He also had a special bear-pit built at Warwick Castle[11]. Among his books were the *Chronicle of John of Brompton*, Aegidius on statecraft, *Of the Rule of Princes* by Giles of Bologna and William of Worcester's Norman documents. He commissioned only one illuminated manuscript, a translation of Vegetius on war. Lighter reading consisted of a volume of tales (including two by Chaucer.) He owned a Lollard bible, indicating an inability to read Latin or French in which the scriptures were freely available. A love of heraldry is revealed by his founding the College of Arms. Fond of music, he employed minstrels and choirs. He enjoyed building, notably a great hall at Middleham Castle and a new chapel at Sheriff Hutton, while during his reign he added towers and a range of lodgings to Warwick Castle, as well as palatial apartments to Nottingham Castle, which became a frequent residence.

He converted Middleham parish church into a college of priests, who daily said Mass for him, his wife and his dead kindred. When he became king, he planned to add a huge chantry chapel to York Minster, with six altars served by a hundred priests, which in size would have rivalled the great chapel that Henry Tudor later built on to Westminster Abbey. Clearly, he intended it to be his burial place.

Constantly on pilgrimage and visiting shrines, Richard developed a cult for St Julian the Hospitaller, a parricide who killed his father and mother but was pardoned by God. (A prayer to Julian by 'thy servant King Richard' in his Book of Hours has a paranoiac quality.) He was prone to moralize, denouncing enemies as fornicators and adulterers – giving substance to More's gibe that he posed 'as a goodly continent prince, clean and continent of himself, sent out of heaven into this vicious world for the amendment of men's manners'.[12]

The coups d'état of 1483

Whatever Gloucester's plans may have been, Edward IV's death took him by surprise and he found himself threatened by the Wydevilles, who formed a majority on the council. They denied his right to be more than a titular Protector, insisting the council as a whole must rule. But the Wydevilles had enemies, the most prominent being Henry Stafford, Duke of Buckingham, with whom Richard immediately forged an alliance. Another ally was Edward IV's treasurer, Lord Howard – later rewarded with the duchy of Norfolk.

He then mounted two coups d'état in quick succession. The young king's governor, Earl Rivers, who was the queen's brother and the Wydevilles' leader, had gone to Ludlow to bring him to London for his coronation on 4 May. Richard and Buckingham met the earl in the most amiable way at Stony Stratford on 29 April, spending the evening carousing together. Next morning, however, despite Edward's tearful protests, their men seized Rivers and his key lieutenants, eventually executing them without trial. The Wydevilles were unpopular, so the Londoners cheered Gloucester when he rode in with the king. Lord Hastings, an old enemy of the Wydevilles, was overjoyed. Terrified, Queen Elizabeth fled to sanctuary in Westminster Abbey, taking her younger son, the Duke of York. As Lord Protector, Richard chose a new date for his nephew's coronation, amid general approval. This was his first coup.

The second coup followed after he had persuaded the queen to give him custody of York, who was sent to join his brother at the Tower of London – still a palace as well as a fortress. Having discreetly summoned troops from the North, at a council meeting on 20 June he suddenly called armed guards into the room and arrested the unsuspecting Lord Hastings, whom he accused of plotting with the Wydevilles and then had beheaded in the yard outside.

Now that Hastings, the one man who might have stopped Richard, had been eliminated, a friar announced at St Paul's that the young king and his brother were bastards because of a marriage contract between Edward IV and Lady Eleanor Butler which predated the Wydeville marriage – he even alleged that the late king had himself been a bastard. Buckingham then made a speech at Guildhall, asking everyone to petition the Protector to take the throne, an invitation repeated by a delegation of peers and gentlemen. On 26 June Richard graciously accepted.

'Richard III'

On 6 July, Richard III and Anne Neville were crowned at Westminster Abbey by Archbishop Bourchier of Canterbury, and every effort was made to make the occasion joyful, with pageants in the London streets. At the end of July, the new king went on progress, visiting the West Country, the Midlands and the North. He spent over a fortnight at York, whose citizens vied in producing displays and tableaux, the corporation giving sumptuous banquets for the royal party. On 8 September the ten-year-old Edward of Middleham was invested in the minster as Prince of Wales, with splendour worthy of a coronation.

'He contents the people where he goes best that ever did prince', wrote Dr Thomas Langton, Bishop of St David's, who accompanied Richard. 'For many a poor man that hath suffered wrong many days have been relieved and helped by him and his commands now in his progress. And in many great cities and towns were great sums of money give to him, which all he hath refused. On my troth, I never liked the condition of any prince so well as his. God hath sent him to us for the weal of us all.' Breaking into Latin, the bishop marred this paean a little by adding, 'I do not take exception to the fact that his sensuality [*voluptas*] seems to be increasing.'[13]

Meanwhile the boy now known as 'Edward Bastard, late called King Edward V' and his brother were taken into the inner rooms of the Tower itself, and seen less and less until they disappeared altogether. They may have been murdered after an attempt to release them in July. The London chronicles suggest they were dead before the end of the year, while across the Channel Louis XI, who died on 30 August 1483, believed that Richard had killed the boys. During an address to the Estates General in January 1484 the chancellor of France referred to the English king having done away with his nephews.

Sir Thomas More has been accused of writing his biography of Richard as Tudor propaganda. Yet Mancini, in London at the time, bears out More. 'The importance of Mancini's narrative lies in the fact that he provides direct contemporary evidence that Richard's ruthless progress to the throne aroused widespread mistrust and dislike, to the extent that at least some of his subjects were willing to believe, within a fortnight of his accession, that Richard had disposed of his nephews by violence.'[14]

Plots

Richard was still in the North when he learned on 11 October that a rebellion had broken out, led by Buckingham. Writing to his chancellor, he described the duke as 'the most untrue creature living: whom with God's grace we shall not be long till that we be in those parts and subdue his malice. We assure you there was never traitor better purveyed for'.[15]

The plot's originators were the former queen and Lady Margaret Beaufort, Lord Stanley's wife, who used Dr John Morton to turn 'Harry Buckingham' against the king. Aghast at Richard's unpopularity, the duke did not wish to share his downfall. Mainly former members of Edward IV's household, but including the Wydevilles and their friends, most of those involved were leading gentry from all over the southern counties, who at first hoped to restore Edward V. The Yorkist establishment had 'imploded'.[16] Suspecting that Edward and his brother were dead, they now planned to replace Richard with Henry Tudor, the son of Margaret Beaufort who was the last heir of the left-handed line of Lancaster. To strengthen his claim, Henry must marry Elizabeth of York, the young king's eldest sister and heiress.

The weather was on Richard's side. Heavy rain prevented Buckingham from joining the rebels in the southern counties, his Welsh retainers deserted him and the rising collapsed almost as soon as it began, while the duke was quickly caught and beheaded. Henry Tudor, who arrived too late, sailed back to Brittany without setting foot on English soil. Many of those involved fled the country.

However, Buckingham's revolt turned the unknown Tudor into a serious pretender, who was soon joined in exile by a substantial number of rebels. At the same time, Richard's narrow political power base became even narrower, restricted to three magnates – the Duke of Norfolk, the Earl of Northumberland and Lord Stanley. Placed under house arrest, Margaret Beaufort set about turning her husband Stanley against him.

When parliament met at Westminster in January 1484, the Lord Chancellor, Bishop Russell, claimed the rebellion violated the laws of God, and a hundred men who had taken part were attainted. Another bill confirmed Richard's right to the Crown. There were legal and economic measures, one particularly appreciated being to abolish benevolences – the arbitrary 'gifts' from wealthy men introduced by Edward IV. Richard was presenting himself to his subjects as a good lawmaker who looked after the common people.

On 9 April his only son Edward died unexpectedly at Middleham after a short illness. 'On hearing the news at Nottingham where they were staying, you could have seen his father and mother in a state bordering on madness, from shock and grief', says the Croyland author.[17] The king's loss looked like divine judgement, while the lack of an obvious successor increased his insecurity. He thought of making Clarence's son Warwick heir presumptive, but this meant reversing Clarence's attainder, which would give the boy a better claim to the throne than his own. Instead, he chose his sister Elizabeth's son, John de la Pole.

A Wiltshire gentleman called William Colyngbourne wrote secretly to Henry, inviting him to invade, and then posted a famous couplet on the door of St Paul's in July 1484:

> The Cat, the Rat and Lovell our Dog
> Ruleth all England under a Hog.

The Cat was Catesby and the Rat Ratcliffe – Richard's principal henchmen – while the Dog alluded to his chamberlain's crest and the Hog to his Boar emblem. The king grew paranoiac. 'When he went abroad, his eyes whirled about; his body privily fenced [secretly armoured], his hand ever on his dagger, his countenance and manner like one always ready to strike again', is what More was told. 'He took ill rest a nights, lay long waking and musing, rather slumbered than slept, troubled with fearful dreams.'[18]

Richard worked feverishly to persuade Duke Francis of Brittany to hand over Henry Tudor, to whom fellow exiles had sworn allegiance as king in Rennes Cathedral at Christmas 1483. Henry had also taken an oath to marry Elizabeth of York. Francis's chief minister, Pierre Landois, agreed to send him to England, but – probably alerted by Lord Stanley – Dr Morton heard of it and warned Henry, who in September 1484 fled to France.

Early in November 1484, the Earl of Oxford was freed by his gaoler at Hammes (a fortress guarding Calais), the pair going off to join Henry in France, followed by members of the Calais garrison. At the same time Sir William Brandon and his sons started a rising at Colchester, escaping to join Henry by boat when it failed. There was trouble in Hertfordshire, part of the same plot.[19] France recognized Tudor as Henry VI's heir, promising 4,000 troops.

Nevertheless, the Twelve Days of Christmas 1484–5 were celebrated at court with dancing and gaiety, according to the Croyland writer. He says that Queen Anne and Elizabeth of York, Edward IV's eldest daughter, wore each other's clothes, as the two 'were of similar colour and form'.[20] This is the only clue to Anne's appearance: she must have been a considerable beauty if she resembled her cousin Elizabeth, who had fine features and an English rose complexion. Richard was presiding over the Twelfth Night revels, wearing his crown, when spies informed him that Henry Tudor would invade England the next summer.

He paid such attention to Elizabeth that it was clear he meant to marry her. Conveniently, Queen Anne died of tuberculosis on 16 March (during an eclipse of the sun) and his far from unwilling niece could give him an heir, removing a key part of Henry's strategy. Her mother encouraged the match, while canon lawyers assured him they could obtain a dispensation for an uncle–niece marriage. However, Ratcliffe and Catesby told him 'to his face' that if he did not publicly deny the plan even the northerners would accuse him of murdering the queen to indulge his incestuous lust.[21] On 30 March 1485 the Mayor and Corporation of London were summoned to the Priory of the Knights of St John at Clerkenwell with many others, to hear the king tell them, 'It never came in his thought or mind to marry in such manner-wise [his niece], nor willing or glad of the death of his queen, but as sorry and in heart as heavy as man might be.' He complained of rumours, presumably of his having poisoned Anne.[22] The speech gives us an idea of what the Londoners thought of him. Henry sent letters to England, asking supporters to join in 'the just depriving of that homicide and unnatural tyrant that now unjustly bears dominion over you'.[23] Increasingly alarmed, Richard spent the spring and most of the summer waiting for an invasion after learning that Tudor would be supplied with funds by the French, who feared the king might intervene in Brittany and try to reconquer Normandy. Yet by midsummer it looked as if Richard was safe. Pierre Landois was ousted by pro-French Bretons and hanged from the ramparts of Nantes. Now there was no longer a threat that Richard might intervene in the duchy, France lost interest in Henry, withdrawing their offer to help.

In desperation, Henry borrowed money from a French courtier to hire 1,000 men and seven small ships – a much less formidable force than the 4,000 troops originally promised by Charles VIII's government. The king's spies believed he would make for Milford, a tiny harbour in Hampshire, and Lovell assembled a fleet at Southampton to intercept him. In June Richard went to Nottingham Castle, at the centre of England, so he could confront his enemy as soon as he landed. In a proclamation, he denounced the followers of 'Henry Tydder'. They were murderers, adulterers and extortioners, who would steal everyone's estates and offices, killing and robbing on an unheard-of scale.

Richard's challenger was an obscure Welshman, 'descended of bastard blood' on both sides whose grandfather, Owain Tudor, Keeper of the Wardrobe to Henry V's widow, Catherine of Valois, had supposedly married her. One of their sons had married Lady Margaret Beaufort, the heiress of John of Gaunt and Katherine Swynford, and it was they who were Henry Tudor's parents. That someone with such a feeble claim to the throne, whom few Englishmen had ever seen, could become a pretender shows how desperate men were to find an alternative to Richard.

On 7 August Henry landed, not at Milford in Hampshire but at Milford Haven in Pembrokeshire. Supporters joined him as he marched so that he had about 5,000 men. Richard assembled 12,000 troops at Leicester, the largest contingents those of Lord Stanley and his brother Sir William, and of the Earl of Northumberland. This was a small army for a King of England with time to prepare, but it looks as if a few people wanted to fight in his defence while so obscure a challenger as Tudor seemed to have little chance of winning.

If Richard felt doubtful about Lord Stanley and his brother Sir William, their contingents were too strong for him to act on mere suspicion. In retrospect, however, it is clear that Margaret Beaufort had converted Lord Stanley to her son's cause. It is also clear that the Earl of Northumberland had no liking for the king, despite having worked closely with him in the North – or perhaps as a result.

Bosworth

On the morning of 22 August 1485 the two armies faced each other near Market Bosworth in Leicestershire. Every reconstruction of the battle that followed is based on Polydore Vergil, who, although he spoke to people who had fought in it, wrote thirty years later. There is no full eyewitness description, just a few scraps to flesh out Vergil's account, but this was scarcely another Towton – neither leader inspired much loyalty and the ruling class were less inclined to risk their lives. Even the topography has been misunderstood, a recent archaeological examination finding it was fought over a 4 mile area around a group of adjoining villages instead of on the traditional site.[24]

The veteran Lancastrian who led Henry's army, the Earl of Oxford, attacked first, despite having fewer troops. However, archaeologists have recently discovered bullets on the battlefield, suggesting they included French arquebusiers, whose new matchlocks were highly effective against cavalry. It is also likely that there were Swiss-style pike-men among them. When the Duke of Norfolk charged at the head of the vanguard, his men-at-arms were held off by long pikes and shot down. Another attack failed, ending in Norfolk's death. Losing his most loyal commander, fear of treachery by the Stanleys and the enemy's weaponry explain Richard's next, desperate move.

Seeing Henry Tudor's dragon banner, he realized that his

rival was near. If he eliminated him he would win, regardless of matchlocks or pikes. Together with the knights and squires of his household, who amounted to about a hundred and sixty men-at-arms, he charged, killing Henry's banner-bearer with his lance, striking another of his enemy's bodyguard out of the saddle with his axe and cutting down several more.

At the last moment, Sir William Stanley changed sides and led his own men to Henry's rescue, overwhelming the royal household. Northumberland made no attempt to rescue the king, but watched him being killed. Richard's horse became bogged down in the marshy ground and he was forced to dismount. Alone, surrounded by enemies, crying 'Treason! Treason!', he fought to the end. Even the hostile Croyland writer admits he died 'like a brave and most valiant prince'.[25] The wounds found on his skull suggest a frenzy of blows.

Stripped naked and slung over a horse, its face disfigured by banging into a bridge, the king's corpse was taken back to Leicester where for three days it was displayed on a church pavement. Men other than valets or tailors were able to see for the first time how much higher one shoulder was than the other, and perhaps too that he had a small hump, which is not uncommon in sufferers from scoliosis. Then he was buried at the Franciscan friary – the beggars' church; his grave was lost when it was demolished in 1538 during the Dissolution of the Monasteries until its rediscovery in a 'long stay' car park in 2012.

Retrospect

Although Richard III is one of the most studied figures in English medieval history, his brief time on the throne was merely a lurid postscript to his brother's reign. Its only lasting significance lies in providing a *raison d'être* for Henry Tudor. He had committed not just political but dynastic suicide. In March 1483 there had been five male Plantagenets; by August 1485 only Clarence's disinherited son was left, the ten-year-old Earl of Warwick. Vergil was stating the obvious when he wrote of Richard 'destroying the house of York'.[26] *The Great Chronicle of London* (written by someone who lived in the City at the time) comments that 'had he continued still Protector and suffered the childer to have prospered according to his allegiance and fidelity, he should have been honourably lauded over all, whereas now his fame is darkened and dishonoured'.[27]

As his namesake had prophesied three centuries before, after being begotten by the devil, the Plantagenets ended by going to the devil. Not even the Borgias killed children. Yet the last Plantagenet sovereign has a strange fascination, not just for his partisans, but for those convinced of his guilt.

15

Postscript – The Kings in the National Myth

For where is Bohun? Where is Mowbray? Where is Mortimer?
Nay, which is more and most of all, where is Plantagenet?
They are entombed in the urns and sepulchres of mortality!

Chief Justice Crewe in 1625

The place of most Plantagenet monarchs in our pantheon is a shadowy one, but once they were proudly remembered. Edward III became a hero to Henry VIII's court through Lord Berners's stately version of Froissart, which he translated at the king's command, and Edward Hall's *Union of the Two Illustre Families of Lancaster and York* (1548) gave some idea of England's rulers from Henry IV onwards. The Elizabethans were familiar with the entire dynasty from Raphael Holinshed's *Chronicles* (1577). They also learned about the Plantagenets from the theatre. While Bishop John Bale's *Kyng Johan*, written in about 1538 and portraying John as a victim of papal tyranny, was performed only once or twice, it is likely that George Peele's bloodstained *King Edward the First* (1593) made more impact.

Still more important, Holinshed gave Shakespeare the material for his plays about Plantagenet kings (as he did for Christopher Marlowe's *Edward II.*) Despite changes for the sake of entertainment – such as exaggerating the wildness of 'Prince Hal' – Shakespeare is often astonishingly near the mark, since he echoes the contemporary chroniclers from whom Holinshed took his information. A famous example is Richard II's lament for his lost crown, which came from Adam of Usk.

But during the reigns of the first two Stuarts, although Edward I was venerated as a lawgiver by jurists who at the same time shuddered at the memory of John, the Plantagenets inspired no new dramas. Curiously, from Shakespeare until comparatively recent times, almost no plays were written about English history or English monarchs, let alone about the Plantagenets. Admittedly, even the most sanguine playwright would find difficulty in convincing himself he could improve on Shakespeare. On the other hand, the seventeenth century learned something of its former ruling family from the cartographer John Speed's *Historie of Great Britaine*. Similarly, the eighteenth century was treated to the whole story in depth by David Hume, whose six solid volumes had a place on the shelves of every respectable library. Even so, most men and women of the eighteenth and early nineteenth centuries discovered the Plantagenets from Shakespeare, whom they read as we do novels – the great Duke of Marlborough once declared he had learned his history exclusively from the Bard.

What this meant for an understanding of the Plantagenets can be gleaned from William Hazlitt's *Characters of Shakespeare's Plays* (1817), in which Hazlitt analysed their portraits. King John was 'more cowardly than cruel', while Richard II was 'a voluptuary, proud, revengeful, impatient of contradiction, and inconsolable in his misfortunes'. Henry IV was 'humble, crafty, bold and aspiring, encroaching by regular but slow degrees, building power on opinion, and cementing opinion by power'. The summary of Henry V is particularly shrewd: 'Because his own title to the crown was doubtful, he laid claim to that of France . . . He was a hero, that is, he was ready to sacrifice his own life for the pleasure of destroying thousands of other lives.' Henry VI 'wished to pass his time in monkish indolence and contemplation'. As for Richard III, he was 'towering and lofty; equally impetuous and commanding; haughty, violent, and subtle; confident in his strength as well as in his cunning'.

Surprisingly, Plantagenets rarely featured in nineteenth-century historical novels. Scott found room only for Richard Coeur de Lion and John. However, Edward IV came into Bulwer-Lytton's costume drama, *The Last of the Barons*, which portrayed him as 'a temporizer – a dissimulator – but it was only as the tiger creeps, the better to spring, undetected, on its prey'. Bulwer-Lytton credited Richard III with a 'soft and oily manner that concealed intense ambition and innate ferocity'. The only other well-known mention in fiction was a vignette of a youthful Richard (when Duke of Gloucester) in Robert Louis Stevenson's 'piece of tushery' *The Black Arrow* – 'slightly deformed, with one shoulder higher than another, and of a pale, painful, and distorted countenance . . . he that rides with Crooked Dick will ride deep'. Even so, the Victorians knew all about the Plantagenet kings from Shakespeare, Charles Dickens's *Child's History of England* and John Richard Green's phenomenally popular *History of the English People*. Another source was Bishop William Stubbs's *Constitutional History of England*, glorifying the Lancastrians as forerunners of the Whigs, which was widely read and not just by scholars.

In the first half of the twentieth century, before the temporary decline of the historical novel, Conan Doyle and Alfred Duggan wrote stirring romances in which Plantagenet monarchs sometimes played a prominent role. But the authors who really kept their memory green during this period were 'patriotic historians' such as Sir Winston Churchill and Arthur Bryant, whose exuberantly written books enjoyed a vast readership, Churchill praising 'this strong race of warrior and statesman kings'. There were also Laurence Olivier's hugely successful film versions of Shakespeare's *Henry V* and *Richard III*.

Today, we are less aware of them. A multicultural world is embarrassed by patriotic history, which it dismisses as 'celebratory' or politically incorrect, and despite the revival of the historical novel and although Shakespeare's plays still work their magic, the Plantagenets have faded from people's memory. Henry II is known as Eleanor of Aquitaine's husband and for Thomas Becket's death, Richard I is recalled for his 'homosexuality', John for Magna Carta, Edward I for persecuting William Wallace and Edward II for the gruesome way in which he was murdered. Richard II, Henry V, Henry VI and Richard III are more familiar because they were fleshed out by Shakespeare.

Yet the Plantagenet kings can recapture popular imagination, now that the Tudors have been almost – if not quite – worked to death. One straw in the wind is the success of Philippa Gregory's historical romances, one of which became a TV 'soap'. They offer a new field for dramatists. Richard III, already a cult, is attracting increased attention since the discovery of his skeleton. We can expect more new novels and soaps about him, which might revive interest in the entire dynasty.

Only a handful of medieval English men and women can be glimpsed, on a tomb or a monumental brass, in an illuminated manuscript – but even then it is stylized representation. Save for one or two rare exceptions, they have not left revealing letters or journals. In contrast, from John's time effigies or portraits provide a vivid impression of the Plantagenet kings, while chroniclers make a point of describing them, in depth. They can be seen as human beings, so that their personalities offer unique windows on to their age.

Some of them were among the greatest Englishmen who ever lived. Presiding over the fusion of French-speaking colonists and

Anglo-Saxon natives into a nation, giving us the Common Law and parliamentary government, they hammered out a kingdom that became Great Britain.

Notes

Introduction: The Demon and Her Heirs

1 Lord Macaulay, *The History of England*, 4 vols (London, 1849), vol. 1, p. 13.
2 O. Guillot, *Le Comte d'Anjou et son entourage aux XIme siècle* (Paris, 1972), p. 25.
3 Gerald of Wales, *Giraldi Cambrensis Opera*, 8 vols, ed. J. S. Brewer et al., Rolls Series (London, 1861–9), viii, p. 301.
4 Walter Map, *De Nugis Curialium: Courtiers' Trifles*, ed. and trans. M. R. James, revised C. N. L. Brooke and R. A. B. Mynors (Oxford, 1983), p. 346.
5 Gerald of Wales, *Giraldi Cambrensis Opera*, viii, p. 301.
6 J. Buchan, *The Path of the King* (London, 1921), p. 10.

1. The First Plantagenets

1. J. R. Green, *History of the English People*, 4 vols (London, 1877), i, p. 148.
2. *Chroniques des Comtes d'Anjou et des Comtes d'Amboise*, ed. L. Halphen and R. Poupardin (Paris, 1913).
3. W. Stubbs, *Select Charters* (Oxford, 1900), p. 84.
4. William of Malmesbury, *Historia Novella: The Contemporary History*, ed. E. King, trans. K. R. Potter, Oxford Medieval Texts (Oxford, 1998), pp. 32–3.
5. *The Anglo-Saxon Chronicle*, trans. and ed. G. N. Garmonsway (London and New York, 1954), p. 263.
6. Henry of Huntingdon, *Historia Anglorum: The History of the English People*, Oxford Medieval Texts (Oxford, 1996), p. 724.

7. *Anglo-Saxon Chronicle*, p. 263.
8. Henry of Huntingdon, *Historia Anglorum*, p. 734.
9. Henry of Huntingdon, *Historia Anglorum*, p. 720.
10. *Anglo-Saxon Chronicle*, pp. 264–5.

2. The Eagle – Henry II

1. Gerald of Wales, *Giraldi Cambrensis Opera*, viii, p. 295.
2. William FitzStephen, *Vita Sanctae Thomae*, in J. C. Robertson, *Materials for the History of Thomas Becket*, Rolls Series, 3 vols (London, 1877) vol. iii p. 65.
3. E. King, *King Stephen* (New Haven and London, 2010), pp. 262–4.
4. *Gesta Stephani*, ed. and trans. K. R. Potter,with new intro and notes by R. H. C. Davis (Oxford, 1976), p. 261.
5. *Anglo-Saxon Chronicle*, p. 267.
6. Richard of Devizes, quoted in *Chronicles of the Reigns of Stephen, Henry II and Richard I*, ed. R. Howlett, Rolls Series, 4 vols (London, 1884–90), iii, p. 402.
7. *Chronicle of Robert de Torigni* in *Chronicles of the Reigns of Stephen* etc., iv, pp. 165–6.
8. William of Malmesbury, *Historia Novella*, i, pp. 277–8.
9. J. Gillingham, *The English in the Twelfth Century* (Woodbridge, 2000), p. 140.
10. William of Newburgh, *The History of English Affairs: Book II*, ed. G. H. Walsh and M. J. Kennedy, Aris & Phillips Classical Texts (Oxford, 2007), p. 15.
11. N. Barratt, 'Finance and Economy in the Reign of Henry II', in C. Harper-Bill and N. Vincent (eds), *Henry II: New Interpretations* (Woodbridge, 2007).
12. R. Barber, *Henry Plantagenet* (Woodbridge, 2001).
13. Gerald of Wales, *Giraldi Cambrensis Opera*, viii, p. 316.
14. William FitzStephen, *Vita Sanctae Thomae*, iii, pp. 103–6.
15. Adam of Eynsham, *Magna Vita Sancti Hugonis*, ed. D. L. Douie and H. Farmer, 2 vols (Clarendon Press: Oxford, 1985), vol. 1, p. 117.
16. Walter Map, *De Nugis Curialium*, pp. 476–86.
17. *Chronicon Monasterii de Bello*, ed. J. S. Brewer (London, 1846), pp. 105–9 (cit. W. L. Warren, *Henry II* (London, 1973), p. 327).

18. Warren, *Henry II*, p. 132.
19. N. Vincent, 'The Court of Henry II', in *Henry II: New Interpretations*, pp. 306–8.
20. J. Southworth, *Fools and Jesters at the English Court* (Stroud, 1998), p. 339.
21. Warren, *Henry II*, p. 630.
22. J. Gillingham, *The Angevin Empire* (Arnold: London, 2001), p. 230.
23. Gerald of Wales, *Giraldi Cambrensis Opera*, viii, p. 159.
24. *The Chronicle of Battle Abbey*, ed. and trans. E. Searle (Oxford, 1980), p. 186.
25. A. J. Duggan, 'Henry II, the English Church and the Papacy', in *Henry II: New Interpretations*, p. 168.
26. William FitzStephen, *Vita Sanctae Thomae*, iii, p. 45.
27. William FitzStephen, *Vita Sanctae Thomae*, iii, p. 430.
28. R. Barber, *Thomas Becket* (London, 1986), p. 273.
29. Ralph de Diceto, *Historical Works*, ed. W. Stubbs, Rolls Series, 2 vols (London, 1876), i, p. 33.
30. Roger of Howden, *Gesta Henrici II et Riccardi I*, ed. W. Stubbs, Rolls Series, 2 vols (London, 1867), i, p. 292.
31. Walter Map, *De Nugis Curialium*, p. 282.
32. K. Norgate, *England and the Angevin Empire*, 2 vols (London, 1889), ii, p. 231.
33. *Histoire de Guillaume le Maréchal*, ed. P. Meyer, 3 vols (Paris, 1891–1901), i, lines 8831–50.
34. Gerald of Wales, *Giraldi Cambrensis Opera*, viii, p. 296.

3. The Lionheart – Richard I

1. *Poetria Nova of Geoffrey de Vinsauf*, trans. M. F. Nims (Toronto, 1967), pp. 28–31; quoted by J. Gillingham, *Richard I* (New Haven and London, 1998).
2. William of Newburgh, *The History of English Affairs: Book IV*.
3. Howden, *Gesta Henrici II*, ii, pp. 146–7.
4. Gillingham, *Richard I*, p. 263.
5. Eynsham, *Magna Vita*, ii, p. 105.
6. Beha ed-Din, *What Befell Sultan Yusuf*, trans. C. W. Wilson, Palestine Pilgrims; Text Society, 13 vols (London, 1897), xiii, pp. 375–6.

7. Beha ed-Din, *What Befell Sultan Yusuf*, xiii, pp. 375–6.
8. Howden, *Gesta Henrici II*, iii, p. 216.
9. Howden, *Gesta Henrici II*, iii, p. 142.
10. Howden, *Gesta Henrici II*, ii, p. 245.
11. *History of William Marshal*, ed. A. J. Holden and trans. S. Gregory (Anglo-Norman Text Society: London, 2002–6), ii, lines 110409–110411.
12. K. Norgate, *Richard the Lion Heart* (London, 1924), p. 322.
13. Howden, *Gesta Henrici II*, iv, pp. 58–9.
14. Howden, *Gesta Henrici II*, iv, pp. 82–3.
15. Eynsham, *Magna Vita*, ii, p. 136.
16. Howden, *Gesta Henrici II*, iv, p. 84.
17. *History of William Marshal*, ii, line 11766.
18. J. France, *Western Warfare in the Age of the Crusades 1100–1300* (London, 1999), p. 142.

4. The Madman – John

1. Macaulay, *History of England*, i, p. 15.
2. *Chronica Majora*, ed. H. R. Luard, 7 vols, Rolls Series (London, 1872), ii, p. 669.
3. J. Gillingham, 'Historians without Hindsight: Coggeshall, Diceto and Howden on the Early Years of John's Reign', in *King John: New Interpretations*, ed. S. D. Church (Boydell Press: Woodbridge, 1999), pp. 1–26.
4. *History of William Marshal*, ed. A. J. Holden, trans. S. Gregory, 3 vols (Anglo-Norman Text Society: London, 2004–6), ii, lines 11904–7.
5. *Annals of Barnwell Priory*, in *Memoriale Walteri de Coventeria*, ed. W. Stubbs, Rolls Series (London, 1872–3), ii, p. 196.
6. *The Historical Works of Gervase of Canterbury*, ed. W. Stubbs, Rolls Series, 2 vols (London, 1879–90), ii, pp. 92–3.
7. *Chronica Rogeri de Wendover liber qui dicitur Flores Historiarum*, ed. H. G. Hewlett, 3 vols, Rolls Series (London, 1886–9), ii, pp. 48–9.
8. D. Power, 'King John and the Norman Aristocracy', in *King John: New Interpretations*, pp. 135–6.
9. *Chronica Rogeri de Wendover*, i, pp. 316–17.

10. *Radulphi de Coggeshall, Chronicon Anglicanum*, ed. J. Stevenson, Rolls Series (London, 1875), p. 144.

11. *Gervase of Canterbury*, ii, pp. 97–8.

12. W. L. Warren, *King John* (Eyre & Spottiswoode: London, 1961), p. 125.

13. Gillingham, *The Angevin Empire*, p. 85.

14. Howden, *Gesta Henrici II*, iii, p. 198.

15. *Gervase of Canterbury*, ii, p. lix.

16. S. Painter, *The Reign of King John* (Johns Hopkins Press: Baltimore, 1949), pp. 231–2.

17. *Chronica Majora*, ii, pp. 560–3.

18. N. Vincent, 'Isabella of Angoulême', in *King John: New Interpretations*, p. 166.

19. Adam of Eynsham, *Magna Vita*, ii, pp. 143–4.

20. Adam of Eynsham, *Magna Vita*, ii, p. 141.

21. Adam of Eynsham, *Magna Vita*, ii, p. 185.

22. C. Harper-Bill, 'John and the Church of Rome', in *King John: New Interpretations*, p. 306.

23. R. V. Turner, 'John and Justice', in S. D. Church (ed.), *King John: New Interpretations*, p. 319.

24. *Chronica Rogeri de Wendover*, ii, p. 50.

25. S. Duffy, 'John and Ireland, the Origin of England's Irish Problem', in *King John: New Approaches*, p. 242.

26. *Annals of Barnwell Priory*, ii, p. 203.

27. *Chronica Rogeri de Wendover*, ii, p. 248.

28. Painter, *The Reign of King John*, pp. 249–50.

29. Warren, *King John*, p. 191.

30. *Chronica Rogeri de Wendover*, ii, p. 263.

31. Holt, *Magna Carta*, quoted by Turner in *King John: New Interpretations*, p. 320.

32. Harper-Bill, 'King John and the Church of Rome', in *King John: New Interpretations*, p. 310.

33. *Chronica Majora*, ii, p. 559.

34. N. Vincent, *Peter des Roches: An Alien in English Politics 1205–1238* (Cambridge, 1996).

35. *Chronica Rogeri de Wendover*, ii, p. 155.

36. Ralph of Coggeshall, *[Radulphi of Coggeshall] Chronicon Anglia-canum*, ed. J. Stevenson, Rolls Series (London, 1875), i, p. 172.

37. *Chronica Majora*, ii, p. 611.
38. *Chronica Rogeri de Wendover*, iii, pp. 320, 321.
39. *Chronica Majora*, ii, pp. 641–2.
40. *Chronica Rogeri de Wendover*, iii, p. 384.

5. The Aesthete – Henry III

1. F. W. Maitland, *The Constitutional History of England* (Cambridge University Press: Cambridge, 1908), p. 70.
2. *Histoire de Guillaume le Maréschal*, ii, lines 1891–1901.
3. Stubbs, *Select Charters*, ii, pp. 102–3.
4. M. Powicke, *The Thirteenth Century, 1216–1307* (Clarendon Press: Oxford, 1963), p. 19.
5. *Chronica Rogeri de Wendover*, iv, p. 263.
6. *Chronica Majora*, iii, p. 272.
7. D. A. Carpenter, 'King, Magnates and Society: The Personal Rule of Henry III', in *The Reign of Henry III* (Hambledon Press: London and Rio Grande, 1996), pp. 75–106.
8. *Chronica Majora*, ii, p. 334.
9. P. Binski, *Westminster Abbey and the Plantagenets* (Yale University Press: New Haven and London, 1995), p. 45.
10. D. A. Carpenter, 'Matthew Paris and Henry III's Speech at the Exchequer in October 1256', in *The Reign of Henry III*, pp. 137–50.
11. *Chronica Majora*, iv, pp. 181–4.
12. N. Vincent, 'Isabella of Angoulême: John's Jezebel', in *King John: New Interpretations*, p. 210.
13. *Chronica Majora*, iv, pp. 209–12.
14. Henry III: letter to Emperor Frederick II, September 1242, *Close Rolls*, 1237–1242, pp. 530–2.
15. D. A. Carpenter, 'What Happened in 1258?', in *The Reign of Henry III*, p. 183.
16. *Chronica Majora*, v, p. 601.
17. *Annals of Barton*, p. 399.
18. *Chronica Majora*, v, p. 457.
19. Carpenter, 'What Happened in 1258?', p. 183.
20. *Annals of Tewkesbury* in *Annales Monastici*, ed. H. R. Luard, Rolls Series, 5 vols (London, 1864–9), i, pp. 163–4.
21. *Chronica Majora*, v, p. 696.

22. *Annals of Barton*, p. 429.
23. *Annals of Tewkesbury*, i, p. 164.
24. Stubbs, *Select Charters*, ii, p. 103.
25. *Chronica Majora*, v, p. 706.
26. *The Chronicle of William de Rishanger of the Barons' War*, ed. J. Halliwell (Camden Society: London, 1840), pp. 32–34.
27. *Chronica de Mailros*, ed. J. Stevenson (Bannatyne Club: Edinburgh, 1835), p. 200.
28. *Narratio de Bellis*, p. 6.
29. *Annals of Osney*, in *Annales Monastici*, iv, p. 160.
30. Stubbs, *Select Charters*, iv, p. 160.
31. J. S. Hamilton, *The Plantagenets, History of a Dynasty* (Continuum: London and New York, 2010), p. 22.
32. Powicke, *The Thirteenth Century*, p. 19.

6. The Hammer – Edward I

1. Powicke, *The Thirteenth Century*, p. 228.
2. *The Chronicle of Pierre de Langtoft*, ed. T. Wright, 2 vols (London, 1868), ii, p. 354.
3. H. G. Robinson and G. Sayes, 'The Scottish Parliaments of Edward I', *Scottish Historical Review*, 25, pp. 311–16.
4. T. F. Tout, *Edward I* (London, 1896), p. 88.
5. Maitland, *Constitutional History*, p. 19.
6. Stubbs, *Select Charters*, ii, p. 104.
7. *Nicolai Triveti Annales*, ed. T. Hogg (London, 1845), p. 282.
8. M. Prestwich, *Edward I* (London, 1988), p. 123.
9. *Chronicle of Walter of Guisborough*, ed. H. Rothwell (London, 1957), p. 216.
10. J. E. Morris, *The Welsh Wars of Edward I* (Oxford, 1901), pp. 110–48.
11. *Langtoft*, ii, p. 169.
12. *Langtoft*, ii, p. 177.
13. M. Prestwich, *Plantagenet England 1225–1361* (Oxford, 2005), p. 163.
14. Maitland, *Constitutional History*, p. 69.
15. 'Peter Langtoft's Chronicle', trans. Robert Mannyng, in *The Works of Thomas Hearne* (London, 1810), iv, p. 252.

16. *Langtoft*, ii, p. 199.
17. *Langtoft*, ii, p. 316.
18. Chaplais, 'Some Private Letters of Edward I', *English Historical Review*, 77 (1962), p. 85.
19. *Langtoft*, ii, p. 289.
20. *Chronicle of Walter of Guisborough*, pp. 289–90.
21. Stubbs, *Select Charters*, ii, p. 141.
22. Prestwich, *Edward I*, p. 257.
23. *Langtoft*, ii, pp. 266–7.
24. *Chronicon de Lanercost 1272–1346*, ed. Sir H. Maxwell (Glasgow, 1913), p. 190.
25 Powicke, *The Thirteenth Century*, p. 229.
26. G. W. S. Barrow, *Robert the Bruce and the Community of the Realm of Scotland* (London, 1965), pp. 181–2.
27. *Chronicle of Walter of Guisborough*, pp. 382–3.
28. *Langtoft*, ii, p. 326.
29. Prestwich, *Edward I*, p. 156.
30. T. F. Tout, *The Place of Edward II in History* (Manchester, 1936), pp. 33–4.

7. The Changeling – Edward II

1. T. F. Tout, 'The Captivity and Death of Edward of Caernarvon', in *Collected Papers of Thomas Frederick Tout* (Manchester, 1934), iii, p. 146.
2. Sir Thomas Gray, *Scalachronica*, trans. Sir H. Maxwell (Glasgow, 1907), p. 69.
3. *Chronicon de Lanercost*, pp. 247–8.
4. Stubbs, *Select Charters*, ii, p. 328.
5. Tout, *The Place of Edward II*, p. 11.
6. R. M. Haines, *King Edward II* (Montreal and Kingston, 2003), p. x.
7. *Vita Secundi, the life of Edward the Second*, ed. W. R. Childs (Clarendon Press: Oxford, 2005).
8. *Annales Paulini*, in *Chronicles of the Reigns of Edward I and Edward II*, ed. W. Stubbs, 2 vols (London, 1882), i, p. 262.
9. *Polychronicon Ranulphi Higden monachi Cestrensis*, 9 vols, Rolls Series (London, 1864–6), vii, pp. 299–301.
10. H. Johnstone, 'The Eccentricities of Edward II', *English Historical Review*, 48 (1933), p. 265.

11. Prestwich, *Plantagenet England*, p. 181.
12. Tout, *Place of Edward II*, p. 156.
13. Tout, *Place of Edward II*, pp. 14–17.
14. *Vita*, p. 16.
15. *Vita*, p. 48.
16. *Vita*, p. 62.
17. Hamilton, *The Plantagenets*, p. 119.
18. J. J. Norwich, *Shakespeare's Kings and Queens* (London, 1999), p. 16.
19. Tout, *Place of Edward II*, p. 17.
20. *Vita*, p. 148.
21. *Vita*, p. 176.
22. P. Doherty, *Isabella and the Strange Death of Edward II* (London, 2003), p. 66.
23. *Vita*, pp. 164, 166.
24. *Vita*, pp. 194, 196.
25. Tout, *Place of Edward II*, p. 135.
26. *Vita*, p. 194.
27. *Vita*, p. 230.
28. *Vita*, p. 230.
29. Tout, *Place of Edward II*, p. 143.
30. *Oeuvres de Froissart: Chroniques*, ed. J. Kervyn de Lettenhove, 28 vols (Brussels, 1867–77), ii, p. 88.
31. Robert of Reading, *Flores Historiarum*, 3 vols, Rolls Series (London, 1890), iii, p. 229.
32. Doherty, *Isabella*, p. 101.
33. A. Weir, *Queen Isabella: Treachery, Adultery and Murder in Medieval Books* (New York, 2006), p. 14.
34. *Vita*, p. 242.
35. *Vita*, p. 242.
36. *Vita*, pp. 244–6.
37. *Annales Paulini*, i, p. 317.
38. R. Fabyan, *New Chronicles of England and France*, ed. H. Ellis (London, 1811), p. 430.
39. Doherty, *Isabella*, pp. 115–25.
40. *Chronicon Galfredi le Baker de Swynebroke*, ed. E. M. Thompson (Oxford, 1889), p. 33.
41. Haines, *King Edward II*, pp. 221–2.
42. Tout, *Edward I*, p. 225.
43. Hamilton, *The Plantagenets*, p. 133.

8. The Paladin – Edward III

1. *The Brut or The Chronicles of England*, ed. F. W. D. Brie, 2 vols (London, 1908), ii, p. 333.
2. *Oeuvres de Froissart*, v, pp. 260–1.
3. Stubbs, *Select Charters*, ii, p. 394.
4. W. M. Ormrod, *Edward III* (London and Newhaven, 2011), p. 577.
5. *Scalacronica: The Reigns of Edward I, Edward II and Edward III as Recorded by Sir Thomas Gray*, trans. Sir H. Maxwell (Glasgow, 1907), p. 85.
6. *Scalacronica*, p. 86
7. *Galfridus le Baker de Swynebroke*, p. 46.
8. Haines, *Edward II*, p. 347.
9. *The Brut*, quoted by C. J. Rogers, in *The Wars of Edward III, Sources and Interpretations* (Woodbridge, 1999), p. 38.
10. *Rotuli Parliamentarum*, quoted by Rogers, in *The Wars of Edward III*, pp. 83–4.
11. R. Horrox, *The Black Death* (Manchester, 1994), p. 147.
12. M. McKisack, *The Fourteenth Century 1307–1399* (Oxford, 1959).
13. *The St Albans Chronicle: The 'Chronica Majora' of Thomas Walsingham*, ed. J. Taylor, W. R. Childs and I. Watkiss (Oxford, 2003), i, p. 43.
14. W. M. Ormrod, 'Who was Alice Perrers?', *Chaucer Review*, 40 (2006), pp. 219–29.
15. *St Albans Chronicle*, i, p. 57.
16. *St Albans Chronicle*, i, p. 11.
17. *St Albans Chronicle*, i, p. 102.
18. Ormrod, *Edward III*, p. 6.

9. The Absolutist – Richard II

1. Maitland, *Constitutional History*, pp. 197–9.
2. *St Albans Chronicle*, i, p. 137.
3. *Oeuvres de Froissart*, ix, p. 386.
4. *St Albans Chronicle*, i, p. 441.
5. McKisack, *The Fourteenth Century*, p. 420.

6. A. Steel, *Richard II* (Cambridge University Press: Cambridge, 1941), pp. 41–2, 203–4.
7. N. Saul, *Richard II* (Yale University Press: New Haven and London, 1997), p. 465.
8. J. Harvey, *The Plantagenets* (London, 1948), p. 96.
9. A. Strickland, *The Lives of the Queens of England*, 12 vols (London, 1840–8), ii, p. 430.
10. Strickland, *Lives of the Queens of England*, ii, p. 430.
11. *Knighton's Chronicle*, ed. and trans. G. H. Martin (Oxford, 1995), p. 360.
12. *Oeuvres de Froissart*, x, p. 235.
13. Saul, *Richard II*, p. 123.
14. *Knighton's Chronicle*, p. 531.
15. *Oeuvres de Froissart*, xvi, p. 5.
16. Strickland, *Lives of the Queens of England*, ii, p. 430.
17. *Oeuvres de Froissart*, xvi, pp. 2–5.
18. *Oeuvres de Froissart*, xvi, p. 136.
19. *Oeuvres de Froissart*, xvi, pp. 15–16.
20. *The Chronicle of Adam of Usk 1377–1421*, trans. C. Given-Wilson (Oxford, 1977), p. 28.
21. *Oeuvres de Froissart*, xvi, p. 83.
22. M. V. Clarke and V. H. Galbraith, 'The Deposition of Richard II', *Bulletin of the John Ryland Library*, 14 (1930), pp. 163–4, cited in Saul, *Richard II*, p. 394.
23. *Chronicle of Adam of Usk*, p. 48.
24. Saul, *Richard II*, pp. 385–7.
25. K. B. McFarlane, *Lancastrian Kings and Lollard Knights* (Oxford, 1972), p. 46.
26. Saul, *Richard II*, p. 403.
27. *Oeuvres de Froissart*, xvi, pp. 156–9.
28. *Chronicle of Adam of Usk*, p. 52.
29. *Oeuvres de Froissart*, xvi, pp. 173, 175.
30. *Oeuvres de Froissart*, xvi, pp. 196–7.
31. *Chronicle of Adam of Usk*, p. 64.
32. *Oeuvres de Froissart*, xvi, pp. 202–3.
33. *St Albans Chronicle*, ii, p. 206.
34. *Chronicle of Adam of Usk*, p. 78.
35. *Oeuvres de Froissart*, xvi, pp. 235–6.

10. The Usurper – Henry IV

1. McFarlane, *Lancastrian Kings*, p. 7.
2. E. de Monstrelet, *La Cronique d'Enguerrand de Monstrelet*, ed. L. Drouët d'Arcq, 4 vols (Paris, 1857–60), ii, p. 338.
3. M. Bennett, 'Henry IV, the Royal Succession and the Crisis of 1406', in *The Reign of Henry IV: Rebellion and Revival* (York, 2008), p. 14.
4. *Chronicle of Adam of Usk*, p. 136.
5. Stubbs, *Select Charters*, iii, p. 9.
6. *Oeuvres de Froissart*, xvi, p. 229.
7. *Oeuvres de Froissart*, xvi, p. 232.
8. C. J. Neville, 'Scotland, the Percies and the Law in 1400', in *The Reign of Henry IV: The Establishment of the Regime 1399– 1406*, ed. G. Dodd and D. Biggs (York Medieval Press 2003), p. 89.
9. *St Albans Chronicle*, ii, p. 334.
10. C. Given-Wilson, 'The Quarrels of Old Women: Henry IV, Louis of Orleans and Anglo-French Chivalric Challenges in the Early Fifteenth Century', in *The Reign of Henry IV: The Establishment of the Regime 1399–1406*, ed. G. Dodd and D. Biggs (York Medieval Press, 2003), pp. 32–6.
11. Stubbs, *Select Charters*, iii, p. 7.
12. Stubbs, *Select Charters*, iii, p. 8.
13. McFarlane, *Lancastrian Kings*, p. 2.
14. J. Capgrave, *The Chronicle of England*, ed. F. C. Hingeston, Rolls Series (London, 1858), p. 291.
15. Stubbs, *Select Charters*, iii, p. 39.
16. McFarlane, *Lancastrian Kings*, p. 23.
17. H. C. Hingeston, *Royal and International Letters during the Reign of Henry IV* (London, 1860), i, p. 149.
18. *St Albans Chronicle*, ii, p. 338.
19. J. Nuttall, '"Vostre Humble Matatyas": Culture, Politics and the Percys', in *The Fifteenth Century*, vol. 5: *Of Mice and Men: Image, Belief and Regulation in Late Medieval England*, ed. L. Clark (Boydell Press, 2005), pp. 79–83.
20. *The Brut*, i, pp. 75–6.
21. W. M. Ormrod, 'The Rebellion of Archbishop Scrope and the Tradition of Opposition to Royal Taxation', in *The Reign of*

Henry IV: Rebellion and Survival, 1403–1413, ed. G. Dodd and D. Biggs (York, 2008), p. 162.

22. Capgrave, *Chronicle of England*, p. 291.
23. *St Albans Chronicle*, ii, p. 326.
24. A. J. Pollard, Introduction to *Henry IV: Rebellion and Survival*, p. 4.
25. D. Biggs, 'The Politics of Health: Henry IV and the Long Parliament of 1406', in *The Reign of Henry IV: The Establishment of the Regime, 1399–1406*, p. 199.
26. J. L. Kirby, *Henry IV of England* (London, 1970), pp. 202–4.
27. *St Albans Chronicle*, ii, p. 534.
28. *Chronicle of Adam of Usk*, p. 242.
29. *Royal Wills: A Collection of All the Wills Known to be Extant of the Kings and Queens of England*, ed. J. Nichols (London, 1780; New York, 1969), p. 203.
30. *The First English Life of King Henry the Fifth*, ed. C. L. Kingsford (Oxford, 1911), p. 14
31. *St Albans Chronicle*, ii, pp. 608–10.
32. *St Albans Chronicle*, ii, pp. 612, 614.
33. *The Brut*, ii, p. 207.
34. Capgrave, *Chronicle of England*, pp. 302–3.

11. The 'Gleaming King' – Henry V

1. *The First English Life*, p. 131.
2. Stubbs, *Select Charters*, iii, p. 77.
3. McFarlane, *Lancastrian Kings*, p. 133.
4. *Chronique du Réligieux de Saint-Denys 1380–1422*, ed. F. Bellaguet, 6 vols (Paris, 1839–54), iv, p. 770.
5. T. B. Pugh, *Henry V and the Southampton Plot of 1415* (Southampton, 1988), p. 80.
6. *St Albans Chronicle*, ii, p. 636.
7. Pugh, *Henry V and the Southampton Plot*, p. 162.
8. McFarlane, *Lancastrian Kings*, p. 131.
9. E. F. Jacob, *The Fifteenth Century 1399–1485* (Oxford, 1961), p. 121.
10. *Chronique du Réligieux de Saint-Denis*, vi, p. 381.
11. *The First English Life*, p. 5.

12. *The First English Life*, p. 14.
13. *The First English Life*, p. 17.
14. Capgrave, *Chronicle of England*, p. 311.
15. Capgrave, *Chronicle of England*, p. 311.
16. *The First English Life*, p. 51.
17. *The Brut*, ii, p. 378.
18. *Chronique de Jean Lefevre, Seigneur de Saint-Rémy*, ed. F. Morand, 2 vols (Paris, 1876–8), pp. 245–6, 251.
19. *The Chronicle of John Hardyng*, ed. H. Ellis (London, 1812), p. 375.
20. E. Halle, *The Union of the Two Noble and Illustre Families of Lancastre and Yorke* (London, [1548] 1809), p. 70.
21. *Chronicle of Adam of Usk*, p. 262.
22. *Chronicle of Adam of Usk*, p. 258.
23. J. Page, 'The Siege of Rouen', in *The Historical Collections of a Citizen of London* (Camden Society: London, 1876), pp. 4–5.
24. *The First English Life*, pp. 131–2.
25. J. Waurin, *Recueil des croniques et des anchiennes istoires de la Grant Bretaigne*, ed. W. Hardy, 5 vols, Rolls Series (London, 1864–91), ii, p. 429.
26. *Chronicle of Adam of Usk*, p. 270.
27. J. Juvénal des Ursins, *Histoire de Charles VI*, ed. J. A. C. Buchon (Paris, 1836), p. 561.
28. *St Albans Chronicle*, ii, p. 772.
29. *Vita et Gesti Henrici Quinti*, ed. T. Hearn (Oxford, 1727), p. 334.
30. *St Albans Chronicle*, ii, p. 772.

12. The Holy Fool – Henry VI

1. Philippe de Commynes, *Mémoires*, ed. J. Calmette, 3 vols (Paris, 1924–5).
2. *Henry the Sixth: A Reprint of John Blacman's Memoir*, trans. M. R. James (Cambridge University Press: Cambridge, 1919), pp. 26, 37.
3. B. Wolfe, *Henry VI* (Eyre Methuen: London, 1985), pp. 3–21.
4. T. S. Freeman, '"*Ut Verus Christus Sequetur*": John Blacman and the Cult of Henry VI', in *The Fifteenth Century*, vol. 5: *Of Mice and Men*, p. 142.

5. A. H. Nicholas, *A Chronicle of London* (London, 1827), pp. 111–2.
6. G. Harriss, *Cardinal Beaufort* (Clarendon Press: Oxford, 1988), p. 209.
7. *The Paston Letters*, ed. G. Gairdner (Sutton: Gloucester, 1986), ii, p. 131.
8. J. M. Harvey, *Jack Cade's Rebellion 1450* (Oxford, 1991), pp. 188–9.
9. *Gregory's Chronicle*, in *The Historical Collections of a Citizen of London in the Fifteenth Century*, ed. J. Gairdner (Camden Society: London, 1876), pp. 190–4.
10. *Henry the Sixth: A Reprint of John Blacman's Memoir*, p. 15.
11. M. Hicks, *The Wars of the Roses* (Yale University Press: New Haven and London, 2010), pp. 77–82.
12. G. Harriss, *Shaping the Nation: England 1360–1461* (Clarendon Press: Oxford, 2005), p. 611.
13. B. André, 'Historia Regis Henrici VII', in *Memorials of King Henry VII*, ed. J. Gairdner, Rolls Series (London, 1858), x.
14. Wolfe, *Henry VI*, pp. 134–5.
15. R. A. Griffiths, *The Reign of King Henry VI* (University of California Press: Berkeley, 1981), p. 242.
16. *Henry the Sixth: A Reprint of John Blacman's Memoir*, pp. 15–16.
17. Sir J. Harington, *Nugae Antiquae*, ed. T. Park (London, 1804).
18. Harriss, *Shaping the Nation*, p. 260.
19. Hicks, *The Wars of the Roses*, p. 118.
20. *Paston Letters*, iii, p. 270.
21. *Paston Letters*, iii, p. 322.
22. Hicks, *The Wars of the Roses*, p. 78.
23. *An English Chronicle 1377–1461: A New Edition*, ed. W. Marx (Boydell Press: Woodbridge, 2003), p. 78.
24. *Rotuli Parliamentorum*, 6 vols (London, 1767), v, pp. 375–9.
25. *Henry the Sixth: A Reprint of John Blacman's Memoir*, p. 22.
26. Harriss, *Shaping the Nation*, p. 649.
27. *Calendar of State Papers and Manuscripts existing in the Archives and Collections of Milan*, ed. A. B. Hinds (HMSO: Hereford, 1912), p. 58.
28. *Henry the Sixth: A Reprint of John Blacman's Memoir*, p. 18.
29. J. Warkworth, *A Chronicle of the First Thirteen Years of the Reign*

of King Edward IV, ed. J. O. Halliwell, Camden Society 10 (London, 1839), p. 11.

30. Hicks, *The Wars of the Roses*, p. 82.
31. P. Vergil, *Three Books of Polydore Vergil's English History*, ed. H. Ellis, Camden Society 29 (London, 1844), p. 135.
32. Warkworth, *A Chronicle of the First Thirteen Years*, p. 21.
33. Shakespeare, *The Life and Death of King Richard III*, Act I, scene i.
34. Stubbs, *Select Charters*, iii, pp. 134–5.
35. A. F. Gasquet, *The Religious Life of King Henry VI* (London, 1923).

13. The Self-Made King – Edward IV

1. Green, *History of the English People*, ii, p. 28.
2. Stubbs, *Select Charters*, iii, p. 226.
3. Sir Thomas More, *The History of King Richard the Third*, ed. R. S. Sylvester (London and New Haven, 1963), pp. 4–5.
4. E. Hall, *Chronicle*, ed. H. Ellis (London, 1809).
5. C. Ross, *The Wars of the Roses: A Concise History* (London, 1976), p. 140.
6. Commynes, *Mémoires*, i, p. 202.
7. G. Goodwyn, *Fatal Colours: Towton 1461 – England's Most Brutal Battle* (London, 2010), pp. 198–9.
8. *Rotuli Parliamentorum*, v, pp. 462–3.
9. *Calendar of State Papers . . . Milan*, pp. 74–7.
10. Stubbs, *Select Charters*, iii, p. 289.
11. A. J. Pollard, *Late Medieval England 1399–1485* (Harlow, 1988), p. 274.
12. D. Mancini, *The Usurpation of Richard III*, trans. and ed. C. A. J. Armstrong (Oxford, 1938), p. 80.
13. *The Great Chronicle of London*, ed. A. H. Thomas and I. D. Thornley (London, 1938), p. 223.
14. More, *History of King Richard the Third*, p. 64.
15. More, *History of King Richard the Third*, p. 53.
16. *Ingulf's Chronicle of the Abbey of Croyland*, trans. and ed. H. R. Riley (London, 1854), pp. 469–70.
17. *Paston Letters*, iii, p. 400.

18. Warkworth, *A Chronicle of the First Thirteen Years*, p. 12.

19. *Historie of the Arrivall of Edward IV in England and the finall Recovery of his kingdomes from Henry VI*, ed. J. A. Bruce (Camden Society: London, 1838), p. 38.

20. S. B. Chrimes, 'The only imp now left of Henry VI's brood?', in *Henry VII* (London, 1972), p. 18.

21. *The Works of Sir John Fortescue, Knight, Chief Justice, Lord Chancellor to King Henry the Sixth of England*, ed. Lord Clermont, 2 vols (London, 1869), ii, p. 474.

22. *Ingulf's Chronicle of the Abbey of Croyland*, pp. 469–70.

23. *Calendar of State Papers . . . Milan*, p. 189.

24. More, *History of King Richard the Third*, pp. 5–6.

25. Mancini, *Usurpation of Richard III*, p. 82.

26. Mancini, *Usurpation of Richard III*, p. 72.

27. D. Grummitt, *The Wars of the Roses* (London, 2013), pp. 112, 130.

28. More, *History of King Richard the Third*, pp. 5–6.

14. The Suicide – Richard III

1. Stubbs, *Select Charters*, iii, p. 232.

2. More, *History of King Richard the Third*, p. 10.

3. Mancini, *Usurpation of Richard III*, p. 100.

4. Stubbs, *Select Charters*, iii, p. 232.

5. C. Ross, *Richard III* (London, 1981), p. 22.

6. Ross, *Richard III*, p. 27.

7. M. Hicks, 'The Last Days of Elizabeth, Countess of Oxford', in *Richard III and his Rivals* (London and Rio Grande, 1991), pp. 97–316.

8. *Ingulf's Chronicle of the Abbey of Croyland*, p. 407.

9. Stubbs, *Select Charters*, iii, p. 231.

10. Whitelaw's speech in George Buck, *The History of King Richard the Third*, ed. A. N. Kincaid (Gloucester, 1979), p. 206.

11. *British Library Harleian Manuscript 433*, ed. R. Horrox and P. W. Hammond. 4 vols (Richard III Society, 1979–82), 2, p. 71.

12. More, *History of King Richard the Third*, p. 55.

13. Quoted in A. Hanham, *Richard III and his Early Historians* (Oxford, 1975), p. 50.

14. H. Ellis, *Original Letters Illustrative of English History*, 11 vols (London, 1824–46), 2nd series, pp. 159–60.
15. Ross, *Richard III*, p. xliii.
16. *Ingulf's Chronicle of the Abbey of Croyland*, pp. 496–7.
17. Grummit, *Wars of the Roses*, p. 103.
18. More, *History of King Richard the Third*, p. 90.
19. R. Horrox, *Richard III* (Cambridge, 1989), p. 278.
20. *Ingulf's Chronicle of the Abbey of Croyland*, p. 498.
21. *Ingulf's Chronicle of the Abbey of Croyland*, p. 499.
22. *Acts of Court of the Mercers' Company 1453–1577*, ed. F. Lyell and F. Watney (Cambridge, 1936), pp. 173–4.
23. C. Halsted, *Richard III as Duke of Gloucester and King of England* (London, 1844), p. 556.
24. G. Foard, 'Bosworth Uncovered', *BBC History Magazine* (March 2010).
25. *Ingulf's Chronicle of the Abbey of Croyland*, p. 504.
26. *Three Books of Polydore Vergil's English History*, p. 14.
27. *The Great Chronicle of London*, p. 238.

Index

Achard of Chalus 42
Acre 36, 37, 38, 92
Adam of Eynsham 51–2
Adam of Murimuth 119
Adam of Usk 185, 188, 189, 207, 221, 290
Adrian IV, Pope 22, 24
Agincourt, battle of (1415) 19–21, 227
Albemarle, Earl of 68
Alexander II, King of Scots 64
Alexander III, King of Scots 93, 108
Alexander III, Pope 22, 23
Alexander IV, Pope 77, 81
Alfred the Great 240
Alice of France 28, 29, 30, 34
Angers xvii, 3
Anglo-Saxon Chronicle 6, 7, 11
Anne of Bohemia, Queen consort of
    England 175–6, 179, 180
Appellant, Lords 178–9, 183–4, 186, 194
Arnulf, Bishop of Séez 9–10
Arthur of Brittany 34, 45, 46–7, 56
Arthurian legend 20, 96, 97, 154
Arundel, Richard Fitzalan, Earl of 158,
    176, 177, 178, 180, 184, 185, 189,
    190, 194
Arundel, Thomas, Archbishop of
    Canterbury 177, 179, 184, 187, 188,
    195, 198, 199, 204, 207, 212
Assize of Clarendon 16
Audley, Hugh 130, 133

Badby, John 211
Badlesmere, Bartholomew, Lord 130, 131,
    133, 133–4, 135
Baibars, Sultan 92, 93
Bale, John, Bishop of Ossory 289

Ball, John 172, 173
Balliol, Edward, King of Scotland 151–3,
    164
Balliol, John, King of Scotland 109–10, 112
Bamburgh 246, 255, 275
Bannockburn, battle of (1314) 117, 127,
    128, 129, 152
Bardolf, Thomas, Lord 205, 206
Barnet, battle of (1471) 263–4, 273
Beatrice of Savoy 73
Beaufort, Henry, Bishop of Winchester
    207, 212, 222, 235
Beaufort, Lady Margaret 281–2, 286
Beaulieu Abbey 52
Beaumont, Louis de, Bishop of Durham 129
Becket, Thomas 14, 21, 22, 23, 23–4, 25,
    26, 96, 122, 199, 209
Bedford, John, Duke of 198, 212, 222,
    225, 226, 229, 234, 235
Bek, Anthony, Bishop of Durham 112
benevolences 266, 282
Bentley, Walter 163
Berengaria of Navarre, Queen consort of
    England 28, 34, 35, 36, 42
Berkeley Castle 142
Berners, Sir James 178
Bertran de Born 27–8
Berwick 126, 127, 132, 152, 246, 276
Black Death 161, 162, 173
Blacman, John 233–4, 239, 240
Blanche of Castile, Queen consort of
    France 63
Blanche of Lancaster 171
Blondel, minstrel 39
Bohun, Mary de 193, 198
Boisratier, Archbishop Guillaume 213, 214

Boniface, Archbishop of Canterbury 73
Boniface VIII, Pope 112, 113
Bosworth, battle of (1485) 286–7
Bourchier, Thomas, Archbishop of
    Canterbury 280
Bracton, Henry de 68
Bramham Moor, battle of (1408) 206
Brandon, Sir William 283
Breauté, Falkes de 68
Bretagne, Gilles de 236–7, 239–40
Briouze, William de 56
Bruce, Mary 114
Bruce, Robert (later, Robert I, King of
    Scotland) 91, 114–15, 116, 117, 126,
    127, 132, 136, 149
Bruton, John 214
Bryant, Arthur 291–2
Buchan, Isabel, Countess of 114
Buchan, John xviii–xix
Buckingham, Henry Stafford, Duke of
    279, 280, 281, 282
Buckingham, Humphrey Stafford, Duke
    of 245
Burgh, Hubert de 60, 64, 67, 68, 70–1, 72
Burley, Sir Simon 178, 179, 185, 194
Burnell, Robert, Bishop of Bath and Wells
    94, 99, 105
Burstwick 122
Bury, Richard 150
Bury St Edmunds 12–13, 53, 60
Bussy, Sir John 184, 188, 195
Butler, Lady Eleanor 257, 280

Cade, Jack 237, 244, 246, 260
Caernarfon Castle 103
Calais 160–1, 162, 166, 168, 205, 228,
    238, 242, 247, 252, 267
Calais, burghers of 160–1
Calveley, Sir Hugh 163
Cambridge, Richard of Conisburgh, Earl
    of 214
Camoys, Lord 219
Camulio, Prospero di 246, 255
canon law 22–3, 46, 99
Capetians 70, 71
Capgrave, John 197, 202, 204, 217, 218,
    257
Carthusians 174, 216, 227, 240
Catesby, William 277, 283, 284
Catherine of Valois, Queen consort of
    England 215, 225, 226, 229, 253
Chandos, Sir John 147, 163
Channel Islands 68
Charles III, King of France (the Simple) 81
Charles IV, Holy Roman Emperor 175
Charles IV, King of France 138, 139, 155
Charles V, King of France 165

Charles VI, King of France 177, 182, 198,
    202, 207, 213–14, 225, 226, 241
Charles VII, King of France 235, 236, 237
Charles of Anjou, King of Sicily 93
Charles the Bold, Duke of Burgundy 259,
    262, 267, 268
Charter of the Forest 67, 108, 111, 157
Château Gaillard 41, 47, 48
Chaucer, Geoffrey 165, 167, 174, 176,
    216, 278
Chauncy, Fra' Joseph de 93
Chinon 4, 19
Churchill, Sir Winston 118, 291–2
Cinque Ports 64, 83
Clare, Elizabeth de 130
Clare, Isabel de 33
Clarence, George , Duke of 255, 260, 261,
    262, 263, 266, 269, 273, 274, 282
Clarence, Lionel, Duke of 153, 171
Clarence, Thomas, Duke of 198, 207,
    208–9, 212, 217, 222, 227
Clarendon 19, 69, 154, 233
Clarendon, Dr William 197
Clement V, Pope 112
Clifford, Lord John 253
Clifford, Rosamund 21
Clisson, Jeanne de 163
coinage 15, 77–8, 104, 163
Colchester, William de 195
Colyngbourne, William 283
Common Law 16, 31, 94, 255
Commynes, Philippe de 233, 256, 267, 268
Comyn, John, Lord of Badenoch 111, 113,
    114
Constance of Hauteville 34
Constitutions of Clarendon 23, 25
Corbridge, Thomas, Archbishop of York 112
Corfe Castle 64
Cornwall, Edmund, Earl of 99
Cornwall, Richard, Earl of 74, 76, 77, 78,
    82, 83, 86, 97
Crécy, battle of (1346) 159–60
Cressingham, Hugh de 110
Cricklade Castle 8
Crusades 25, 29, 30, 32, 33–9, 60, 74, 77,
    92–3, 156, 194
Culpeper, Sir Walter 134
customs duties 40–1, 266
Cyprus 35–6, 43, 194

Dafydd ap Gruffydd 100, 101, 102–3
Dagworth, Sir Thomas 159, 160, 163
Damory, Roger 130, 133
David I, King of Scotland 10
David II, King of Scotland 152, 160, 164
Despenser, Hugh (elder) *see* Winchester,
    Hugh Despenser, Earl of

Despenser, Hugh (younger) 131, 132, 133, 135–6, 137, 138, 139, 140, 141, 149
Despenser, Lady (Constance of York, Countess of Gloucester) 203
Diceto, Ralph de 26
Dickens, Charles 291
Dictum of Kenilworth 85
Disinherited (Anglo-Scottish magnates) 151, 152
Divine Kingship 174, 185
Dorset, John Beaufort, Earl of 184, 212, 218
Douglas, Sir Archibald 152
Dover Castle 64
Droxford, John 111
Dunheved, Thomas 142
Dupplin Moor, battle of (1332) 152

Edgar Atheling 5
Edington, William, Bishop of Winchester 162–3
Edmund II, Ironside 5, 13
Edmund of Abingdon, Archbishop of Canterbury 72
Edmund, St 70
Edward the Confessor 58, 70, 76, 86, 175, 195
Edward I 66, 70, 73, 77, 86, 91–116, 153
  appearance 95
  castle building 103
  character and qualities 95, 96
  coronation 93
  Crusader 92–3
  death of 116
  early years 92
  expulsion of the Jews 104
  financial policies 104, 107, 108
  First Statute of Westminster 98
  Gascon campaign 105–6, 107
  lawmaker 92, 94, 98–9, 116, 290
  relations with the Church 99, 111–12
  Scottish campaign 108–11, 112–14, 116
  spouses *see* Eleanor of Castile; Margaret of France
  Statute of Merchants 104
  tomb of 119
  truce with France 106
  Welsh campaigns 100–4
Edward II 117–43, 170
  administrative reforms 136
  alleged homosexuality 121–2, 137
  alleged survival 143
  appearance 121
  and Bannockburn 117, 127, 128, 129
  capture of 140
  character and qualities 118, 121–2
  and civil war 125, 130, 134–5
  coronation 120

death of 142–3
deposition of 141–2, 177
and the Despensers' tyranny 135–6, 137, 138, 139
early years 118–19
imprisonment 140–2
Isabella's plot against 138–41
Ordinances of 1311 124, 128, 129, 130, 131, 135, 136
and Piers Gaveston 119–22
Prince of Wales 115
Scottish campaign 126–7
spouse *see* Isabella of France
tomb 143
Edward III 125, 147–69, 188, 199
  appearance 153
  and Arthurian legend 154
  and capture of Calais 160–1
  character and qualities 148, 153, 154–5
  claims French crown 156
  coronation 148
  coup against Isabella and Mortimer 150–1
  and Crécy 159–60
  gain and loss of Aquitaine 164–6
  in literature and national myth 289
  invasion of France 156–9
  and Mortimer's execution 151
  nationalist sentiments 165
  old age and death 167–8
  Order of the Garter 154, 162
  relations with the Church 154, 158
  Scottish campaign 151–3, 164
  and Sluys 157, 158
  spouse *see* Philippa of Hainault
  treatment of Isabella 151
Edward IV 244, 246, 247, 248, 249, 251–70, 273, 280
  appearance 256
  birth and early life 252–3
  character and qualities 251–2, 256–8, 269–70
  claims the throne 253–4
  coronation 254–5
  death of 269
  defeats last Lancastrian army at Tewkesbury 264
  defeats Somerset's rebellion 255–6
  flees to Holland 261–2
  Hundred Years War 266–8
  invades France 266–8, 274
  makes peace with Louis XI 267–8
  relations with the Church 258
  Scottish campaign 275–6
  spouse *see* Wydeville, Elizabeth
  and Towton 251
  Wars of the Roses 252–4, 255–6, 259–65
  Warwick and Clarence plot against 260–2

womanizing 257–8, 268
Edward of Lancaster, Prince of Wales 261, 264, 273
Edward of Middleham, Prince of Wales 274, 277, 280, 282
Edward of Woodstock, Prince of Wales (Black Prince) 153, 163, 164–5, 166, 168, 174
Edward V 279, 280–1
Eleanor of Aquitaine, Queen consort of France and England 11–16, 20, 26–7, 28, 29, 34, 45, 46, 48, 52
Eleanor of Castile, Queen consort of England 93, 95, 97, 105
Eleanor of Provence, Queen consort of England 72–3, 76, 77, 82, 84
Elizabeth of York, Queen consort of England 282, 283, 284
Epiphany Plot (1399–1400) 195, 203, 212
Eric VII, King of Denmark 206
Estreby, Roger de 25
Eton 240, 268
Eugenius, Pope 11
Eustace IV, Count of Boulogne 6, 7, 10, 11, 12–13
Exchequer 15, 54, 94, 108, 136, 159, 162–3, 167
Exeter, Henry Holland, Duke of 262, 263, 264, 268
Exeter, John Holland, Duke of 184
Exeter, Thomas Beaufort, Duke of 222

Ferdinand III, King of Castile 96
Ferrer, Vincent 224
feudalism 5, 16
Fieschi, Manuel 142–3
First Statute of Westminster 98
FitzPeter, Geoffrey 58
FitzWalter, Robert 55–6, 58, 60
Fortescue, Sir John 265
Fotheringhay Castle 257, 272
Francis II, Duke of Brittany 267
Frederick II, Holy Roman Emperor 77, 81
Frescobaldi, Amerigo de 124
Frisby, Dr William 187
Froissart, Jean 137, 147, 148, 155, 168–9, 172, 176, 185, 187, 188, 189, 190, 257
Fulk the Red, Count of Anjou (Fulk I) 3
Fulk the Black, Count of Anjou (Fulk III) ix–xviii, 3–4
Fulk V, Count of Anjou, King of Jerusalem 4
Fusoris, Jean 214, 215

Gascony 49, 59, 68, 77, 80, 98, 103, 104, 105–6, 116, 120, 138, 151, 156, 160, 165, 180, 233, 238, 241

Gaucourt, Raoul de 217
Gaveston, Piers 115, 119–25, 128, 134
Geoffrey of Anjou 11, 12, 16
Geoffrey of Gâtinais 4
Geoffrey of Monmouth 20, 112–13
Geoffrey of Norwich 53–4
Geoffrey Plantagenet, Archbishop of York 50
Geoffrey Plantagenet, Count of Anjou 4–5, 9–10, 11
Geoffrey II, Duke of Brittany (1158–1186) 21, 25, 26, 27, 28, 29, 30
Geoffrey the Hammer xvii, 4
Gerald of Wales xviii, 8, 17, 19, 20, 27, 29, 35
Giffard, John 130
Giles of Rome 185
Gisors 39
Glastonbury 154
Gloucester Abbey 143
Gloucester, Gilbert de Clare, 7th Earl of 84, 85, 97–8, 101
Gloucester, Gilbert de Clare, 8th Earl of 123, 125, 126–7, 132
Gloucester, Humphrey, Duke of 198, 212, 222, 225, 226, 229, 234, 235, 236
Gloucester, Isabella, Countess of 46
Gloucester, Robert, Earl of 6, 7, 9, 10, 17
Gloucester, Thomas of Woodstock, Duke of 177, 178, 179–80, 181–3, 189, 193
Glyndwr, Owain xix, 196, 200, 201, 202, 203, 205, 206, 211, 214
Gower, John 174, 176, 199
Grandson, Othon de 98
Gray, John de, Bishop of Norwich 52–3
Great Council (Curia Regis) 14
Great Famine (1315–22) 129
Great Parliament (1265) 83
Great Schism 181, 222
Great Slump (1440–80) 241, 261, 268
Green, Sir Henry 188, 195
Green, John Richard 291
Gregory VII, Pope 22
Gregory IX, Pope 77
Gregory X, Pope 93
Grey, Sir Thomas 214
Grosseteste, Bishop Robert 81, 85
Guala Bicchieri, Cardinal 64
Guesclin, Bertrand du 165–6
Gurdon, Sir Adam 92

Halidon Hill, battle of (1333) 152, 156
Hampstead Marshall 154
hanging, drawing and quartering 103, 116
Harclay, Sir Andrew 134, 136
Harfleur 217–18, 222, 237
Harlech Castle 103, 202, 206
Harvey, John 174

Hastings, William, Lord 258, 262, 263, 279–80
Hazlitt, William 290–1
Henry I 4, 5, 15
Henry II xix, 8–31, 92
    appearance 13–14
    and Arthurian legend 20
    at war with Louis VII 11–12
    at war with Stephen 10, 12
    bastard children 21
    birth and early life 9
    character and qualities 17–18
    claims English throne 8–9, 12
    conflict with sons 21–2, 25–6, 29, 31
    coronation 13
    death of 31
    Duke of Brittany 16
    Duke of Normandy 10–11
    erudition 20
    financial reforms 15
    heir to Stephen 13
    invasion of Ireland 24–5
    legal administration 15–16
    marries Eleanor of Aquitaine 11
    rages 21
    relations with Becket 22, 23–4, 25
    relations with Richard 30–1
    and the Young King's rebellion 25–6, 27
Henry III 66–87
    and the barons' war 78–9
    appearance 68–9
    character and qualities 69–70
    coronation 67, 68
    Crusading plans 77
    cult of Edward the Confessor 76
    death of 86
    French campaigns 70–1, 74–5
    homage to Louis IX 80
    piety 70
    and the Provisions of Oxford 79–80, 81, 82, 85
    and Simon de Montfort 66, 74, 77, 78–9, 80, 81, 82, 83–5
Henry IV Bolingbroke xix, 178, 179, 184, 185–6, 192–209
    appearance 197
    and Archbishop Scrope's rebellion 204
    and the Armagnac–Burgundian dispute 206–7, 208
    banished by Richard II 186–7, 198, 211
    character and qualities 193, 197–9
    claims the throne 187–8, 190, 192, 197
    coronation 195
    Crusader 194
    illness and death 204, 205–6, 207, 209
    in literature and national myth 290–1
    Percy rebellions 199–202, 206

    plots and risings against 195, 196–7, 199–202, 203, 204, 206
    and Richard II's deposition 189–90
    Scottish expedition 196
    spouses *see* Bohun, Mary de; Joan of Navarre
    Welsh campaigns 196, 198, 202, 203, 204, 205, 206
Henry V 210–30
    Agincourt 19–21, 227
    appearance 215–16
    character and qualities 215
    claim to the throne 211
    coronation 212
    death of 229–30
    Hundred Years War 210–11, 213–14, 217–25, 228–9
    in literature and national myth 291
    Lollard persecution 211–12, 213, 216
    Lollard plot against 213
    Normandy invasion 223–4
    Prince of Wales 198, 200, 201, 202, 206, 207, 208, 211
    recognised as 'Heir and Regent of France' 225–6
    relations with the Church 216, 227–8
    Southampton Plot (1415) 214
    spouse *see* Catherine of Valois
    Welsh campaigns 211
Henry VI 229, 233–50, 255, 260, 261, 262
    appearance 238–9
    asceticism 240
    character and qualities 239–41
    coronation 234
    crowned King of France 235
    death of 248–9, 273
    Duke of York's protectorate 241–2, 243
    and Duke of York's rising 238
    flees to Scotland 246
    Hundred Years War 234–7, 238
    imprisoned in the Tower 247–8
    in literature and national myth 291
    mental breakdown 241, 242
    posthumous cult of 249
    Readeption 247–8, 262
    'Rout of Ludford' 244
    spouse *see* Margaret of Anjou
    Wars of the Roses 241–7, 248, 249
Henry VI, Holy Roman Emperor 34, 39
Henry VII (Henry Tudor) 281–2, 283, 284
    Bosworth 286–7
    claim to the throne 285
    lands in England 285
Henry the Young King, son of Henry II 21, 23–4, 25, 26, 27, 28
Henry of Huntingdon 7

Hereford, Humphrey de Bohun, Earl of
98, 107, 133, 134
Hexham, battle of (1464) 256
Higden, Ranulph 121, 199
Hoccleve, Thomas 154
Holinshed, Raphael 166, 289
Holland, Sir Thomas 154
Howden, Roger 34–5, 42–3
Hugh, Bishop of Lincoln 17, 35, 42, 52
Hugh of Hereford 14
Hume, David 290
Hundred Rolls 94
Hundred Years War xix, 155, 156–61, 162,
163–6, 177, 182, 209, 234–7, 238,
256, 259, 266–8
Hywel Dda code 101, 103

Ingelger 3
Innocent III, Pope 53, 57, 58, 60, 63, 71
Isaac Komnenos, 'Emperor' 35, 36
Isabeau of Bavaria, Queen of France 225
Isabel of Gloucester 33, 46
Isabella of Angoulême, Queen consort of
England 46, 50–1, 75
Isabella of France, Queen consort of
England 120, 121, 123, 125, 128–9,
132–4, 137, 138–9, 140, 141, 142,
143, 148–9, 150, 151
Isabella of Valois, Queen consort of
England 182

Jaffa 37, 38
James III, King of Scotland 275, 276
James of Savoy 103
Jerusalem 29, 32, 37–8, 194
Jews 15, 25, 27
under Edward I 104
under Henry III 78, 79, 85
under John 54, 61
under Richard I 33
Joan of Arc 234–5
Joan of England, Queen of Sicily34 35, 38
Joan of Kent 154
Joan of Navarre, Queen consort of England
198, 227
John, King 21, 28, 30, 31, 33, 39, 40, 41,
44–65, 67, 69
administrative reforms 54
appearance 50
character and qualities 50, 51, 56
civil war 62–3
conflict with barons 55–7, 58, 60–3
coronation 45
crosses the Wash 64–5
death of 65
and the death of Arthur of Brittany 46–7
excommunication 53–4, 57
French campaigns 46–9, 58–9

grants Magna Carta 61–2
in literature and national myth 289–90
and invasion of Prince Louis (Louis VIII)
63–4
Irish campaign 55
loses Normandy 45–8, 49, 59
papal vassal 57
quarrel with the Church 51–2, 53
Scottish policy 55
spouses *see* Gloucester, Isabella, Countess
of; Isabella of Angoulême
wealth 54–5
John II, Duke of Burgundy 224, 225
John II, King of France 162, 164
John XXII, Pope 150
John of Brittany, Earl of Richmond 97,
113, 117, 133, 134, 139
John of Gaunt, Duke of Lancaster 153,
166, 167, 168, 171–2, 174, 176, 177,
179, 180, 181, 183, 186, 193, 194
John of Montfort 158–9
John of Powderham 131

Kenilworth Castle 85, 140, 243
Kent, Edmond, Earl of 138, 139, 149, 154
King's Evil (scrofula) 96
King's Langley 122, 128, 196
Knights Hospitallers 37, 93
Knights Templar 36, 105, 129
Knolles, Sir Robert 163

La Rochelle 68, 106
Lacy, Hugh de 26
Lancaster, Edmund Crouchback, Earl of
70, 73, 77, 78, 79, 81, 82, 83, 84, 86,
97, 106, 181
Lancaster, Henry, Earl of 140, 148, 149
Lancaster, Henry of Grosmont, Duke of
159, 160, 162, 163–4
Lancaster, John of Gaunt, Duke of *see* John
of Gaunt
Lancaster, Thomas, Earl of 122, 123, 124,
125, 126, 129–31, 132–3, 134, 199
Landois, Pierre 283, 284–5
Langland, William 167
Langtoft, Peter 110, 115–16
Langton, Stephen 53, 54, 57, 58, 60, 61,
62, 68
Langton, Dr Thomas 280
Langton, Walter, Bishop of Lichfield 105,
111, 115, 119
Latimer, Lord 167, 168
le Baker, Geoffrey 119
le Fartère, Roland 20
Leeds Castle 133, 227
legal system
under Edward I 94, 98–9
under Henry II 15–16

under John 54
Welsh 101, 103
Leopold, Duke of Austria 37, 39
Les Espagnols-sur-Mer, battle of (1350)
    147–8, 162
Lincoln, Henry de Lacy, Earl of 98, 122,
    123, 129
Llewelyn ap Gruffydd 81, 86, 100, 101–2
Llewelyn ap Iorwerth 55
Llewelyn Bren 128, 133
Lollards 174–5, 181, 196, 211–12, 213,
    216, 226
longbows 152, 201
Longchamp, William 40
Losecoat Field, battle of (1470) 260–1
Louis IV, Emperor 156
Louis VII, King of France 10, 11, 12
Louis VIII, King of France 63, 64, 65, 67,
    68, 70
Louis IX, King of France 73, 75, 76, 77,
    80, 81, 82, 92, 96
Louis XI, King of France 247, 256, 259,
    261, 262, 267–8, 269, 274, 281
Lovell, Viscount 277, 285
Ludlow Castle 252
Lusignan family 70, 76, 78, 79, 80, 81, 82
Lusignan, Guy of, King of Jerusalem 36
Lusignan, Hugh of, Count of La Marche
    46, 74, 75
Lyons, Sir Richard 167, 168, 172

Mad Parliament (1258) 79, 86
Madog ap Llewelyn 103–4, 108
Magna Carta 44, 61–2, 67, 72, 78, 98, 99,
    108, 111, 157
Malcolm III, King of Scotland 5
Malemort, Hélie de, Archbishop of
    Bordeaux 49
Malmesbury Castle 12
Maltravers, Sir William 84
Mancini, Domenico 256–8, 272, 281
Manfred, King of Sicily 77, 78
Manny, Sir Walter 162, 163
Manuel II Paleologus, Emperor 185, 196
Map, Walter xviii, 6, 11, 17–18, 19, 20,
    27
March, Edmund Mortimer, 3rd Earl of 171
March, Edmund Mortimer, 5th Earl of
    188, 199, 201, 203, 211, 212–13,
    214, 217, 226
Marcher lords 81, 84, 100, 102, 133, 134
Mare, Sir Peter de la 168
Margaret, Fair Maid of Norway 108–9
Margaret of Anjou, Queen consort of
    England 233, 236, 239, 242–4,
    245–6, 247, 253, 261, 263, 264, 265
Margaret of France, Queen consort of
    England 106–7, 116

Margaret of Wessex, Queen consort of
    Scotland (St Margaret) 5
Marlborough 69, 86
Marsh, Adam 81
Marshal, William, Earl of Pembroke 29, 30,
    33, 43, 45, 49, 52, 57, 60, 65, 67,
    68, 70
Matilda, Empress 4, 5–6, 7, 9, 10
Matilda, Queen consort of England 6–7, 13
Mauléon, Savaric de 49, 63, 64
Meaux, siege of (1421) 228–9
Melusine xviii
Mercadier (French mercenary) 41, 42
Merciless Parliament (1388) 179
Middleham Castle 273, 275, 278
Mistlebrook, William 271–2
Model Parliament (1295) 104
Moleyns, Adam, Bishop of Chichester 237
Monstrelet, Enguerrand de 192
Montague, John Neville, Marquess of
    255–6, 261, 263, 264
Montague, Sir William 150, 151
Montferrat, Marquis of 36, 39
Montfort, Eleanor de 100, 101
Montfort, Simon de 66, 74, 77, 78–9, 80,
    81, 82, 83–5, 92, 131
More, Sir Thomas 252, 268, 271, 272,
    278, 281, 283
Mortimer, Hugh de 14
Mortimer, Sir Edmund 200–1, 203, 206
Mortimer, Sir John 226
Mortimer, Roger 102, 133, 136, 139, 140,
    141, 142, 143, 148, 149, 150–1
Mortimer's Cross, battle of (1461) 253
Morton, Dr John 265, 283

Netter, Thomas 212, 216, 229
Neville, George, Archbishop of York 248,
    256, 259, 262
Neville, Hugh de 50, 51
Neville, Lady Anne, Queen consort of
    England 261, 266, 273, 277, 280,
    284
Neville, Thomas, Bastard of Fauconberg
    264–5, 273
Neville's Cross, battle of (1346) 160
Norfolk, Hugh Bigod, Earl of 26
Norfolk, John Howard, Duke of 279, 286
Norfolk, John Mowbray, Duke of 254
Norfolk, Roger Bigod, Earl of 98, 99, 107
Norfolk, Thomas Mowbray, 4th Earl of 204
Norfolk, Thomas Mowbray, Duke of
    (earlier, Earl of Nottingham) 178,
    183, 184, 185–6
Northampton 25, 60, 83
Northumberland, Henry Percy, 1st Earl of
    188–9, 199, 200, 201, 202, 203, 204,
    205, 208

Northumberland, Henry Percy, 2nd Earl of
    (Harry Hotspur) 199, 200, 201, 202
Northumberland, Henry Percy, 4th Earl of
    261, 285, 287
Norwich 26
Nottingham 25–6, 55, 56, 156, 168, 257,
    278, 285

O'Connor, Rory 24
Old Byland, battle of (1322) 117–18, 136,
    137
Oldcastle, Sir John 213, 214, 226
Olivier, Laurence 292
Order of the Garter 154, 162
Ordinance of Labourers 161
Ordinances of 1311 124, 128, 129, 130,
    131, 135, 136, 151, 158
Otto IV, Holy Roman Emperor 58–9, 59
Outremer 36, 38
Oxford, Dowager Countess of 274
Oxford, John de Vere, Earl of 262, 263,
    265, 266, 273, 283, 286
Oxford, Robert de Vere, Earl of 178–9

Paris, Matthew 44, 50–1, 62, 65, 70, 73,
    74, 76, 77, 79, 92
Paston, John 237
Peasants' Revolt 171, 172–3, 193
Pecham, John, Archbishop of Canterbury
    99
Peele, George 290
Pembroke, 1st Earl of *see* Marshal, William
Pembroke, Aymer de Valence, Earl of 97,
    116, 122, 123, 124, 125, 126, 130,
    131, 133, 134, 135
Pembroke, Jasper Tudor, Earl of 253
Pembroke, Richard de Clare, Earl of
    ('Strongbow') 24
Pembroke, Richard, Earl of 72
Perrers, Alice 166–7, 168
Peter of Blois 18, 20
Peter of Savoy 73
Peter the Hermit 57
Peverell, William 14
Philip II, King of France 27, 29, 30, 33,
    34, 37, 39, 40, 41, 45, 46, 47, 48, 49,
    52, 57, 58, 59, 68, 70
Philip III, King of France 93, 96
Philip IV, King 105, 106, 108, 109, 111,
    120, 123, 128, 129
Philip VI, King of France 155, 156–7, 158,
    159, 160
Philip of Flanders 26
Philip the Good, Duke of Burgundy 224,
    226, 229, 235
Philippa of Hainault, Queen consort of
    England 139, 153, 160–1, 166
Pipe Rolls 15

Pizan, Christine de 199
Plantagenet family
    diabolical genes xviii–xix
    in literature and national myth 289–93
    name xix
poaching 19, 40, 61
Poitevins 72, 75, 79, 80
Poitiers, battle of (1356) 164
Pope, Alexander 249–50
Portsmouth 40, 156
Potyer, Richard 271–2
'Princes in the Tower' 272
    see also Edward V; York, Richard of
        Shrewsbury, Duke of
Provisions of Oxford 79–80, 81, 82, 85
Puddlicott, Richard 112
Purton Castle 8, 9

Radcot Bridge, battle of (1387) 179, 186,
    194
Ragman Rolls 98
Ralph of Coggeshall 47–8, 61
Ratcliffe, Sir Richard 277, 283, 284
Raymond Berenguer IV, Count of Provence
    72–3
Raymond of Toulouse 29
Reynolds, Walter, Archbishop of
    Canterbury 121, 128, 141, 148
Rhys ap Griffith 142
Richard I xviii, 21, 25, 26, 27, 28–31,
    32–43, 50
    appearence 34
    captivity and ransom 39
    character and qualities 35, 42–3
    coronation 33
    Crusader 32, 33–9
    death of 42
    Duke of Normandy 33
    Lionheart 35, 43
    popularity 33
    spouse *see* Berengaria of Navarre
    war with Philip II 41
Richard II 170–91, 202, 212, 290
    appearance 175
    banishes Bolingbroke 186–7
    character and qualities 173–5
    coronation 171
    death of 195–6, 209
    deposition 189–90
    despotism 183–5
    imprisoned in the Tower 189
    in literature and national myth 290
    Irish campaigns 180–1, 187
    and the Lords Appellant 178–9, 183–4,
        186
    and the Peasants' Revolt 171, 172–3
    relations with the Church 174–5, 182
    Scottish campaign 177

spouses *see* Anne of Bohemia; Isabella of Valois
Richard III 249, 271–88
  appearance 259
  birth and early life 272–3
  Bosworth 286–7
  and Buckingham's revolt 281–2
  character and qualities 277–8
  coronation 280
  death of 287
  discovery of grave in Leicester 272, 287
  Duke of Gloucester 255, 266, 271, 273
  hostile propaganda 272
  in literature and national myth 291
  in the North 275–6
  and the 'Princes in the Tower' 272
  scoliosis 272, 277, 287
  Scottish campaign 275–6
  spouse *see* Neville, Lady Anne
  warden of the Western Marches 276
Richard of Devizes 11
Rishanger, William 83, 85
Rivaux, Peter de 71, 72
Rivers, Anthony Woodville, Earl 279
Rivers, Richard, Lord 258, 259, 260
Robert III, King of Scotland 196
Robert of Artois 156
Robert of Reading 119, 137
Robert the Bruce (younger) *see* Bruce, Robert (later, Robert I, King of Scotland)
Robert Bruce (elder), Earl of Carrick 109, 111, 113
Robin of Redesdale 260
Roches, Peter des 59, 60, 67, 70, 71, 72
Roches, William des 45, 46, 48
Rochester Castle 63
Roger, Bishop of Worcester 17
Roger of Wendover 56, 62, 71
Rouen 223–4, 237
Round Table 97, 154
'Rout of Ludford' (1459) 244, 252
Russell, John, Bishop of Lincoln 282
Rustichello da Pisa 97

St Albans, battle of (1455) 242
St George's Chapel, Windsor 257
Sainte-Chapelle 77
Saladin 29, 36, 37, 38
Saladin Tithe 39
Salisbury, John Montague, Earl of 184, 188
Salisbury, Ralph Neville, Earl of 216, 241, 244, 245
Salisbury, William Longespée, Earl of 57, 59, 64
Salle, Sir Robert 163
Sanchia of Provence 76
Saumur 4

Scarborough 275
Scott, Sir Walter 291
Scrope, Henry, Lord 214
Scrope, Richard, Archbishop of York 204, 209
Scrope, Richard, Lord 176
Segrave, Stephen de 71
Shakespeare, William xix, 290, 292
Sheen 168, 174, 180, 216, 258, 273
shield money (scutage) 16, 54, 61
Shore, Jane 268
Shrewsbury, John Talbot, 1st Earl of 238, 241
Shrewsbury, battle of (1403) 201–2
Sigismund of Hungary 221–2, 224
Sluys, battle of (1340) 157, 158
Somerset, Edmund Beaufort, 2nd Duke of 236, 238, 241, 242
Somerset, Edmund Beaufort, 4th Duke of 262, 263, 264
Somerset, Henry Beaufort, Duke of 243, 255, 256
Southampton Plot (1415) 214
Stanley, Thomas, Lord 285–6
Stanley, Sir William 285–6, 287
Stapledon, Walter, Bishop of Exeter 136, 138, 140
Statute of Gloucester 98
Statute of Merchants 104
Statute of Mortmain 99
Statutes of Wales 103
Stephen, King xix, 5, 6–7, 9, 10, 11, 12
Stephen of Blois *see* Stephen, King
Stevenson, Robert Louis 291
Stirling Bridge, battle of (1297) 110
Stirling Castle 113–14, 126, 127
Stone of Scone 110, 149
Stratford, Archbishop 157, 158
Straw, Jack 173
Strongbow *see* Pembroke, Richard de Clare, Earl of
Stubbs, Bishop William 32, 33, 69, 80, 85, 93, 118, 148, 155, 193, 197, 209, 210, 249, 251–2, 271, 272, 275, 291
Suffolk, John de la Pole, Duke of 83
Suffolk, Michael de la Pole, 1st Earl of 176, 177, 184
Suffolk, Michael de la Pole, 2nd Earl of 217
Suffolk, William de la Pole, Duke of 236, 237
Surrey, John de Warenne, Earl of 97, 109, 110, 122, 126, 130
Surrey, Thomas Holland, Duke of 184
Swinehead Abbey 65
Swynford, Katherine 181, 198

Tancred, King of Sicily 34
Tany, Luke de 102

taxation 15, 39
  clerical taxation 107, 112
  papal tax-gatherers 77
  under Edward I 104, 107, 108, 112, 116
  under Edward II 136
  under Edward III 156, 157, 158, 163
  under Edward IV 266
  under Henry III 77
  under Henry V 227
  under John 50, 54–5, 56, 57, 60
Tertulle the Forester 3
Teutonic Knights 194, 225
Tewkesbury, battle of (1471) 264, 273
Theobald, Archbishop of Canterbury 10,
    13, 14, 22
Toulouse, Raymond, Count of 75
tournaments 40, 96, 97, 120, 149, 155
Tours 4, 30
Towton, battle of (1461) 246, 251, 255
Treaty of Brétigny (1360) 164–5
Treaty of Leake (1318) 131, 132
Treaty of Troyes (1420) 225, 227
Trivet, Nicholas 95
Trokelowe, John 119
Tudor, Owen 253, 285
Tunstall, Sir Richard 240, 247, 248
Tyler, Wat 172–3

Urban II, Pope 181
Urban III, Pope 28

Vendôme, Elisabeth of xvii
Vergil, Polydore 286, 287
Vesci, Eustace de 50, 55–6, 58, 60

Wace 20
Wakefield, battle of (1460) 245, 253
Wallace, William 110–11, 114
Wallingford Castle 12
Walsingham 70, 154, 168
Walsingham, Thomas 166, 167, 170, 176,
    184, 185, 196, 201, 213, 229–30
Walter, Hubert, Archbishop of Canterbury
    41, 45, 49, 52, 53, 58
Walter of Amersham 110
Walter of Coutances, Archbishop of Rouen
    40
Walworth, William 173
War of Saint-Sardos 138
ward-money 16
Wars of the Roses xix, 241–7, 248, 249,
    252–4, 255–6, 259–65
Warwick, Edward, Earl of 287
Warwick, Guy Beauchamp, Earl of 122,
    123, 125, 126
Warwick, Henry Beauchamp, Duke of 239

Warwick, Richard Beauchamp, Earl of 234
Warwick, Richard Neville, Earl of 241, 243,
    244, 246, 247, 248, 253, 254, 255–6,
    259–60, 261, 262, 263, 264
Warwick, Thomas Beauchamp, Earl of 184,
    185
Warwick, William Beauchamp, Earl of 98
Welles, Sir Robert 260, 261
Westminster Abbey 69, 76, 78, 86, 95,
    119, 154, 174, 175, 180, 195, 209,
    230, 255, 263, 279
Westminster Hall 79, 174, 181
Westmorland, Ralph Neville, Earl of
    199–200, 204
William I, the Conqueror 5
William the Lion, King of Scotland 26, 55
William of Aumale 14
William, Bishop of Valence 73
William of Malmesbury 13
William of Newburgh 14–15
William of Valence 78, 82
Willikin of the Weald 64
Wilton Diptych 174–5
Wiltshire, William le Scrope, Earl of 187–8,
    195
Winchelsea 104
Winchelsey, Robert, Archbishop of
    Canterbury 107, 108, 111–12, 120,
    123, 124
Winchester 69, 70, 76
Winchester, Hugh Despenser, Earl of 130,
    135, 138, 139, 140, 149
Windsor 69, 154
Woodstock 21
wool trade 15, 104, 156, 177
Worcester, John Tiptoft, Earl of 255
Worcester, Thomas Percy, Earl of 199, 201,
    202
Wycliffe, John 167, 174, 181
Wydeville, Elizabeth, Queen consort of
    England 258–9, 263, 268, 279
Wydeville family 258, 259, 260, 279, 281
Wykes, Thomas 85

York, Cicely Neville, Duchess of 252
York, Edmund of Langley, 1st Duke of
    177, 181, 183, 187
York, Edward of Langley, 2nd Duke of
    203, 219, 221
York, Richard of Shrewsbury, Duke of 279,
    280–1
York, Richard Plantagenet, 3rd Duke of
    235, 236, 238, 241–2, 243, 244, 245,
    252, 260
York Minster 278